FROMMER'S
1985-86 GUIDE TO NEW ORLEANS

by Susan Poole

Copyright ©1981, 1983, 1985
by Simon & Schuster, Inc.

All rights reserved
including the right of reproduction
in whole or in part in any form

Published by Frommer/Pasmantier Publishers
A Division of Simon & Schuster, Inc.
1230 Avenue of the Americas
New York, NY 10020

ISBN 0-671-52415-1

Manufactured in the United States of America

*Although every effort was made to ensure the accuracy
of price information appearing in this book,
it should by kept in mind that prices
can and do fluctuate in the course of time.*

CONTENTS

Chapter I	Introducing New Orleans	1
Chapter II	The Practicalities	8
Chapter III	Where to Stay in the French Quarter	19
Chapter IV	Where to Stay Outside the Quarter	30
Chapter V	Dining in the French Quarter	38
Chapter VI	Dining Outside the Quarter	59
Chapter VII	Things to Do in New Orleans	70
Chapter VIII	Seeing French Quarter Sights	82
Chapter IX	Sightseeing Outside the Quarter	114
Chapter X	The Festivals	142
Chapter XI	Shopping in New Orleans	157
Chapter XII	Side Trips	170
Appendix	$25-a-Day Travel Club—How to Save Money on All Your Travels	217

MAPS

New Orleans in Brief	10
The French Quarter	84
The French Quarter and Environs	117
Plantations	171
Cajun Country	191

ACKNOWLEDGMENTS

Seldom if ever, have I met with such cooperation—to say nothing of friendliness and downright eagerness to help—as in the preparation of this guide. By rights, the first acknowledgment should be simply to New Orleans herself, for once again taking me in and seeing to it that I found what I was looking for. So, although the following were *specifically* my guiding angels in this project, I'd also like to make an up-front blanket statement of thanks to taxi drivers, doormen, waiters and waitresses, sales clerks, artists, bartenders, fellow tourists imbued with a love of this city, and the scores of others who pointed me in the direction of yet another "find" to pass along to readers.

My very first thanks must go to Mrs. Junius Underwood, a gracious hostess and landlady who knows and understands New Orleans with an enthusiasm and passion she readily shares with her guests. Similarly, Beverly Gianna, of the Greater New Orleans Tourist and Convention Commission, serves up warm affection for the city along with any and every sort of information requested. Gayle Burchfield, Audrey Krust, and Mary Sue Griffith, of the Louisiana State Office of Tourism, made sure I found my way around New Orleans's environs via little-known restaurants, interesting people, and background facts that added vibrancy and color to my journey. And Jim Monaghan, a good friend and dedicated New Orleans Booster, has again proven an unfailing source of places to go and things to do I might otherwise miss on every trip.

*To Bill,
the lagniappe
of my life*

Inflation Alert

It is hardly a secret that inflation continues to batter the countries of the world. The author of this book has spent laborious hours attempting to ensure the accuracy of prices appearing in this guide. As we go to press, we believe we have obtained the most reliable data possible. Nonetheless, in the lifetime of this edition—particularly its second year (1986)—the wise traveler will add 15% to 20% to the prices quoted throughout these pages.

Chapter I

INTRODUCING NEW ORLEANS

THERE'S NO OTHER PLACE quite like it in our country. Call it the "Crescent City" (because it sits in a deep bend of the Mississippi River); call it "The City That Care Forgot"; call it "America's Most Interesting City"—by any name, New Orleans holds a unique place among American cities.

It also holds, I'm quick to confess, first place in my affections. I've never been able to put my finger on exactly why this should be so. Maybe it's the intriguing architecture of the French Quarter or the Old South appeal of the Garden District or the food that is so special it can make me homesick just remembering when I'm far away or the uninhibited gaiety of Bourbon Street or the joyous jazz of Preservation Hall. Maybe it's a little of all those things. But I think perhaps it is really the *people* of New Orleans who first won my heart many years ago and have held it captive ever since. Although I grew up in the tradition of hospitality that is the hallmark of the South, I've found over the years that the word "hospitality" takes on richer meaning in this city. It isn't only that you're warmly welcomed—New Orleanians seem *overjoyed* that you've chosen to come, and they can't wait to make sure you enjoy your stay! Tales abound of those who have come on a "passing through" basis and remained to join the ranks of residents. It's unlikely you'll escape a similar inclination after only a day or two!

Who can resist that sense of history as you walk narrow streets lined with centuries-old buildings fairly dripping with fancy ironwork and still as functional today as when they were built. The imagination would have to be nonexistent not to people sidewalks, courtyards, and restaurants with frock-coated gentlemen and ladies in swaying hoops. Visions of black women in calico balancing baskets of sugary pralines on their heads, or swashbuckling privateers swaggering through the streets while their leader, Jean Lafitte, huddles with Gen. Andrew Jackson in the Old Absinthe House deep in plans for a cooperative defense against the British, or glittering, candlelit ballrooms in the very buildings you pass by, dine in, or call "home" during your visit—all come as automatically as a reflex.

But don't for one instant imagine you'll be stuck in New Orleans's past. That brassy jazz sound filling the streets is very much of the 20th century. And if it occasionally turns into the low moan of blues that echo past sorrows, you're likely to hear a very modern echo in your heart. A look across Canal Street from the French Quarter will propel you even further into the present and the future, with skyscrapers once thought impossible to build on this swampy site sharing the skyline with skeleton-like frameworks of others yet to come. The Superdome pays homage to a modern-day preoccupation with sporting events, while the towering International Trade Mart and sprawling Rivergate Exhibition Center serve the interests of commerce.

And then there are those people! Artists "on the fence" around Jackson Square; musicians sitting in at jazz clubs or Preservation Hall; shopkeepers displaying exquisite imports alongside inexpensive souvenirs; taxi drivers who hop out to open doors (unheard of nowadays); natives happily sharing tables with tourists at the Café du Monde for an any-hour café au lait and beignets (more about those later)—they come in all occupations, shapes, sizes, nationalities, colors, and accents. The population "stew" that comes from this marrying of flavors is a natural result of New Orleans's long history, a past which has seen widely differing groups gather here to oppose each other in the beginning, only to join hands in mutual self-interest in the end.

A LOOK BACKWARD: It was in 1718 that a Canadian-born Frenchman, Sieur de Bienville, set out to find a suitable location for a French settlement to protect that country's holdings in the New World from British expansion. His brother, Sieur d'Iberville, had planted a cross at the great bend of the Mississippi River in 1699, and Bienville found it a strategic point for his "city." Although it was almost 110 miles inland from the gulf by river, there was an easy portage route to a little stream (Bayou St. John) which provided easy water transportation directly into Lake Pontchartrain. From a military standpoint, this was a convenient "back door" for defense or escape, depending on the fortunes of war should the British get serious. And, of course, it was a perfect trade route for the fabled Indian gold Bienville hoped to ship back home. Following the plan of a late French medieval town, a central square (the Place d'Armes) was laid out, with streets forming a grid around it, a church, government office, priest's house, and official residences fronting the square and earthen ramparts dotted with forts on its perimeter. In honor of the then Regent of France, the Duc d'Orléans, the little town was named New Orleans.

Today, we know that section of the modern city as the Vieux Carré (it means Old Square and is pronounced vyew-ka-ray) and the Place d'Armes as Jackson Square. Rude huts of cypress filled in with moss and clay were erected, and a tiny wooden levee was raised against the mighty river, which persisted in flooding periodically to turn streets into rivers of mud.

The fabled gold turned out to be just that, a fable. But there were furs aplenty, and Bienville needed settlers to trap them, run farms to feed the colony, and fight off hostile Indians. The French government saw this as a perfect opportunity to rid itself of all its misfits at home and sent out the dregs of its prisons, some bonded servants, and slaves from French Caribbean settlements. They were the first ingredients of New Orleans's population "stew." Among them were "fallen women" who somehow managed to leave no direct descendants—if you can believe today's New Orleanians, who proudly trace their ancestry to French or Spanish nobility and the respectable "casket girls" brought over by Ursuline nuns in 1727 (carrying all their worldly goods in casket-like trunks), with never a mention of those earlier women of the streets!

Lured by the first real estate scam in this country's history (a flamboyant speculator named John Law painted the appealing picture of a virtual paradise on earth in the new settlement), wealthy Europeans, aristocrats, merchants, exiles, soldiers, and a large contingent of German farmers arrived to find only mosquitoes, a raw frontier existence, and swampy land that resisted all but the most heroic efforts to put it to productive use. But the Europeans stayed on, and as they tamed the land, the colony prospered and attracted more and more members of the aristocratic class. Social life began to take on the complexion of European court life. By 1763, yet another seasoning was added to the pot—Acadians from Nova Scotia fleeing British rule. You'll find their descendants living a little to the west of New Orleans, still engaged in farming and trapping, still speaking their unique brand of French, and proudly calling themselves "Cajuns."

French to the core from the very beginning, New Orleanians were horrified to learn in 1764 that Louis XV had secretly given their city—and them—to his cousin, Charles III of Spain. Their resentment forced the first Spanish governor to leave, and it wasn't until "Bloody O'Reilly" was dispatched by the Spanish crown with 3000 soldiers in 1769 that revolutionary ideas were firmly squelched (after the execution of five French patriots) and Spanish rule accepted as a reality. With a Gallic shrug, French aristocracy mingled with Spanish nobility, intermarried, and created a new "Créole" culture.

Tragedy struck in 1788 when a disastrous fire destroyed more than 850 buildings, and again in 1794 in the midst of rebuilding. From the ashes emerged a completely new city, dominated by the proud Spanish style of brick and plaster buildings replete with arches, courtyards, balconies, and, of course, attached slave quarters. Even today, you'll see tile markers giving Spanish street names at every corner in the "French" Quarter.

The new city was much coveted by both the English and the Americans. France, recognizing her blunder in giving it away, wanted it back. Control of the Mississippi River was at stake, and with all sorts of plots flying about, Governor Carondelet reinforced the wall around the city and armed its five forts with cannons pointing outward to fend off invaders and inward to ward off any internal uprising. France finally regained possession in 1800, with a surprisingly quiet transfer of ownership, and held on for three years when Napoleon negotiated the Louisiana Purchase with the United States for the paltry (as it turned out) sum of $15 million. To the Créole society, this was almost as appalling as Spanish rule had been to French settlers, for they considered all Americans barbarians who would surely bring about the end of the sophisticated Vieux Carré lifestyle.

Shunned by existing New Orleans society, newly arrived Americans settled across Canal Street (so named because a drainage canal was once planned along its route, although never actually constructed) and set about showing the "downtown" snobs that they were no strangers to culture. Splendid mansions sprang up in what is now the Garden District and a segregated social life took shape. But not for long. Yankee commercialism (which took on a boom-town air "uptown") brought industry and wealth much needed by downtowners, and the vitality of warm-blooded downtown society drew uptowners like a magnet.

Besides, both were forced to join forces against hurricanes, yellow fever epidemics, and floods. A spirit of unity grew between the two sections, so much so that when Andrew Jackson needed volunteers to protect New Orleans against British attack in 1814, some 5000 citizens responded—from both sides of Canal Street. Even the infamous (but much revered in New Orleans) privateer Jean Lafitte joined in, supplying cannons and ammunition that swung the balance in favor of the Americans. Ironically, the battle—which left some 2000 British casualties as opposed to only a small number of American dead and wounded—was fought two weeks *after* a peace treaty had been signed, unbeknownst to either side at New Orleans!

From then until the Civil War, New Orleans gloried in a prosperity unmatched anywhere in the country. Wealthy cotton and sugar planters left upriver mansions from time to time to occupy luxurious town houses and attend festivals, opera, theater, banquets, parades, and spectacular balls (including "Quadroon Balls," where beautiful mulatto girls were displayed to the gentry as possible mistresses). Hardworking Irish and German immigrants arrived in vast numbers to add their own dash of spice to the already exotic culture. Canals and levees were built to keep the city alive and a little drier; steamboats plied the river serving King Cotton and pleasure-seeking passengers; politics and gambling became passionate pastimes; and there was a lively trade in the slaves who supported the plantation economy on their oppressed backs. Federal troops put an end to all that when they marched in during 1862 to stay through a bitter Reconstruction period until 1877. New Orleans would never again be quite so flamboyant, but she was far from dead.

Like the rest of the defeated South, the city went about the business of rebuilding its economic life without the dependency on slavery which had been its downfall. By 1880, port activity had begun to pick up and industrial activity drew more and more visitors from the business world, many of whom became residents. And a new group of immigrants, Italians, came to put their special mark on the city. Through it all, there survived an undiminished enthusiasm for fun. By 1880, gambling again thrived in over 80 establishments, there were almost 800 saloons, and scores of "bawdy houses" openly engaged in prostitution (illegal, but uncontrolled). New Orleans was earning a reputation for open vice, and there were some who felt something should be done to counteract such publicity. Alderman Sidney Story, in 1897, thought he had the answer. He moved all illegal (but highly profitable) activities into a restricted district along Basin Street, next door to the French Quarter. Quickly nicknamed "Storyville," the district boasted fancy "sporting palaces" with elaborate decor, musical entertainment, and a variety of ladies of pleasure. Visitors and residents could purchase a directory (the "Blue Book") which listed alphabetically the names, addresses, and race of more than 700 prostitutes, ranging from those in the "palaces" to poorer inhabitants of wretched, decaying shacks called "cribs" on the blocks behind Basin Street. Black musicians came into their own when they moved from the streets into ornate bordellos to entertain patrons with the music we know as jazz. While jazz itself predates Storyville, it was here that it gained the popularity which sent it upriver and into this country's musical heritage. When the secretary of the navy decreed in 1917 that our armed forces should not be exposed to so much open vice (without, it might be added, any visible support from the troops) Storyville was closed down and has now disappeared without a trace.

IN RECENT YEARS: Today, New Orleans has built its port into the largest in the United States and the second busiest in the world (Amsterdam is first). It ranks third in tourism in this country (conventions alone bring in more than 800,000 visitors each year) and is one of the top three travel destinations for foreign visitors (San Francisco and New York are the other two). Drainage and epidemic problems have been conquered by means of high levees, canals, pumping stations, and great spillways which are opened to direct flood water away from the city.

Outside the French Quarter, the city's face has changed considerably over recent years. The 1984 World's Fair left a legacy of high-rise luxury hotels and a reconstructed waterfront on the Fair's site in what was a derelict warehouse district. New Orleans's emergence as a major financial center (more than 50 commercial banks!) has brought with it the construction of soaring office buildings, mostly in the Central Business District. Thus it once more has shown its traditional ability to hold on to the best of the old while embracing all that is new and exciting in the present, all the while looking to the promise of things to come in the future.

Yesterday lives on in the architecture and lifestyle of the French Quarter, Garden District mansions, and colorful steamboats ferrying fun-loving passengers around the harbor—and, as always, it joins hands happily with today's Yankee entrepreneurs in a friendly, heart-warming collaboration that makes New Orleans an exciting travel experience not to be missed.

Chapter II

THE PRACTICALITIES

NEW ORLEANS IS AN EASY CITY to get to. No fewer than ten **airlines** serve its international airport: American, Continental, Delta, Eastern, Lacsa, Northwest Orient, Ozark, Pan American, Republic, and USAir. *As we go to press,* average round-trip coach fares are $604 from New York, $410 from Chicago, and $734 from Los Angeles. With the current yo-yo airline fares situation, these may change, sometimes overnight. And, of course, you should *always* check for Super Saver and special promotional packages—New Orleans is a favored destination for seasonal and advance-booking discount rates with some airlines. For example, in 1984 Delta offered an "Old Man River & Grand Old Lady" three-day, two-night package (with discounted airfares) of $155 to $190 per person, double occupancy, which included city and paddlewheel tours as well as accommodations. Be sure to check on what's available when you plan your visit. *Special Note:* Delta, in conjunction with the Days Inn motel chain, offers airfare discounts of 25% to 40% for members of the Days Inn September Club (55 years and older)—a substantial savings well worth looking into.

From the airport, you can reach the Central Business District by bus for 90¢, by limousine for $7 per person (direct to leading hotels), and by taxi for about $19 ($7 per person for over three passengers).

Amtrak trains reach New Orleans's Union Passenger Terminal, centrally located at 1001 Loyola Ave., from Los Angeles and intermediate points; New York, Washington, and points in between; and Chicago and intermediate points. Average round-trip coach fares are: from New York, $406; from Chicago, $244; from Los Angeles, $400. Amtrak, too, frequently offers special family rates and other packages, some with a rental car, so be sure to check when you reserve.

Amtrak does an especially good job with tour packages, which can be arranged through your local Amtrak Tour Desk. In 1984, options ranged from one-night "Escapades" no-frills hotel accommodations at $44, to five-day extravaganzas which included escorted sightseeing tours, top-rated hotel accommodations (double occupancy), and other extras at $521. All tour prices are in addition to rail fares. Prices will change, of course, during the life of this book, but from past experience, it is safe to say that Amtrak tours will be genuine moneysavers.

Greyhound and Trailways buses also come into the Union Passenger Terminal from points throughout the country. Round-trip fares at the time of writing are: from New York, $223; from Chicago, $163; from Los Angeles, $283.

Trailways offers attractive group package rates (individuals should check with travel agents about joining groups already formed) which in 1984 ranged from $97 to $175 for two days and two nights, depending on hotel selection and extras. These prices are in addition to bus fares.

By automobile, you can drive to New Orleans via I-10, U.S. 90, U.S. 61, and across the Lake Pontchartrain causeway on La. 25. Most hotels provide parking, and these public garages are open 24 hours a day: French Market Parking Lot, Decatur Street at St. Peter Street (tel. 529-5708); International Rivercenter, Poydras Street at the Mississippi River (tel. 561-0500); and Rivergate Convention Center, entrance on St. Peter Street (tel. 529-2861). The AAA Louisiana is located at 3445 N. Causeway, Metairie, LA 70002 (tel. 504/838-7500), and will assist members with trip planning, service aids, and emergency services.

For banking services such as foreign money exchange, money transfers, and travelers checks, visit the Hibernia National Bank, 313 Carondelet St., 9 a.m. to 3 p.m. weekdays, where several foreign languages are spoken.

GETTING TO KNOW NEW ORLEANS: Before you do anything else (indeed, before you even leave home, write ahead for information), stop by the **Visitor Information Center** at 334 Royal St. (tel. 504/566-5011) in the French Quarter. They are open Monday through Saturday from 9 a.m. to 5 p.m. and have excellent walking and driving tour maps, booklets on restaurants, accommodations, sightseeing, special tours, and almost anything else you want to know. The staff is multilingual, friendly, and a veritable fount of valuable information.

From those maps you pick up at the Visitor Center, you'll see

10 □ ARTHUR FROMMER'S NEW ORLEANS

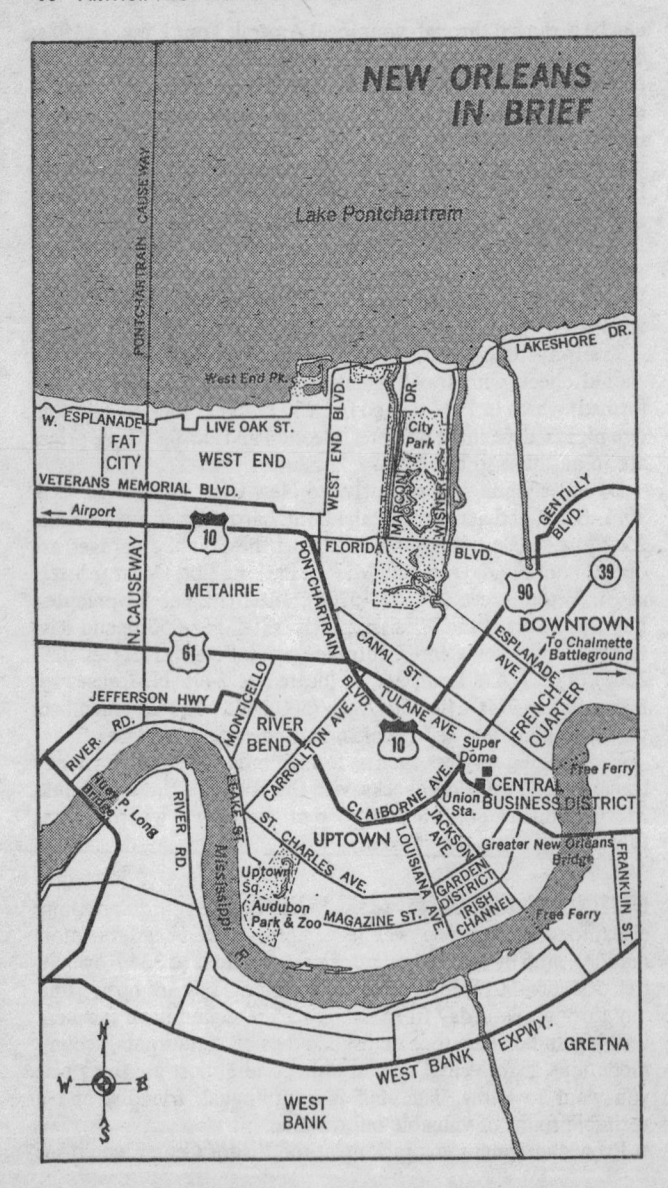

that the **French Quarter,** where the city began, is a 13-block-long area between Canal Street and Esplanade Avenue running from the Mississippi River to North Rampart Street. You'll also see that because of the bend in the river, much of the city is laid out at angles which render useless such mundane directions as north, south, east, and west. Never mind. New Orleans solved the geographical problem long ago by simply substituting "riverside," "lakeside," "uptown," and "downtown." It works, and you'll catch on quickly if you keep in mind that North Rampart Street is the "lakeside" boundary of the Quarter, Canal Street marks the beginning of "uptown," and the Quarter is "downtown." As for building numbers, they begin at 100 on either side of Canal. In the Quarter, they begin at 400 at the river (that's because four blocks of numbered buildings were lost to the river before the levee was built). Another reminder of Canal Street's boundary role between new and old New Orleans is the fact that street names change when they cross it (i.e., "downtown" Bourbon Street becomes Carondelet "uptown").

The **Central Business District** lies directly above Canal from the Mississippi River, stretching toward the lake to Loyola Avenue 11 blocks away and over to the elevated expressway ten blocks from and parallel to Canal. There are pleasant plazas, squares, and parks sprinkled among all those commercial highrise buildings, and some of the most elegant of the luxury hotels are located in this area.

The beautiful **Garden District** lies between St. Charles Avenue and Magazine Street toward the river, and Jackson and Louisiana Avenues. Incidentally, the area past Magazine Street nearer the river is sometimes called the "Irish Channel" because it was home to hundreds of Irish immigrants during the 1800s. Audubon Park and Loyola and Tulane Universities are a little farther out on St. Charles Avenue. "Fat City" is bounded by North Causeway and Veterans Boulevard, extending to Division Street and West Esplanade. The map on page 10 will help you locate other sections of New Orleans and to see the layout of the city as a whole.

AND THE LANGUAGE: Well, it's English, of course—but it may come in tones, accents, and pronunciations that surprise you. Don't expect to hear a lot of "you-alls" or other Deep South expressions; be prepared instead for a sort of southern Brooklynese! Unless you stick to the Garden District and university

12 ARTHUR FROMMER'S NEW ORLEANS

campuses, you should know before you come that "erl" means "oil," "toin" translates to "turn," and even the most cultured downtowner is likely to slip in a "de" or two for "the." There are, of course, all sorts of dialects around town, as you'd expect from the ethnic backgrounds represented in New Orleans, but somehow they *all* seem to have caught a little bit of New York's Brooklyn in their speech. Various theories have been raised to explain this phenomenon: that the same ethnic groups immigrated to both cities in the 1800s; that both are seaports; or that *most* foreigners who learn English later in life adopt this kind of talk (although I have my doubts about that). Whatever the reason, it seems to be a permanent part of the New Orleans scene, and believe it or not, actually becomes a part of the city's charm.

As for the pronunciation of certain, rather ordinary street names and other commonly used words, there is simply *no* explanation—except that New Orleanians have decided (using some obscure logic, no doubt) that they should be said a certain way and that's the way they're said in New Orleans! To help you sound less like a "foreigner" as you move around town, here are some of those with the native twist:

Conti Street	CON-teye
Burgundy Street	Bur-GUN-dee
Carondelet	Car-ONDE-let *(not* "lay")
Caliope	CAL-i-ope *(not* "Cal-I-opee")
Chartres Street	Charters
Dauphine Street	daw-FEEN
Iberville Street	EYE-bur-vill
Bienville Street	Bee-EN-vill
Orleans Street	Or-LEENS
but	
New Orleans	Noo OR-lyuns (or, better yet, NOR-luns!)

You're sure to hear others that sound peculiar—don't question, just follow the lead of those who live there.

And speaking of pronouncing words, here are a few others you should know to complete your New Orleans vocabulary:

lagniappe	lan-yap (a little something extra you've neither paid for nor deserve—like the 13th doughnut when

NEW ORLEANS ORIENTATION 13

	you order a dozen)
bayou	by-you (a marshy, sluggish stream, usually feeding into a river or lake)
beignet	baan-yaa (a cross between a doughnut and a cruller, liberally sprinkled with powdered sugar—yummy!)
banquette	ban-KET (a French word for bench which means "sidewalk" in New Orleans, since early wooden sidewalks were elevated above muddy streets)
dressed	In New Orleans this means "served with the works"—as when ordering a sandwich.
pralines	praw-lines (a *very* sweet confection made of brown sugar and pecans—they come in creamy and brittle styles)
crayfish	CRAW-fish (sometimes spelled "crawfish" and *always* pronounced that way—a tiny, lobster-looking creature plentiful in the waters around New Orleans and used in every conceivable way in cooking)
étouffée	ah-too-fay (a Cajun dish—a kind of smothered stew served with rice, which may contain crayfish and always contains *something* very good)
café brûlot	cah-fay brew-low (coffee mixed with spices and liqueurs and served flaming—gorgeous!)

14 ARTHUR FROMMER'S NEW ORLEANS

DRINKING LAWS: Alcoholic beverages are available in New Orleans around the clock, seven days a week. But be warned, while the police may look the other way if they see a pedestrian who's had a few too many (as long as he's peaceful and not bothering anyone else), they have no tolerance at all for those who are intoxicated behind the wheel. If you find yourself in that condition far from your hotel, you'd best take a taxi!

WHAT TO WEAR: It's a little hard to say. True, the average mean temperature is 70°, but it is also true that the thermometer can drop or rise several degrees in a single day. And because of the humidity you can be uncomfortably cold or uncomfortably warm at relatively mild temperatures. However, I've found that lightweight clothing is usually enough, supplemented by a medium-weight raincoat (although from December through March it's a good idea to carry along an extra sweater). The almost subtropical climate keeps this a good place to visit almost any time of year, but July and August can be exceptionally muggy. If you do come during those months, you'll quickly learn to follow the natives' example and stay out of the noonday sun and duck from one air-conditioned building to another. And even in the rain (which averages 63 inches annually), you'll be able to get around without difficulty—to borrow a phrase from the Irish, it's a "soft rain" hereabouts.

TELEPHONE AREA CODE: The area code for all sections of the city is 504.

USEFUL TELEPHONE NUMBERS: Should you become ill during your New Orleans visit, most major hotels have in-house staff doctors on call 24 hours a day. If there's not one available in your hotel or guest house, call or go to the Emergency Room at **Charity Hospital,** 1532 Tulane Ave. (tel. 568-3291) if you're downtown; the **Touro Infirmary,** 1401 Foucher (tel. 897-8423), uptown. For dental emergencies, call the **New Orleans Dental Association** (tel. 834-6449). Other useful numbers: **Greater New Orleans Tourist and Convention Commission** (tel. 566-5011); **Travelers Aid Society** (tel. 525-8726); **Union Passenger Termi-**

nal, 1001 Loyola Ave., for bus and train information (tel. 528-1610); local **transit information** (bus routes and schedules) can be obtained from the New Orleans Public Service, Inc. (tel. 486-6338); Time (tel. 529-6111); Weather (tel. 525-8831); Marine/Recreational Forecast (tel. 522-2686); Passport Agency (tel. 589-6728).

GETTING AROUND NEW ORLEANS: Rental cars are available from Hertz, Avis, Budget, American International Rent-a-Car, Dollar, Greyhound, Econo-Car, Holiday, and National. Driving can be difficult in New Orleans, and I've been told by locals that while traffic patrolmen are fairly tolerant of moving violations, they're absolute murder on illegal *parking,* handing out tickets right and left. For that reason, I strongly suggest that you put the car away for any French Quarter sightseeing (it's more fun, anyway, on foot or by minibus—see below) and use it only for longer jaunts out of congested areas.

By Bus

New Orleans has an excellent public bus system, and you can get complete information on which numbers run where by calling 486-6338 or by picking up an excellent city map at the **Visitor Information Center,** 334 Royal St. in the French Quarter, which shows all bus routes. All fares at the moment are 60¢ (you must have exact change) except for expresses, which are 75¢.

A very special bus ride for your first, farewell, or "tired-feet" tour of the French Quarter is the **Vieux Carré Minibus.** Quaint little vehicles leave Canal and Bourbon Streets from 6 to 9:30 a.m. and 4 to 6 p.m. on weekdays, or you can board at Bourbon and Iberville from 9:30 a.m. to 4 p.m. and 6 p.m. to 12:30 a.m. weekdays (all day Saturday, Sunday, and holidays). It'll cost you just 60¢ to see all of the French Quarter in comfort, although certainly not in as much detail as via the hoof-it route.

Outside the Quarter, you can park at the Superdome and ride a **Central Business District shuttle bus** which for 30¢ takes you down Poydras Street to the Rivergate Exhibition Center, then back up Canal to the Superdome. If you're interested in Canal Street shopping, this is by far the most convenient and economical way to do it, making as many stops along the way as you want without the bother of finding that elusive parking space. It's another fare, however, each time you board. Shuttles run from 6:30 a.m. to 7:30 p.m. daily except Sunday and holidays.

By Foot

For my money, the *only* way to see the **French Quarter** and the **Garden District** is by foot. They're both small areas, crammed with things you won't want to miss, and easy to find your way around. Only by strolling can you really soak up the charm of both these sections. In the Quarter, look through iron gates or down alleyways for glimpses of lovely patios and courtyards and above street level for interesting facades and incredibly fragile, lacy iron railings. Along Bourbon Street, intersperse strolls with stops to listen to live jazz groups playing at open-door saloons—there's nonstop music most of the day. In the Garden District, be sure to allow enough time to drink in the beauty of formal gardens surrounding the fine old mansions.

By Taxi

Taxis are plentiful and respond quickly to telephone calls in New Orleans. They can be hailed easily on the street in the French Quarter and some parts of the Central Business District, and are usually in place at taxi stands at the larger hotels. Otherwise, telephone and expect a cab to appear in three to five minutes. In my experience, at least two out of three drivers will get out to open doors for you at both ends of the ride. Rates are $1.10 when you enter the taxi and 25¢ for every one-tenth of a mile thereafter. Two reliable companies are: **United Cab** (tel. 524-9606) and **Pelican Cab** (tel. 821-5474).

Touring Tip: Most taxis can be hired for about $20 per hour for up to five passengers—a hassle—free and economical way for a small group to tour far-flung areas of the city (the lakefront, for example). Out-of-town trips cost double the amount on the meter.

By Trolley

One treat you really should allow yourself is the hour-and-a-half ride down St. Charles Avenue on the famous old streetcar line which has been named a National Historic Landmark. The trolleys run 24 hours a day at frequent intervals, and the fare is just 60¢. Board at Canal and Carondelet Streets (directly across Canal from Bourbon Street in the French Quarter), sit back and look for landmarks in this part of town. Lafayette Square is at the 500 block of St. Charles, and across from it is Gallier Hall, built in the 1840s, which was the seat of the city's ruling fathers for 100 years.

At Lee Circle, a little farther on, you'll see a huge statue of the general (Robert E., that is) which was erected in 1884—take note that he's facing *north* (that's so his back will never be to his enemies!). From here on, it's fun to watch the homes that line the avenue as they change from Greek Revival to Victorian to early 1900s. The Garden District begins at Jackson Avenue, and you may want to get off the trolley to explore it fully. Even while riding by, however, you'll see many lovely homes in their garden settings. Loyola and Tulane Universities are at the 6000 block, across from Audubon Park. The park itself is worth a visit—there are huge old live oaks, a zoo, lagoons, a children's amusement park, tennis courts, and a municipal golf course. It extends all the way to the levee at the Mississippi.

The end of the line is at Palmer Park and Playground at Claiborne Avenue, but if you want to mount a shopping expedition at the interesting Riverbend Shopping Area (see "Shopping"), get off at Carrollton. It will cost you another 60¢ for the ride back to Canal Street, and it's a good idea to sit on the opposite side for the return to watch for things you missed going out. As a New Orleans friend once told me proudly, "The St. Charles trolley has to be the best 60¢ tour in the world!"—I'm inclined to agree with him.

By Horse and Carriage

If you have even one romantic bone in your body, you'll find it hard to resist the authentic old horse-drawn carriages that pick up passengers at Jackson Square. Each horse is decked out with a flower- and ribbon-trimmed straw hat, and each driver is apparently in fierce competition with all other drivers to win a "most lavishly decorated carriage" award. No matter which one you choose, you'll get a knowledgeable, nonstop monologue on historic buildings, fascinating events of the past, and a legend or two during the 2¼-mile drive through the French Quarter. They're at the Decatur Street end of Jackson Square from 9 a.m. to midnight in good weather, and the charge is $8 per adult, $4 for children.

By Ferry

One of New Orleans's nicest treats is absolutely free. It's the 25-minute (round-trip) ferry ride across the Mississippi from the foot of Canal Street, and it's a joy, whether you go by day for a view of the busy harbor or at night, when the lights of the city reflect in the mighty river. If you'd like to do some West Bank driving between trips, the ferry carries both car and foot passengers.

By Boat

If the horse-drawn carriages represent romance on land, they are matched on the river by several oldtime steamboats that leave from the foot of Canal or Toulouse Streets for river cruises. You'll find details of the cruises at the end of Chapter IX.

Chapter III

WHERE TO STAY IN THE FRENCH QUARTER

FROM THE BEGINNING a city which welcomed visitors with open arms and warm hospitality, New Orleans today carries on a long tradition of providing comfort for travelers wide-ranging in taste, style, and price. And in spite of the annual influx of hundreds of thousands in search of a place to stay, this spirited city has managed to keep historic districts like the French Quarter free of that modern disease, "progress" in the form of high-rise monstrosities that stick out like a sore thumb and deface many an old, formerly gracious part of the American heritage. Indeed, it is almost impossible to tell if some of the newer French Quarter hotels have been built from scratch or lovingly placed inside the shell of an older building, so faithful has been the dedication to preserving the Quarter's architectural style. Even motor hotels (which eliminate the ever-present problem of off-the-street parking) have the look that is distinctly New Orleans's. Oh, you'll find those high-rises, of course, but they're uptown in more appropriate, commercial sections, where they seem to "fit" just fine. In fact the proliferation of slick new hotels brought on by the 1984 World's Fair has done a lot to ease New Orleans's chronic hotel room shortage.

As for guest houses, they really *do* make you feel like a guest. Presided over by New Orleanians imbued with a special brand of hospitality, many are furnished with antiques and all are outstanding in terms of a home-like atmosphere. Such is their appeal for me that I haven't even considered staying anywhere else in years.

A relative newcomer on the New Orleans scene is **New Orleans Bed & Breakfast** (contact: Mrs. Sarah Margaret Brown, 3658 Gentilly Blvd., P.O. Box 8163, New Orleans, LA 70182; tel. 504/949-6705, or toll free 800/541-9852 outside Louisiana).

Mrs. Brown can book you into any one of some 200 private homes, guest houses, inns, and plantations in New Orleans, the state of Louisiana, or the Mississippi Gulf Coast. Prices range from a low of $25 to $65 a day, double occupancy.

But whatever your preference—be it hotel, motel, guest house, or bed-and-breakfast—one thing is certain: you're sure to find much more than a place to lay your head in any of the New Orleans accommodations.

One word of warning, however. In spite of the thousands of rental rooms in New Orleans, there are times when there isn't a bed to be had. Advance reservations are a must during fall and winter months when the city is crowded (a good idea whatever the season), and if you're planning your trip to coincide with Mardi Gras it isn't an exaggeration to say that you should book as far as a year ahead. Sugar Bowl week and other festival times also flood New Orleans with visitors and require advance planning for accommodations. That's not to say that you might not run across a cancellation and get a last-minute booking, but the chance is remote, to say the least. A good time to visit New Orleans is almost anytime, but if you want to miss crowds and hard-to-find lodging, consider coming in the month immediately following Mardi Gras (it begins soon after Christmas with the opening of Carnival season and lasts until "Fat Tuesday," the last day before Lent) or in the summer months (which can be muggy, but not unbearable) when streets are not nearly so thronged.

One more caution—the prices quoted here are those *in effect as of the time of writing* and, like everything else these days, subject to change. However, even with inevitable changes, you can expect the categories to remain the same, i.e., "moderate" will remain moderate even if at a slightly higher level.

Since I am personally convinced that the only place to stay is in the French Quarter—the very heart and soul of New Orleans —I'm listing accommodations there first. But if circumstances make another location more desirable for you, you'll find outside-the-Quarter listings in the next chapter. All rates quoted are for double occupancy.

Special Note: You will almost always be asked to guarantee your reservation either by a deposit or credit-card charge, no matter what type of accommodation you decide on. Also, rates frequently jump more than a notch or two for Sugar Bowl week, Mardi Gras, and other festival times, and in some cases there's a four- or five-night minimum requirement.

Hotels

THE UPPER BRACKET: Unique among New Orleans's luxury hotels is the small, European-style **Hotel Maison de Ville**, 727 Rue Toulouse (tel. 504/561-5858). Dating back prior to 1742 (it appears on every early map of New Orleans), the Maison was restored several years ago to an elegance created by marble fireplaces, fine French antiques, gilt-framed mirrors, rich swagged drapes, and matching quilted bedspreads. Guest rooms surround a brick courtyard (one of the loveliest in the Quarter) with a tiered fountain and palm trees. It was here, working on one of the wrought-iron tables, that Tennessee Williams reworked *A Streetcar Named Desire* while staying in one of the converted slave quarters. Another famous tenant, John Audubon, lived in one of the seven cottages now operated by the Maison while painting the Louisiana portion of his *Birds of America*. The cottages, with brick walls, beamed ceilings, and slate or brick floors, are furnished with antiques and reflect a warm country elegance. The Maison's very personal service includes a breakfast of fresh orange juice, croissants or brioche, and steaming chicory coffee served on a silver tray in your room, in the parlor, or on the patio. Complimentary sherry and port are served in the afternoon and evening, morning and evening newspapers are delivered to your room, and that almost-vanished shoe-polishing service is available (just leave them outside your door at night and notify the desk). Double-room rates run from $95 to $135, and cottages are $275 for one bedroom, $375 for two bedrooms.

Another very special small hotel right in the heart of the Quarter is the **St. Louis**, 730 Rue Bienville (tel. 504/581-7300). Sophisticated elegance reminiscent of Parisian luxury hotels is the keynote here, and there's even a concierge on hand to render very specialized service. Built around a lovely courtyard which is centered by a marble fountain, the St. Louis is done in true French decor, with antique furniture, elegant crystal chandeliers, and gilt-framed original oil paintings. Some rooms have private balconies overlooking the courtyard, and suites have *private* courtyards. Doubles run from $130 to $160 with suites starting at $195. Children under 12 stay free in their parents' room.

The **Royal Sonesta**, 300 Bourbon St. (tel. toll free 800/343-7170; or 504/586-0300), is adorned with those lacy New Orleans balconies. Its 500 rooms are furnished with elegant period pieces, and many overlook inner patios or the pool. There's a restaurant named Begue's which carries on the tradition of an older New Orleans eating spot of the same name, and the Greenhouse, an indoor-outdoor café, features soups, salads, crêpes, and Créole specialties. This is an ideal French Quater location—within walking distance to almost everything. Doubles are $95 to $170, and there are money-saving vacation plans available from time to time.

Considered by many veteran New Orleans visitors as "the" place to stay (and certainly one of the most beautiful French Quater hotels), the **Royal Orleans,** 621 St. Louis St. (tel. 504/529-5333), is very, very elegant. That is as it should be, for the present-day hotel opened its doors in 1960 on the site of the 1836 St. Louis Exchange Hotel, one of this country's most elegant hostelries of that era. The St. Louis Exchange (whose rates in 1842 were an astounding $2.50 per day!) was a center of New Orleans social life until the final years of the Civil War, when it became a hospital for wounded from both the North and the South, served for a time as the state capitol building and meeting place of the carpetbagger legislature, and was finally destroyed by a 1915 hurricane. In its heyday of gala soirees and grandee visitors, it was also the innovator of the "free lunch" for noontime drinkers, creating a tradition of top-notch cuisine that survives even today. The Royal Orleans has proved a worthy successor, with a lobby of shiny marble, gleaming brass, and sparkling crystal chandeliers. Furnishings are truly sumptuous in the guest rooms, and there are extra touches such as a "goodnight mint" and beds turned down at night. The classic, gourmet Rib Room is a favorite dining spot for many natives (see Chapter V), and there's informal dining in the Café Royale's beautiful garden setting, soft music after 8 p.m. in the Esplanade Lounge (just right for the evening's last drink, no matter where you stay). Doubles are in the $130 to $175 range, and there are several attractive package specials available.

Take seven crumbling mansions on a historic French Quarter site, rebuild with bricks that date back to the founding of New Orleans, construct 225 guest rooms and furnish them with country French provincial, add a year-round, heated swimming pool in the center of a tropical courtyard, and you come up with the **Maison Dupuy,** 1001 Rue Toulouse (tel. toll free 800/535-9177; or 504/586-8000). Just a short walk from Bourbon Street, the Central Business District, and many of the city's best restaurants, the hotel is the ultimate in comfort and near-elegance, with one of the friendliest and most accommodating staffs in the Quarter. There's live entertainment in the Cabaret Lautrec, where walls are decorated with life-size Toulouse-Lautrec murals, and fine Cajun eating in the beautiful LeBon Créole restaurant. All guest rooms have either two double beds or a large king-size bed, and many courtyard rooms have private balconies. Exterior rooms overlook Toulouse or Burgundy Streets. There's a heated pool, and delightful thought, you can have breakfast, lunch, or dinner in the "Fountain of the Arts" Courtyard. Doubles go for $110 to $160, suites for $170 to $800. The Maison Dupuy also offers some of the most attractive package deals in the French Quarter, especially during Mardi Gras and other festival times.

MODERATE: The "Grand Old Lady" of French Quarter hotels is its largest and has been family operated by three generations of Monteleones. Covering almost an entire block, the 600-room **Monteleone Hotel,** 214 Royal St. (tel. toll free 800-535-9575; or 504/523-3341), seems to keep growing and expanding over the years without losing a trace of the charm that has been a trademark since its beginning. Room decors cover the spectrum, from luxurious, antique-filled suites to more modern, very comfortable family rooms. The trellis-trimmed, green and white Le Café restaurant is a favorite with native New Orleanians, and the Carousel Bar, which slowly revolves under its red-and-white-striped canopy, also draws the locals. Up on top, the fabulous Sky Terrace has to be seen to be believed; there's a heated swimming pool, a putting green, the 9-to-5 Bar, and the exquisitely elegant Sky-lite Lounge, really a rooftop club which features top-notch live entertainment such as the famous "Dukes of Dixieland." Rates for a double room run from $95 to $140. Ask about their attractive package deals, which in 1984 ran as low as $215 per person for four days and three nights, plus several extras.

The lovely **Place d'Armes Hotel,** 625 St. Ann St. (tel. 504/524-4531), has one of the most magnificent courtyards in the Quarter, as well as the largest swimming pool. Rooms are homey, many of them wallpapered, and all are furnished in traditional style. Be sure you ask, however, for a room with a window when you reserve—there are some interior rooms without them (not all that bad, but still, a window is better). There's a Parisian-style coffeehouse which serves a complimentary continental breakfast for guests and lunch at moderate prices, and the location, just off Jackson Square, makes sightseeing a breeze. Guest rooms start at $85 double occupancy, and run to $115.

A continental breakfast is served in your room at the **Prince Conti Hotel,** 830 Rue Conti (tel. toll free 800/535-7908; or 504/529-4172), and there's free valet parking. But the nicest things here are the friendly, helpful staff and the comfortable guest rooms, many furnished with antiques and period reproductions. Prince Armand de Conti, the French nobleman who helped back Bienville's expedition to found New Orleans, would be proud of his namesake, with its small lobby beautifully furnished in the French château fashion and delicate iron grillwork lining second-story rooms. Doubles will cost anywhere from $70 to $150.

Many rooms at the **Marie Antoinette,** 827 Rue Toulouse (tel. toll free 800/535-9111; or 504/525-2300), have private balconies overlooking the courtyard garden and pool. All are tastefully furnished with traditional pieces (although not antiques). This is the home of the stately Louis XVI French Restaurant (see "Dining in the French Quarter," Chapter V). Double-room rates run from $85 to $140.

The **Hotel Villa Convento,** 616 Ursulines St. (tel. 504/522-1793), is really a small inn and in many respects resembles a guesthouse because of the personal touch of its owner/operators, the Campo family. The building is a restored Créole town house, and its 24 rooms have been luxuriously furnished. Some open to the tropical patio, some to the street; many have balconies; and the lovely "loft" rooms are unique. A continental breakfast is served just off the lobby in a small, cheerful breakfast room or on the patio. Tropical plants and a three-tiered fountain are focal points of that patio. Doubles run from $65 to $85, suites begin at $100, and children under 15 stay free in the same room with their parents.

Motels

THE UPPER BRACKET: A friend urged me to inspect the **Château LeMoyne French Quarter,** 301 Dauphine St. (tel. 504/581-1303), saying "it's not like any Holiday Inn you've ever seen." She was right—although it is, in fact, a member of that chain, it is so distinctly French Quarter you'd never, ever associate it with any of those highway stopover hostelries. Housed in buildings over a century old, with arched colonnades and winding staircases, the place exudes character and charm. Patios and converted slave quarter suites add to the Old New Orleans flavor, and bedrooms are furnished in a comfortable traditional style. There's a restaurant on the premises and free off-street parking. If you plan to do much sightseeing or business outside the French Quarter, the Château LeMoyne's location is ideal—only minutes away from the Central Business District and the trolley that takes you to the Garden District. And, of course, anything in the Quarter is within easy walking distance. Double rooms here cost from $85 to $125.

The **Landmark Inn Bourbon Street**, 541 Bourbon St. (tel. 504/524-7611), sits on the site of the 1859 French Opera House, the first ever built in the U.S., which burned to the ground in 1919. It's hard to tell, however, that the present building hasn't been here for just that many years, so well have the planners integrated its design into New Orleans traditional architecture. All rooms have a Deep South decor and oversize double beds, and some have balconies overlooking Bourbon Street. Both the lounge and Le Market (a restaurant specializing in "the freshest food in the world") are open 24 hours a day. Prices hinge on whether or not your room faces Bourbon Street or has a balcony. Doubles without same begin at $85; those with, at $120.

Right in the heart of the Quarter is the **Hotel de la Poste**, 316 Chartres St. (tel. 504/581-1200). Its 100 rooms are spacious and comfortable, and most overlook either the Grande Patio and pool or face onto one of the more interesting French Quarter streets. The courtyard, incidentally, has a magnificent staircase leading up to a second-level outdoor patio. Parking is free, there's a babysitting service, and children under 12 stay free in the same room with their parents. Double-occupancy rooms begin at $95; location, accommodations, and service all qualify as deluxe.

There's a sort of casual elegance at the **Dauphine Orleans**, 415 Dauphine St. (tel. toll free 800/238-6161; or 504/586-1800). All 100 rooms are nicely furnished with modern or period pieces (some have king- or queen-size beds) and wrought-iron balconies overlook the patio and pool or Dauphine Street. Suites are housed in two separate, completely restored historic buildings with private patios. There's a complimentary continental breakfast, free in-room movies, and the morning paper delivered to your door. Double rooms run from $95 to $125.

Just two blocks from Jackson Square, the **Best Western French Market Inn**, 501 Decatur St. (tel. toll free 800/528-1234;

or 504/561-5621), is a historic building which has been lovingly restored to its former old-world beauty. Rooms have individual charm, with 18th-century European country-style furnishings. Some have exposed brick walls and cypress beams, and each has a view of the lush tropical patio or French Quarter streets. There's complimentary coffee and the morning newspaper. Rates for doubles range from $90 to $110.

MODERATE: Another restoration is the **Le Richelieu Motor Hotel**, 1234 Chartres St. (tel. 504/529-2492), which is housed in what was once a row mansion and a macaroni factory. They're proudest here of their VIP suite, which has three bedrooms, a super kitchen, and even a steamroom (and rents for a whopping $300 a night!) but the "ordinary" guest rooms I saw were all exceptionally nice and much less expensive (doubles are $75 to $95). There's a pool in the large courtyard and lunch service poolside. Most rooms have balconies and all overlook either the French Quarter or the courtyard. Le Richelieu is the only French motel with a free self-park on the premises—you keep your car keys, so there's no wait for an attendant to bring your car.

There are no fewer than five patios—and each a jewel—at the family-owned **Provincial Motor Hotel**, 1024 Chartres St. (tel. 504/581-4995). Rooms in the 1830s building are high-ceilinged, and each is decorated in a distinct style with imported French and authentic Créole antiques. My own favorite holds a huge carved mahogany double bed with a high overhanging canopy topped by a carved tiara. Gaslights on the patios and the overall feeling of graciousness make this one a real delight, a tranquil refuge from the rigors of sightseeing or nighttime revelry. The pleasant restaurant serves breakfast and lunch at moderate prices. Rates for double occupancy rooms range from $65 to $100, and bargain package rates are available during summer months.

Not much elegance, but a good deal of charm and just plain comfort at the **Château Motor Hotel**, 1001 Chartres St. (tel. 504/524-9636), one of the best buys in town pricewise. Its flagstone-paved courtyard is bordered by an awning-covered café, where breakfast and lunch are served outdoors. There are a few four-poster beds, as well as bed-living room combinations. Parking is free. Doubles run from $60 to $80.

FRENCH QUARTER HOTELS 27
Guest Houses

My personal "home" is with Mrs. Junius Underwood at the **French Quarter Maisonnettes**, 1130 Chartres St. (tel. 504/524-9918). It would be my choice because of Mrs. Underwood's gracious personality and dedication to the welfare and happiness of her guests, if for no other reason. There are, however, many other attractions. The Maisonnettes are in an 1825 mansion entered through a lovely iron gateway leading to the arched carriage drive and flagstone courtyard in the rear. A wrought-iron balcony rings the second story, overlooking that courtyard and its three-tiered, 17th-century French cast-iron fountain, tropical plants, and vines. Guest units on the ground floor open through wide French doors onto the courtyard or carriage drive, and second-floor rooms overlook the courtyard. All have modern, very comfortable furnishings, and Jesse, who is a delightful part of your stay here, keeps them impeccably clean (he's also always on hand to lend cheerful assistance with luggage). Each has a private bath, air conditioning and heat (individually controlled), and the morning newspaper delivered to your door every morning. The location is a sightseer's dream—across the street is the historic Beauregard House, next door is the Ursuline Convent built in 1734 and said to be the oldest building in the Mississippi Valley, and just a few blocks away is the old French Market, so handy for coffee and beignets to begin or end the day. Best of all, there's Mrs. Underwood, whose thoughtfulness extends to furnishing a privately printed brochure of tips on dining, sightseeing, shopping, and almost anything else to make your visit more entertaining and comfortable, all gleaned from her intimate, longtime association with New Orleans. Children over 12 are welcomed, as are "well-behaved" pets. Rates of $38 to $48 make this one of the best bargains in New Orleans, and it is very, very popular, making advance booking an absolute must. There's private parking at an additional charge.

At **623 Ursulines St.** (tel. 504/529-5489), Jim Weirich and his partner, Don Heil, have created five suites in old slave quarters, leaving some in near-original state, and making all thoroughly modern as far as comfort goes. Each has a living room, bedroom, and private bath, and opens onto a courtyard that holds azaleas, towering crape myrtle trees, and magnolias. Three suites of comparable size are in the main house, and rates range from $46 to $48. A decided plus here is the warm hospitality—Jim and Don know New Orleans intimately and are a gold mine of tips on how to make your stay more fun. Jim and Don don't give their guest house a name, but simply use the street number. If you plan to visit New Orleans and are a guest house devotee, I heartily recommend that you call in advance for reservations—this is a very popular spot. Garage parking is available at an additional charge.

If you think a Bourbon Street address automatically means a noisy, honky-tonk environment, think again. The **Lafitte Guest House**, 1003 Bourbon St. (tel. 504/581-2678), is far enough down to be in a quiet, pleasant residential neighborhood, yet close enough to walk anywhere in the Quarter. The three-story brick building, with its typical New Orleans wrought-iron balconies on the second and third floors, was constructed in 1849 and restored in the last few years. There are marble fireplaces, exposed brick walls, and 14-foot-high ceilings, and 13 of the guest rooms are furnished with a blend of modern upholstered pieces and massive Victorian antiques. The 14th, on the top floor, is huge, with four dormer windows affording a splendid French Quarter view and modern furnishings. All guest rooms have telephones (unusual for most guest houses), and there's a continental breakfast of fresh juice, croissants, jam and butter, and coffee or tea, all included in the room rate. Doubles here run $78 to $125, and there's a charge of $10 for each extra person in a room. There's no charge, however, for the friendly hospitality dispensed by Steve Guyton, the personable owner/manager.

Not far from Jackson Square, you'll find the **Maison Chartres**, 508 Rue Chartres (tel. toll free 800/475-2386; or 504/529-2172), in a building constructed in 1835 to house the Pacific Concert Saloon. The original flagstone flooring and slave-made bricks (the same as those in the Pontalba Apartments) were carefully preserved during renovation in recent years. The 16 rooms are somewhat small, but beautifully furnished in French decor, and most have balconies which look out over Chartres Street or over the small, lushly planted patio centered by a beautiful little pool. You can have the complimentary continental breakfast out on the patio or in your room while reading the morning newspaper that's been delivered to your door. Another extra is the shoe-shining service—just place your shoes outside the door when you retire at night. Rates run from $85 to $105 for double-occupancy rooms.

A FRENCH QUARTER HOSTEL: One of the best accommodation buys in the French Quarter is to be found at **L'Auberge Hostel**

and Guest House, 717 Barracks St. (tel. 504/523-1130). And don't be misled by the name "hostel"—L'Auberge just misses being a full-fledged guest house. This is a "double shotgun" Créole house which is Nancy Saucier's home. She lives in one side and accommodates eight guests in the other five bedrooms. There's a fully equipped kitchen for the use of guests and a bath which everyone shares. The rooms are furnished with antiques, and there's a patio sometimes used for cookouts. Nancy also has bicycles for hire—a lovely way to see the French Quarter. She doesn't take reservations, but if readers of this book will telephone a day in advance of arrival and mention the book by name, she will hold space if it's available. There is a two-night minimum stay (three during July and August), and the rate is $25 per person per night. Not your usual hostel, but a genuine travel bargain!

Chapter IV

WHERE TO STAY OUTSIDE THE QUARTER

THERE ARE MANY CONSIDERATIONS that could lead you to find accommodations outside the French Quarter, and you will find a wide price range of hotels and motels in almost any section, whether you wish to be near the universities, in the Central Business District, or on the outskirts of town. While guest houses are concentrated for the most part in the French Quarter, there's a lovely one on St. Charles Avenue that I'll tell you about.

One thing I should add: with the advent of the 1984 Louisiana World Exposition came a flood of new hotels outside the French Quarter. In fact the bulk of the city's 20,000 hotel rooms are now outside the French Quarter. To their credit, most of the new establishments reflect a distinct New Orleans flavor. However, even with all these additional rooms, there will be times when booking could be a problem—the sooner you reserve, the better.

Hotels

IN THE UPPER BRACKET: The New Orleans Hilton, Poydras Street at the Mississippi River (tel. 504/561-0500), has perhaps integrated itself most successfully into the lifestyle of the city. Located in what some are coming to call the "River Quarter," the Hilton sits right at the riverfront, adjacent to the International Trade Mart, and somehow manages to avoid the sterile impersonality projected by so many large hotels. Maybe it has to do with a decor that makes use of warm colors like tea rose and emerald green, Italian oak and Pomele mahogany paneling, Travertine marble and deep-pile, hand-woven carpeting. The 90-foot, nine-story, multilevel atrium creates a feeling of space, but is so well designed that there is none of that rattle-around boxiness that always makes me a little nervous. While no one could describe it as "cozy," it is broken up into attractive centers like the English Bar, the Café Bromeliad, the French Garden Bar and Oyster Bar, Le Croissant Coffee Shoppe, and the elegant Winston's. There are in fact ten restaurants and lounges within the 1600-room complex (see "Dining Outside the Quarter," Chapter VI). You will know without doubt that the Hilton has won New Orleans's approval when you learn that Pete Fountain moved his jazz club from the Quarter to a third-floor replica here! There's also a swinging dance club, the Rainforest, on the 29th floor, with glass walls, gnarled cypress trees and lush greenery (as well as a simulated "rainstorm"), that serves a very nice weekday luncheon.

Guest rooms are, of course, the primary concern of travelers, and those at the New Orleans Hilton are spacious, most have fabulous views of the river or the city, and all are furnished in a country French manner, using muted colors and French treatment draperies keyed to the etched toile of wall coverings. Light-softening sheer glass curtains let you take full advantage of those gorgeous views. The epitome of luxury is to be found on the 25th, 26th, and 27th tower floors, which hold 132 guest rooms, including 13 sumptuous suites, and boast a bevy of "concierge" ladies ready to take care of the nitty-gritty details of your stay, as well as a private club and honor bar. The newest Hilton addition is its 456-room, low-rise Riverside complex perched right on the edge of the Mississippi. There are six luxurious suites and eight courtyards with fountains and lush tropical foliage, open to the river.

In short, just in case you haven't already guessed, the Hilton is my personal choice if you must stay outside the French Quarter. Rates range from $118 to $160 for doubles, with suites running $270 to $480, and guests are eligible for membership in the Hilton's tennis club, which includes the use of a gym, saunas, whirlpools, and a jogging track.

"Elegant" is the word for the **Pontchartrain Hotel**, 2031 St. Charles Ave. (tel. 504/524-0581), located in the Garden District. Rooms are beautifully furnished, many with mini-bars, and the service will make you feel like a pampered favorite within minutes of your arrival (i.e., you'll find your bed turned down and bedclothes laid out at night). Everything in this 52-year-old New Orleans institution is in the continental tradition at its finest, and the gourmet cuisine of the Caribbean Room (see "Dining Outside the Quarter," Chapter VI) is internationally known. Double room rates are in the $100 to $145 range.

New Orleanians remember it as the Roosevelt, and today's **Fairmont Hotel,** on University Place (tel. toll free 800/527-4727; or 504/529-7111), upholds the tradition of elegance left by its predecessor. There's the feel of luxury from the moment you enter the lobby, with its deep carpeting, dark-red velvet chairs and sofas, magnificent chandeliers, and impressive oil paintings. Rooms are spacious, with marvelous high ceilings and such extras as Irish linen hand towels, an electric shoe buffer, and evening maid service. On the rooftop recreation area there's a swimming pool, two tennis courts, and a cozy bar that serves beverages and sandwiches. For more elegant recreation, there's the Blue Room, which has been presenting top-name entertainers for as long as I can remember. (Remember those old radio broadcasts "from the Blue Room of the Hotel Roosevelt in downtown New Orleans"?) I'm happy to report that although it is as spiffy as if just done up today, that lovely, very elegant decor of blue and gold and French period furnishings hasn't changed since the days of my visits years ago. An addition since those days, however, is Bailey's, a casual, 24-hour Irish bar which serves light foods and drinks. In short, the Fairmont is a "grand hotel" in the old manner which offers midtown convenience as a bonus. Double rooms range from $110 to $150.

Of the newer hotels, one of the loveliest is the high-rise **Windsor Court,** 300 Gravier St. (tel. 504/523-6000). Centrally located between Poydras and Canal Streets, the hotel has some 330 accommodations, of which 280 are deluxe suites that go for amazingly moderate prices. A nice touch is the English tea served in a pretty lobby lounge, and corridors are mini-galleries displaying works of art. Italian marble and antique furnishings distinguish the two lobbies. The Windsor Court Bar is a clubby sort of gathering place, and the restaurant overlooks the courtyard. Among guest facilities are a health club sporting a resort-size pool, sauna, and steamroom. Numerous conveniences are available for business travelers, who might well want to conduct business conferences in the privacy of their own suite or in especially planned meeting spaces.

As for those suites, each features its own individual decor, large bay windows looking out over the river or the city, private foyer, large living room, bedroom entered through french doors, marble baths, separate his-and-her dressing rooms, a "petite kitchen," and a wet bar. They, as well as the guest rooms (all of

HOTELS OUTSIDE THE FRENCH QUARTER 33

which come with a wet bar), are exceptionally spacious and beautifully furnished. All this at rates of $135 for guest rooms, $160 to $180 for suites. This one is truly a standout.

The **Hotel Inter-Continental**, 444 St. Charles Ave. (tel. toll free 800/327-0200; or 504/525-5566), rises in red granite splendor within walking distance of Canal Street shopping and the central business and financial district. Its 500 deluxe rooms and suites feature separate conversation seating, dressing areas, mini-fridges and bars, built-in hair dryers, and even safes. Furnishings in guest rooms as well as public areas are a nice blend of classic and contemporary styling, and the large marble lobby holds a lounge serving afternoon tea as well as drinks. Gourmet meals are served in Les Continents Restaurant, and Pete's Pub combines rich paneling with art deco touches. Other facilities include a health club, pool, and several services for business travelers. Rates are in the $130 to $170 range for doubles, and $285 to $775 for suites.

MODERATE: Out on St. Charles Avenue, the **St. Charles Hotel**, 2203 St. Charles Ave. (tel. 504/529-4261), is a small, homey place to stay, and the trolley makes it accessible to the Garden District, the Central Business District, and Canal Street. Rooms are pretty standard, but comfortable, and the staff here is especially friendly and helpful. Doubles run from $70 to $90.

A little farther out the avenue, the **St. Charles Inn**, 3636 St. Charles Ave. (tel. 504/899-8888), is only five minutes away from Tulane and Loyola Universities and ten minutes from the French Quarter or Superdome via the trolley. All rooms have either two double or king-size beds. There's a lounge and restaurant, and extras include a complimentary continental breakfast served in your room and the morning newspaper. Doubles start at $65.

The gracious mahogany-paneled drawing room (complete with comfortable sofas and chairs, and a large fireplace) of the **Avenue Plaza Hotel**, 2111 St. Charles Ave. (tel. toll free 800/535-9575; or 504/566-1212), sets the tone at this small hotel that was once an apartment building. All 100 rooms are nicely furnished and have a wet bar, coffee maker, and fridge. There are excellent health club facilities, a courtyard swimming pool, rooftop sun deck, and a lovely, window-lined dining room overlooking St. Charles Avenue. Doubles run $95 to $160, and suites from $225 to $425.

It's hard to know whether to label the **Prytania Park**, 1525

34 ARTHUR FROMMER'S NEW ORLEANS

Prytania St. (tel. 504/524-0427), a hotel or a guest house. The first of several adjoining old New Orleans residences opened with a dozen beautifully restored and nicely furnished guest rooms, both in the main house and attached slave quarter wing, and the Prytania Park operated for nearly two years on a guest-house basis. But as the attractive, enthusiastic owner, Mrs. Theone Halpern, took on more renovations and opened 50 additional guest rooms, it has become a charming small hotel run with the same personal attention as a guest house. My personal preference is for those rooms in the original restoration, some of which open onto the narrow coutryard while others overlook Prytania Street. There's no quarrel, however, with the latest additions, many of which have microwave ovens and fridges that may be used for in-room snacking with the blessings of the management. Connecting courtyards join the two sections, and the New Orleans flavor has been carefully preserved throughout. Although the area is presently in the throes of urban renewal, it presents an interesting mix of historic buildings badly in need of repair alongside those such as the Prytania Park that have been taken in hand by the likes of the Halperns. St. Charles Avenue is only a block away, making streetcar transportation an added convenience. There's also off-street parking, a decided plus for drivers. Rates for doubles range from $40 to $60, with family suites running from $75 to $110 (as with most New Orleans accommodations, rates increase during special events).

You'll find convenience and comfort at budget prices at the **Hotel LaSalle,** 1113 canal St. (tel. toll free 800/521-9450; or 504/523-5831). No frills here, but plainly furnished, clean, and comfortable rooms that come with or without private baths. There's an old-fashioned air to the small lobby with its high ceilings, overhead fans, carved Austrian wall clock, and an old-time wooden reception desk. Free coffee is always available in the lobby, and a continental breakfast can be served in your room for a small additional charge. Roland and Pat Bohan own and operate the LaSalle, and have been known to arrange such extras as practice rooms for out-of-town musicians come to audition for the New Orleans Symphony. This is a favorite with European visitors who appreciate bathroom-down-the-hall savings, as well as with jazz musicians just arriving in the city. Doubles run from $44 to $46 with private bath, $30 to $33 without.

Motels

MODERATE: For motel convenience and comfort, you simply cannot beat the **Days Inn Canal Street**, 1630 Canal St. (tel. toll free 800/325-2525; or 504/586-0110). The French Quarter is only eight blocks away, Poydras Plaza shopping mall only one block, and the Rivergate convention center also one block. The motel's 216 comfortably furnished and nicely decorated rooms all have double beds and the spaciousness typical of this dependable chain. There's a pool with cabana, same-day dry-cleaning service, and a good restaurant. Double rooms range seasonally from $55.88 to $68.88. *Special Note:* If you're 55 or older, be sure to look into Days Inn's September Club membership, which offers discount room rates and airfare discounts of 25% to 40% with Delta Airlines.

The **Quality Inn Midtown**, 3900 Tulane Ave. (tel. toll free 800/228-5151; or 504/486-5541), is not quite so centrally located, but is still only about five minutes from the Central Business District. All rooms have balconies, many facing the courtyard and swimming pool, are spacious, and have double beds. Doubles are in the $65 to $155 range.

The 17-story **Downtown Howard Johnson's**, 330 Loyola Ave. (tel. toll free 800/535-7830; or 504/581-1600), is centrally located, with easy access to New Orleans's business and financial centers, as well as the Superdome and French Quarter. Each of the 300 rooms has a balcony and city view. Guest rooms are large enough for a "sitting room" area, and are furnished with modern, comfortable fittings. The dining room boasts some of the renowned Audubon prints, and there's an "ice cream parlor" which also serves light meals. Rates for double rooms are in the $77 to $85 range.

BUDGET: My favorite budget chain, Day's Inn, has a motel in Slidell, the **Day's Inn-New Orleans East Motel**, 1645 Gause Blvd., Slidell (tel. toll free 800/325-2525; or 504/641-3450). In my travels around the Southeast, I've learned to rely on this chain for accommodations that go beyond mere comfort (i.e., each room has two double beds, the rooms are spacious, the decor is usually pleasing; there's usually a restaurant, swimming pool, and play area for the kids; etc.), and this one is no exception. The Tasty World restaurant is here, as well as an outdoor pool. Doubles here cost $38.88, and if you plan to stay on the outskirts of town, this one has my heartiest recommendation.

Guest Houses

If you're in New Orleans to visit Tulane, Loyola, or Dominican Universities, you'll want to know about this ideally located guest house.

On the far edge of Audubon Park, the **Parkview Guest House,** 7004 St. Charles Ave. (tel. 504/861-7564), is a rambling old Victorian structure built in 1884 as a hotel for the Cotton Exposition. It has been in the National Register of Historic Places since 1981. There's a feeling of another era from the minute you enter the wide central hall with its gleaming crystal chandeliers through a front door that sparkles with etched-glass panels. A lovely old stained-glass window is the focal point of the large lounge, with its comfortable sofas and chairs, and all the rooms are furnished in antiques. I immediately fell in love with the room on the first floor just to the right of the front door—it has floor-length windows and a carved walnut bed and dresser that made a strong appeal to the romantic in my soul. Other rooms are not as elegant as the three on the first floor, although all reflect an old-fashioned comfort that's hard to resist. Some have balconies. There's a large dining room, with windows overlooking the park, where a complimentary continental breakfast is served daily—a pleasant way to start the day. All guests have the use of a refrigerator and ice machine anytime. Most of the 25 rooms have private baths, although three have baths connecting with another room, and there's individually controlled heat and air conditioning in all. Double rooms go for $55 to $70. At this time they don't allow pets, but this policy may be relaxed and it wouldn't hurt to check when you book.

Campgrounds

If you arrive in New Orleans in your own recreational vehicle, you'll have no trouble finding a campground—there are several excellent facilities with easy access to the city.

The **Riverboat Travel Park,** 6232 Chef Menteur Hwy. (that's U.S. 90; tel. 504/246-2628), is located in the southwest cloverleaf of the I-10 and U.S. 90 intersection. It has full hookups, a heated swimming pool, game room, and laundry and shower facilities. There is transportation to and from the French Quarter, as well as tours (for a fee) of the city, nightclubs, and harbor (aboard

HOTELS OUTSIDE THE FRENCH QUARTER

riverboats) which leave from the park daily. Rates are $17 for two, $4 for each additional person.

Three-quarters of a mile east of the I-10 and U.S. 90 junction, you'll find the **New Orleans Travel Park**, 7323 Chef Menteur Hwy. (tel. toll free 800/535-8632; or 504/242-7795). Most of the 150 sites are shaded, and there are full hookups, two swimming pools (one just for the kids), a game room, laundry, and showers. There's bus service to the French Quarter, downtown New Orleans, and the riverfront. Tours of the city and Superdome leave three times daily (stay three days and you get one free!), and there's a pickup for riverboat tours. You'll pay $17 for two, $4 for each extra person.

One of the newest travel parks is **Parc d'Orléans I**, 7676 Chef Menteur Hwy. (U.S. 90; tel. 504/241-3167). It's just one mile east of the I-10 exit from U.S. 90 and only seven minutes' driving time from the French Quarter. The park has paved streets, showers, full hookups, and parking for motor homes, travel trailers, campers, and tents. Picnic tables dot the grounds and there's a swimming pool. City bus service reaches the park, but free transportation is provided to and from the French Quarter. Rates are $16 for two, $4 for each additional person.

There are two KOA campgrounds, one on each side of town. The **KOA New Orleans West**, 11129 Jefferson Hwy. (La. 48; tel. 504/467-1792), is the closest campground to the west of the city and welcomes tenters as well as vehicles, for which there are full hookups. The lounge provides games, and you can swim in the pool, as well as buy provisions in the on-site store. City and boat tours are available, and if you want to "do" the French Quarter on your own, there's city transportation to and from. The **KOA New Orleans East**, Rte. 16, Box 100 E. Slidell (tel. 504/643-3850), is a half mile east of I-10 on La. 433. Full hookups here, too, in a country setting that includes two pools, a recreation room, and miniature golf. Riverboat and city tours are available. Rates at both campgrounds are $17 for two, $4 for each additional person.

Chapter V

DINING IN THE FRENCH QUARTER

IF NEW ORLEANS'S POPULATION is an exciting "stew" of nationalities and cultures, her cuisine is a rich, tasty "gumbo" of French provincial, Spanish, Italian, West Indian, African, and American Indian cooking flavored with a liberal dash of full-fledged southern. Those who return time after time do so as much for her food as for jazz, the Mardi Gras, or sightseeing. Indeed, dining out in New Orleans rightly falls under the heading of entertainment.

Provincial French recipes brought to the New World by early settlers fast acquired a subtle change with the use of native herbs and filé (ground sassafras leaves) from native Indians. Saffron and peppers arrived somewhat later along with the Spanish. From the West Indies came new vegetables, spices, and sugarcane, and when slave boats arrived, landing many a black woman in a white kitchen, an African influence was added. Out of all this came the distinctive "créole" culinary style unique to New Orleans. Italian touches later on added yet another dimension to the city's tables, and through it all, traditional Old South dishes were retained virtually intact.

As a rule of thumb (but remember, rules are made to have exceptions!), when it comes to New Orleans food, "créole" means hot and "Cajun" will be spicy. But both can mean hot *and* spicy. Spices much loved here are onions (both green and regular), bay leaf, thyme, parsley, cloves, allspice, cayenne pepper, filé, and Tabasco (a red-hot sauce made of red peppers fermented in brine and vinegar). There is a whole family of sausages: boudin (boo-dan) contains onions, spices, pork, and rice, and comes in white or red; chaurice (cho-reece) is a hard sausage used chiefly for flavoring beans or soups; andouille (ahn-dwe-ye) is also hard and a bit saltier than chaurice; and delicious smoked sausages. Seafood is everywhere—in fact, I find it next to impossible to order anything else when I'm in town. Oysters on the half shell (usually simply called "raw oysters" in New Orleans) are just the beginning of an oyster feast that includes soups, stews, pies, baked specialties like oysters Rockefeller (on the half shell in a creamy sauce and spinach—so named because that was the only name rich enough for the taste), an oyster loaf (which elevates "sandwich" into the realm of a delicacy), and a host of other creations. Crabs, shrimp, and crayfish are used in imaginative recipes or served plain, hot or cold. "Gumbo" is a thick soup, always served with rice, usually containing crab, shrimp (sometimes oysters), and okra in a tomato base. Jambalaya is made with meat and seafood combined with rice and seasonings. Beef and veal (you may see either on a menu as "daube," pronounced "dohb") take on added luster in New Orleans restaurants, as do classic French and Italian dishes. There's also a special quality to the French bread baked here, with its crisp, flaky crust and its insides as light as a feather. Two mainstays of any native's diet are red beans and rice (don't knock it, try it!) and "po-boy" sandwiches (they once cost a nickle, are made with a long, skinny bread loaf, and can contain anything from roast beef and gravy to ham and cheese to fried fish, shrimp, soft-shell crabs, or oysters, in which case they become an "oyster loaf").

And never let it be said that New Orleanians neglect the libations that precede, accompany, and follow a proper meal! As a matter of fact, they lay claim to adding the word "cocktail" to our modern vocabulary (that came about when a Monsieur Peychaud, who presided over the bar at 437 Rue Royale, took to serving small drinks in egg cups—"coquetiers" in French—and Americans took to ordering them by a mangled version of the word). Since then, more than a few inspired concoctions have appeared on the scene, among them the Sazerac (bourbon or rye with bitters), the Ramos gin fizz (gin, egg whites, and orange flower water), and the Hurricane (rum and passionfruit punch). If you're a cocktail drinker, take my advice and try the local fare—martinis you can drink anywhere!

As for coffee, you'll find it strong, hot, and black, with or without chicory (which adds a slightly bitter flavor—it was first used to stretch scarce coffee beans during the War Between the States). It's served straight or "au lait" (mixed half and half with hot milk). And at least once during your stay, do end a meal with café brûlot (cah-fay brew-low), a lovely mixture of coffee, spices,

40 ARTHUR FROMMER'S NEW ORLEANS

and liqueurs served in special cups, with ladle and chafing dish, and flamed at your table.

Restaurants pride themselves on their wine lists. If you are doubtful as to what to order with your entree, not to worry—your waiter will know.

Along with their love of exciting combinations of international cooking, the people of New Orleans have inherited an appreciation for fine service in elegant surroundings as well as a sense of fun that delights in gourmet dishes which appear in the plainest of settings and the plainest of meals (like boiled crayfish or red beans and rice) which show up in the fanciest of eateries. Many New Orleanians eat out at least three times a week, and with their native sense of festivity, they may stretch out an evening to include cocktails at a favorite spot, appetizers (like oysters Rockefeller) at another, the entree at still another, and dessert perhaps in a favorite courtyard setting. And for many, the evening is not complete without a stop by the Café du Monde for café au lait. In other words, dining out is an occasion, no matter how often it occurs. Incidentally, you can follow their example and double the number of restaurants you get to sample during even a short stay! Keep in mind, however, that if your evening's itinerary includes the upper-bracket restaurants, most will require jackets and ties. Another tip for sampling the better spots with an eye to the budget is to plan your main meals at lunch, when prices are lower and menus often identical to those at dinner.

A few last words about New Orleans restaurants: They number in the hundreds; service will almost always be efficient, friendly, and relaxed; and if your budget keeps you out of the most famous, you'll have no trouble at all finding very good samples of New Orleans specialties in less formal (many times, very inexpensive) places that are just as much fun. I might add that no matter how many restaurants I list in this book, you will surely find at least one on your own that is so great you'll wonder how I missed it.

And because it really doesn't fit any "restaurant" category, I'd like to spotlight right up front one of my favorites—the **Café du Monde** in the French Market, an indispensable part of the New Orleans food scene. Across from Jackson Square, and absolutely habit-forming, this delightful spot has been a favorite with New Orleanians for years. There are only four items on the menu—coffee (black or au lait), milk, hot chocolate, and beignets (three to a serving)—and each item costs 60¢. Beignets ("baan-yaas") are square, doughnut-like confections that come hot, crisp, and covered with confectioner's sugar—one order and a cup of café au lait have served as breakfast, lunch, or a light dinner (after one of those "splurge" lunches) for me at one time or another, for the incredible price of $1.20. There's an indoor dining room, but I wouldn't miss sitting outside under the awning to take advantage of that Mississippi River breeze and unexcelled people-watching. Besides your fellow diners, there's all of Jackson Square, with horse carriages lined up across from the café, as well as shoppers headed for the French Market a little farther along Decatur Street. It's open around the clock every day but Christmas, and you'll find many a native as your neighbor if you show up in the dawn or predawn hours.

As in the case of hotel rates, it must be said that restaurant prices quoted here are those *at the time of writing*. In these uncertain times, they will probably differ to some degree by the time you visit New Orleans. The categories, however, should remain the same, i.e., budget will still be budget, even if dollar amounts are a little higher.

The Top Restaurants

Any preferential listing of New Orleans's top restaurants is bound to be subjective, so let's start with my favorite. And there's a bit of history that goes with it. Some 20 or more years ago, when I was a frequent visitor to the city, I always headed straight for **Arnaud's,** 813 Bienville St. (tel. 523-5433), for some of the finest dining to be found anywhere. Housed in historic old buildings dating back to the 1700s, the restaurant was opened in 1918 by "Count" Arnaud Cazenave (the fictitious title was bestowed by locals in recognition of his grand manner and great love of life), and after his death in 1948 the old traditions were carried on for many years by his daughter. Then a decline set in that eventually led to its desertion by even the most loyal of its wide clientele. But in late 1978, an Egyptian-born "newcomer" to the city (he arrived in 1966) fell in love with the old restaurant as he had with the New Orleans girl who became his wife. Archie Casbarian bought Arnaud's and set about a restoration that would have gladdened the old count's heart. The lovely mosaic tile floors were patched and polished; lighting fixtures, dark-wood paneling, original ceiling medallions, and antique ceiling fans were refurbished; the Richelieu bar was restored; a delightful Grill Bar was added; and when wood was stripped from interior columns, beautiful old iron fluted posts were revealed. Flickering gaslights now welcome you into the large dining room where potted palms, beveled-glass windows, and crystal chandeliers recreate the turn-of-the-century air that has always been Arnaud's. There is also an upstairs exhibition room for a marvelous collection of Mardi Gras costumes, another fixture of the restaurant as I remember it.

Best of all, of course, is what has happened in the kitchen and with the dining service itself. The food is once more something to dream of in far-away places, and formally dressed waiters who are as knowledgeable, efficient, and friendly as they are stylish see to your needs at tables laid with classic linen cloths and set with sterling silver, original Arnaud china, fine crystal, and original water decanters. Executive chef Christian Gille has retained old specialties like shrimp Arnaud, trout meunière, and a superb caramel custard, and is constantly creating exciting new dishes. The menu is à la carte, with prices that range from $8.95 to $19. Lunch is served from 11:30 a.m. to 2:30 p.m. Monday through Friday, and dinner hours are 6 to 10 p.m. seven days a week. Le Richelieu Bar is open from 11 a.m. to 3 p.m. and 5:30 p.m. to closing Monday through Friday, 5:30 p.m. to closing on Saturday and Sunday. There's a terrific Sunday Brunch featuring eggs Benedict, eggs Forestier, eggs Mirabeau, omelets in several versions, crêpes, quiche, and other specialties, along with the jazz of Sal Alcorn, Jr.'s Trio. Hours are 10 a.m. to 2:30 p.m., and entree prices range from $12 to $16. If you're dining, reservations are an absolute must (not necessary at the bar)—this has been a favored place to eat, especially during Carnival season, with New Orleanians over the years and I rejoice to report that now it is reclaiming their devotion, which had (like mine) flagged in the recent past.

Chances are that **Antoine's,** 713 St. Louis St. (tel. 581-4422), is high on your list of places you have wanted to visit for at least one meal. The legendary restaurant that has been run by the same family for more than 130 years is indeed a landmark, and it's popular with locals as well as visitors. Most natives prefer the large, dimly lit back dining room, but you may be seated in any one of 14 rooms, where the decor runs the gamut from plainness to grandeur, although all have white tile floors and slowly turning antique ceiling fans. As for the food, choose from such classics as oysters Rockefeller, pompano en papillote, chicken Rochambeau, or filet de boeuf Robespierre en casserole; or settle for something simpler from a menu that lists more than 150 selections (although not all are available at all times). To accompany your choice, there's one of the richest wine cellars in this country. Be sure to bone up on your French before you come, however, for there's not a word of English on the à la carte menu (or resign yourself to asking for help from the waiters, some of whom can be quite condescending about it). I must confess to a tinge of disappointment recently in this fine restaurant, and I think it has to do with those waiters—Antoine's waiters have always been respectfully informal, even when busy, and about the most individualistic you'll find anywhere. Many are from family groups (fathers and sons, sons-in-law, a nephew or uncle or cousin), and in the past all have known their jobs and the food, making it a real pleasure to dine here. Not so with some of the newer personnel. For years, no matter how high the check or how long the wait for a table (even with reservations you'll have about a 30-minute to an hour wait), I left convinced that both time and money had been well spent. Sad to say, it's sometimes a different story these days, and you'll have to decide for yourself if a visit to one of America's most famous eating places is, in itself, compensation for expensive, what may turn out to be less-than-perfect meals, and service that can be indifferent. Prices on the à la carte menu run from $10 to $18 at lunch and $15 to $35 at dinner. Lunch hours are noon to 2 p.m., dinner from 5:30 to 9:30 p.m., and it's closed on Sunday. Do reserve ahead.

Don't worry about reservations at **Galatoire's,** 209 Bourbon St. (tel. 525-2021)—they don't accept them (even the visiting Duke and Duchess of Windsor had to wait in line!). So unless you take a tip from the natives and go to lunch before noon or dinner before 6, you'll line up with everyone else. But, believe me, it's worth the wait. This is another family-run restaurant (since 1905), and one critic describes it as one of the most magical eating experiences in town. With its mirrored walls and gleaming brass fixtures, it is certainly one of the loveliest. And the food—ah, the food! The seafood dishes simply have no match: try trout amandine, trout Marguery, or the perfectly broiled pompano meunière. At lunch, you might opt for oysters en brochette, eggs Sardou, or stuffed eggplant. Any, or all, come to table in a state of perfection. This is a restaurant that draws its charm from a comfortable sense of its age, good unfussy service, and a way with seafood that will leave you beaming. The à la carte menu is the same at lunch and dinner, and hours are 11:30 a.m. to 9 p.m. (from noon on Sunday); it's closed on

Monday and holidays. (*Tip:* If you go on a Sunday afternoon, you'll find yourself in the company of New Orleans family groups who have made Sunday dinner here a ritual for generations.) Prices are in the $10 to $20 range.

One of the greats among New Orleans restaurants is **Brennan's**, 417 Royal St. (tel. 525-9711). It occupies an 1801 building that was once the home of Paul Morphy, international chess champion, and although the restaurant has only been here since 1946, it has from the start won a place in the hearts of residents and visitors alike. The Brennan family seems dedicated to providing fine food, good service, and exceptional atmosphere. The lush tropical patio here has to be seen to be believed, and there's a view of it from any table in the downstairs rooms. "Elegance" is the only word for the interiors, but it is elegance with warmth, not the cold, sterile kind. "Breakfast at Brennan's" has, of course, become internationally famous, and you can breakfast here even in the evening. But if that's what you have in mind, take heed and don't plan another meal that day—you'll want to be able to do justice to the sumptuous dishes listed on a menu that tempts you with items like eggs Hussarde (poached eggs atop Holland rusks, Canadian bacon, and marchand de vin sauce, topped with hollandaise sauce and accompanied by grilled tomato) or pompano Pontchartrain amandine (sauteed in butter with grilled almonds, lump crabmeat, and lemon-butter sauce). Even their omelets are spectacular. You see, this is not your typical bacon-and-eggs breakfast, but breakfast in the old tradition of antebellum days in the Quarter, so if you really want to do it right, order one of their complete breakfast suggestions. A typical one begins with eggs Sardou (poached eggs atop creamed spinach and artichoke bottoms, served with hollandaise sauce), followed by quail in burgundy sauce (served over wild and white rice), and topped off by crêpes Fitzgerald (served with a sauce of crushed strawberries flamed in maraschino) and hot chicory coffee. A marvelous eyeopener to begin the whole thing with is an absinthe Suissesse (a legendary Brennan's drink that has the faint flavor of anisette). Well, you get the idea—this is a very special restaurant serving very special meals. Breakfast and lunch prices will run from about $12 to $22, dinner from $17 to $32, depending on whether your selections come from the table d'hôte or à la carte menu. Brennan's is open every day except Christmas from 8 a.m. to 2:30 p.m. and 6 to 11 p.m., and it's best to reserve ahead.

Reserve ahead also—and as far in advance as possible—at

Broussard's, 819 Conti St. (tel. 581-3866). This venerable old (it's been here 50 years) New Orleans restaurant has recently been redecorated and the three dining rooms vary from opulent elegance in the largest (the Bonaparte Room) to Italian rustic in a smaller room overlooking the courtyard (the Sicilian Room). The third is a delightful French country provincial decor. And you'll find some of the city's best French-Créole cooking in these surroundings. Along with old standbys, you can choose between such innovative dishes as crabmeat and oysters à la Burton (fresh crabmeat en coquille, prepared with cream cheese, green pepper, pimientos, dry mustard, fines herbes, mayonnaise, and served with oysters that have been grilled in stock, their own liquor, cream sauce, and shallots) and trout Conti (fresh filet of speckled trout served with a creamy sauce of butter, lemon, and parsley). The flaming desserts are simply glorious, with absolutely perfect crêpes and perfectly blended fillings (try the crêpe Brulatour, filled with strawberries, pecans, and whipped cream), and the bananas Foster have a marvelous caramelized syrup. Broussard's opens for dinner only every day (5 to 11:30 p.m.), and prices range from $15 to $35, either table d'hôte or à la carte.

Ask almost any New Orleans native for a list of favorite restaurants and chances are that the Royal Orleans Hotel's **Rib Room,** 621 St. Louis St. (tel. 529-5333), will be at or very near the top. It's a pretty room, with arched windows, high ceilings, natural brick, lots of wood, and open rotisserie ovens in the back of the room. As you might guess, specialties are beef, and they've raised its cooking to an art. Roasts are exceptional and served piping hot. Prime ribs rank highest in most patrons' esteem, but there are also filets, sirloins, brochettes, tournedos, and steak au poivre. Veal, lamb, and duckling also appear on the menu, as do trout, crab, oysters, and shrimp. At lunch, a variety of egg dishes and salads are also offered. The Rib Room is open every day for lunch from 11:30 a.m. to 3 p.m. (prices from $7.50 to $15.50) and for dinner from 6 to 11:30 p.m. (prices $17.75 to $22.50). At least one meal at the Rib Room is a *must* for any New Orleans visit!

K-Paul's Louisiana Kitchen, 416 Chartres St. (tel. 524-7394), has, in its short life, become beloved by New Orleanians and a real "find" for tourists. Opened in mid-1979 by Kay Henrichs and Paul Prudhomme (an award-winning Cajun chef who used to run the kitchen at Commander's Palace), the plain, luncheonette-style place serves the kind of Louisiana food you couldn't hope to find unless you managed an invitation from somebody's grandmother! Dishes like chicken and andouille sausage gumbo, crawfish étouffée, blackened redfish (*do* try this!), or—well, the list could go on and on. It does, in fact, go on beyond the menu, so be sure to ask the waitress what else is available unless you're captivated by what's shown. This is another place where waitresses like Sandy add to the pleasure of good eating—the entire staff is friendly and efficient, and there's an air very akin to festivity, even when things get rushed. And prices? Well, they're reasonable. Appetizers run from $3.50 to $8; entrees (which include vegetable, or salad and bread), $14 to $22. Open Monday to Friday from 5:30 to 10 p.m.

The Next Best

Set in the small, stylish Marie Antoinette Hotel, the **Louis XVI**, 829 Toulouse St. (tel. 581-7000), is a fine French restaurant. The two elegantly appointed dining rooms, with fan-lighted windows looking onto the courtyard separating the main part of the hotel from the restaurant, manage to create a "grand European" manner and still retain a feeling of intimacy. Crystal chandeliers and wall sconces bathe diners in a soft, relaxing glow, and everything seems designed to put you in a proper mood for the excellent cuisine.

Russian caviar and burgundy escargots are among the stars of a five-page menu, as are beef Wellington, oysters Bienville, rack of lamb, and delicious creamed soups. Luncheon is served Monday through Friday from 11:30 a.m. to 2:30 p.m., dinner every day of the week from 6:30 to 11:30 p.m. Prices on the à la carte menu range from $10 to $18 for lunch, $20 to $35 for dinner, and reservations are a good idea, although not always necessary.

You can dine à la carte or table d'hôte at the elegant **Andrew Jackson,** 221 Royal St. (tel. 529-2630). This beautiful restaurant across from the Monteleone Hotel is decorated with crystal chandeliers, a life-size wall sculpture of its namesake, and a marble fireplace that once was part of the Paris Opera House. There are two really exquisite dishes here I can heartily recommend: veal Ferdinand VII (veal, crabmeat, and an unusually good béarnaise sauce), and crabmeat Lafitte hollandaise. Other seafood on the menu is usually very good also, as is the entrecôte of chicken Rochambeau Rachel (broiled ham in mushroom and wine sauce topped with tender chicken breasts sauteed in toasted crumbs and enveloped in that great béarnaise sauce—makes me hungry just remembering!). This is true elegance at slightly lower prices than some of the other grand establishments, with a complete meal running about $10 to $15 at lunch (11 a.m. to 2:30 p.m.) and $15 to $25 at dinner (6 to 10:30 p.m., on Sunday 5:30 to 10 p.m.). It's closed on holidays, and I strongly recommend that you make reservations.

Authentic old family Cajun and Créole dishes are featured at **Le Bon Créole**, 1001 Toulouse St. (tel. 586-8008), in the Maison Dupuy Hotel. Everything's fresh, and every dish is prepared to order, always the sign of a good kitchen. In addition to an unbelievable variety of seafood (channel catfish, crayfish, crabmeat, shrimp étouffée, barbecued shrimp, and live Maine lobster), the finest U.S. prime steaks and fresh-cut lamb chops are offered. The dining room itself is lovely, and in good weather you may also dine (or at least have cocktails) in the beautiful courtyard. The menu is table d'hôte, with prices in the $12 and $25 range at dinner, lower for lunch. Hours are 11:30 a.m. to 11 p.m. Breakfast southern style is served from 7 to 10:30 a.m. and there's a delightful brunch on Saturday and Sunday.

One of the loveliest and most atmospheric of French Quarter restaurants is the **Court of Two Sisters**, 613 Royal St. (tel. 522-7261). There are entrances from both Royal and Bourbon Streets into a huge courtyard filled with flowers, fountains, and low-hanging willows, with a wishing well at its center. The building and its grounds were designed by an early French territorial governor of Louisiana to create the atmosphere of his homeland, and the unusual name comes from a Shop of the Two Sisters which was operated here in the late 1800s by two maiden ladies (sisters, of course). You can dine outside amid all that lush planting or in the Créole Patio Room. Créole and French cuisine are specialties. You'll know you've found a friendly establishment from the very first, for a sign just outside the door lists their hours as: "Breakfast 8:30-11 a.m., Brunch 11 a.m.-3 p.m., Dinner 5:30-11 p.m. Visiting and browsing allowed 3:30-5 p.m. Have a nice day." You can accept that invitation to browse and enjoy a cocktail in the courtyard while you're about it. An innovation here that is gaining increasing popularity is the daily Jazz Brunch Buffet (from 9 a.m. to 3 p.m.), which features over 50 dishes (meat, fowl, fish, vegetables, fresh fruits, homemade bread, and pastries) and strolling jazzmen. Reservations are necessary for dinner, where delicacies like shrimp Toulouse, crabmeat Rector, and sirloin tips à la Créole are good bets. Prices begin at $12 and are for a complete meal. (The Jazz Brunch Buffet is $15.)

You may have to look a bit for **Moran's Riverside Restaurant**,

44 French Market Place (tel. 529-1583). It's hidden away on the second floor of the Bazaar Building of the renovated market complex. The site is just opposite the crescent bend of the river, and Moran's makes full use of it by providing an outdoor terrace with a sweeping view of the French Market and the Mississippi River. It's a terrific place for a before- or after-dinner drink. Inside, the dining room is done in low-key elegance, with a window wall that lets you enjoy that river view during dinner (incidentally, there's no need to insist on a window table—the view's great from any position in the room). It's French-Italian cooking here, with all sorts of pasta offerings (they make their own and even operate a "pastaficcio" on the main floor where you can make purchases to take home), seafood, steak, chicken, lamb, and veal. I found seafood sauces—like the lemon-butter sauce on shrimp scampi "Don Josey"—light and well seasoned, and the salad with house dressing was exceptional. Another favorite is chicken majestic (chicken in a sauce of chives, mushrooms, shallots, and sprinkled with cognac). And if you've any room left, do try the delicious amaretto parfait for dessert. Moran's is open every day but Sunday from 6 to 11 p.m. (later on weekends), and reservations are advisable. The menu is à la carte, with prices ranging from $10 to $19 for entrees.

"If you don't want to wait at Galatoire's and you want good seafood at lower prices," the taxi driver told me, "then go next door to Ralph & Kacoo's." Well, **Ralph & Kacoo's**, 215 Bourbon St. (tel. 523-0449), a relative newcomer on the New Orleans scene, turned out to be every bit as good as he predicted. The large, attractive restaurant sports a long bar up front where you can wait for a table (they don't take reservations either, but because of its size, the wait is usually a short one), exposed brick walls, friendly, prompt service, and some of the most generous portions you'll find in the city. Louisiana seafoods, both fresh- and saltwater varieties, are the specialties here, and if you can't make up your mind from the large menu, why not try a seafood platter, with perhaps a bowl of crayfish bisque as an appetizer. One thing is certain—you'll leave satisfied as to both quality and quantity. The menu is à la carte, and you can put together a complete meal for something like $7 to $15. Hours are: Monday to Thursday, 11:30 a.m. to 10 p.m.; Friday and Saturday, to 10:30 p.m.; and Sunday, to 9 p.m. The same hours, prices, and menu prevail at a second location, 519 Toulouse St.

Another of the Moran brothers owns **Tony Moran's**, 240 Bourbon St. (tel. 523-8833), on the second floor of the Old

Absinthe House. As at Moran's Riverside Restaurant, pasta is revered here and comes fresh daily from the Moran-owned pastaficcio shop in the French Market. According to Tony, his fettuccine Alfredo is the best to be found anywhere, and after one taste I'm not about to challenge that boast—it's delicious, cooked to exactly the right consistency and dressed with butter, cream, and cheese. At Tony's it goes by the name of fettuccine al burro, and you really shouldn't miss it. Among the seafood dishes, I especially like shrimp Moran, which comes with a lemon, butter, and herb sauce so good I found myself dredging the last little bit with the hot Italian bread that comes with every order. Beef, lamb, veal, and chicken also appear on the menu. Prices are in the $10.50 to $25 range and hours are 7 p.m. to 2 a.m., Tuesday through Saturday. Incidentally, the decor in the inner dining room features a wall-size painting of the Battle of New Orleans, and my favorite spot out in the side room overlooking Bienville Street is a cozy retreat of old brick, frosted glass, mahogany, and sheer embroidered curtains at the floor-to-ceiling windows.

Moderate Choices

One of the delights of exploring New Orleans is discovering the many small, inexpensive places to eat, some just as exciting as the better known restaurants. What you'll find here is a sort of thumbnail sketch of some of my own favorites—it simply isn't possible to list them all or to tell you all I'd like to about these in this limited space. But do explore on your own—you'll be certain to find others.

Across from the French Market at the **Café Sbisa**, 1011 Decatur St. (tel. 561-8354), you're likely to run into some of New Orleans's best artists and writers, along with other natives entertaining guests from all over the world. It's an old building and the interior is casually elegant, with mirrors reflecting ceiling fans and potted greenery and the tile floor reminding you of its humble beginnings. Seafood here is freshness itself, with such specialties as swordfish, smoked fish, salmon, mussels, clams, and an excellent bouillabaisse. Steak, lamb, and duckling round out the menu. Prices are in the moderate range ($9 to $20). Dinner hours are 6 to 11 p.m. Monday through Thursday, until midnight on Friday and Saturday. On Sunday there's a champagne brunch from 11 a.m. to 3 p.m. and dinner from 6 to 11 p.m.

50 ARTHUR FROMMER'S NEW ORLEANS

The **Olde N'Awlins Cookery**, 729 Conti St. (tel. 529-3663), symbolizes several of the city's food traditions. First of all, it's located in an 1849 building whose history includes having begun as two private residences, a later resurrection as a large rooming house which combined the two, a probable short stint as a brothel, and service for a time as bistro bars, then a disco, before lying idle nearly two years prior to becoming a restaurant. Most important, however, its kitchen staff boasts three members of co-owner George Rhode III's immediate family. Indeed, son George IV gained much of his culinary expertise under the tutelage of world-famous Cajun chef Paul Prudehomme. Since its opening in mid-1983, the family-operated restaurant has dished up traditional New Orleans favorites and attracted a loyal clientele from the ranks of city residents. Using the freshest of Louisiana seafood and local seasonings, the kitchen turns out specialties like Cajun jambalaya, grilled redfish and barbecued shrimp, as well as soups, salads, and great desserts. Its blackboard menu changes daily, featuring whatever is freshest each day. In a rather plain setting that makes use of the original old brick and a delightful courtyard, informality is the keynote. No reservations, but with hours of 11 a.m. to 11 p.m. seven days a week, a price range of $5 to $15, and a lively, distinctly New Orleans ambience, this is one place where you won't mind a short wait to be seated.

You'll think the **Four Seasons**, 505 Royal St. (tel. 523-1149), should be listed under budget restaurants if you go in for a light breakfast or lunch. For instance, luscious croissants in five varieties (from plain to almond to ham and cheese, spinach and feta cheese or andouille) from 60¢ to $2.50 and other luncheon items at prices just as reasonable. But it's the fixed-price dinner, at $12, that makes it one of the best moderate-priced restaurants around. The four courses include appetizer, salad, a choice of three entrees (chicken, fish, or beef), and dessert from a choice of 20. It's an attractive, casual place with dining inside or on the patio. Hours are 7:30 a.m. to 11 p.m. daily, making it one of the best "drop in" spots in the Quarter.

Mr. B's Bistro and Bar, 201 Royal St. (tel. 523-2078), is owned and operated by Ella, Adelaide, Dottie, Dick, and John Brennan and is one of the most attractive restaurants in town. The decor is one of polished oak floors, warm wood paneling, marbletop tables, and large bay windows that look out onto Royal Street. In keeping with the bistro spirit, you can drop in for an espresso or a casual glass of wine, or enjoy a full meal.

Traditional New Orleans dishes are featured from the open kitchen, and both espresso and cappuccino come from espresso machines on the 65-foot-long bar. A treat here is the charcoal-grilled fish (grilled over hickory and pecan logs) and shrimp Chippewa. Dinner entrees are priced from $8.50 to $17, complete dinners from $13 to $18. All prices are a little lower at lunch. There's continuous service from 11 a.m. to 11 p.m., seven days a week. Besides being a great place for a moderately priced meal, this is a superb "rest the feet" break when wandering about the Quarter.

Tujague's ("two-jacks"), at 823 Decatur St. (tel. 523-9462), is the second restaurant to occupy this site. The first was run by Madame Bergue, who began in 1856 cooking huge "second breakfasts" for the butchers who worked in the French Market across the way. So well loved were her elaborate, leisurely meals that even today her name lives on in a modern eatery in the Royal Sonesta Hotel. Today, Tujague's serves only lunch and dinner, but continues the original cook's tradition of simply serving whatever she was cooking up that day. This is a favorite with New Orleanians, who seem to mind not at all that there's a very limited menu. At lunch, you have a choice of three entrees (which might include a traditional specialty here like brisket of beef with horseradish sauce, their terrific shrimp remoulade, and the freshest fish available that day), but the five-course meal will consist of soup, salad, entree, vegetable, dessert, and beverage for no more than a modest $7.50 to $10.50. If something lighter appeals to you, choose gumbo served with a side dish of shrimp salad at just $6. Six courses at dinner will run about $15.50 to $18.50. Hours are 11 a.m. to 2:30 p.m. and 5 to 10 p.m. daily.

Early on during your New Orleans visit you're likely to develop an itch to duplicate some of these great dishes in your own home. Well, you can scratch that itch by dropping in at the **New Orleans School of Cooking**, 835 Conti St. (tel. 525-3034), where native New Orleanian Joe Cahn (sometimes called the "Créole guru") offers a 2½-hour class in basic Créole cooking. Not one to simply stand up and lecture, Joe conducts a lively, entertaining discussion which involves the development of New Orleans's unique cuisine, detailed instructions for preparing as many as four dishes cooked during the session, and sampling the results in a mouthwatering lunch. You'll learn how to season red beans and rice, jambalaya, gumbo, etc., and leave the "home kitchen" setting with printed recipes for all the dishes and a burning ambition to go home and put your lessons to immediate use. The

$15 charge would be a good buy for either the cooking demonstration or the huge lunch—when it covers both, it becomes a downright bargain! Hours are 11 a.m. to 3 p.m., and it's a good idea to call ahead, although if it's not booked up, you're welcome to just drop in. *Note:* As we go to press, there is a possibility that the school will be moving into the new Jax Brewery complex on Decatur Street—be sure to check.

In one of the only five buildings to survive the disastrous fire of 1788, the **Gumbo Shop,** 630 St. Peter St. (tel. 525-1486), is just one block off Jackson Square. There's a lovely informal atmosphere both in the small patio and the warm indoor dining room. Murals of Old New Orleans, ceiling fans, lots of brass, a fireplace with an antique mirror hung above the mantel, and red-checked tablecloths create a charm that seems to make the excellent Créole food taste even better. Their seafood gumbo is a meal in itself, and if you haven't yet tried jambalaya, this is the place. Red beans and rice are also featured (there's a marvelous combination plate with red beans and rice, shrimp créole, and jambalaya for just $7, and there are salads, sandwiches, and homemade desserts. From 9 to 10 a.m. you can get a hearty Créole breakfast in the $5 to $9 price range; lunch and dinner are served from 11 a.m. to 10 p.m. at prices that range, à la carte, from $7 to $12.

The **Original Melius Bar,** 622 Conti St. (tel. 523-9820), is an attractive, rather large place with lots of exposed brick, dark wood, and overhead fans. It's a great lunch favorite of lawyers, bankers, and—surprisingly—waiters from some of the more elegant restaurants in the neighborhood. The menu features American food (e.g., roast pork with baked potato), and hot lunches are served Monday through Friday from 11 a.m. to 3:30 p.m. The bar stays open until 2 or 3 a.m., however, and there's a game room and disco dancing nightly. On Wednesday, draft beer goes for 25¢ a glass after 8 p.m. Lunch prices are in the $5 to $8 range.

I have New Orleans friends to thank for introducing me to **Port of Call,** 838 Esplanade Ave. (tel. 523-0120). With my strong penchant for seafood when I get anywhere near this city, I didn't feel especially drawn to a hamburger place. Not, that is, until I stepped inside the cozy wooden interior, met some of the friendliest people in the city, and feasted on mushrooms in wine, as well as one of the best hamburgers I've ever had. Now I understand my friends' enthusiasm and why this place stays so packed at lunch and dinnertime. Other times, the bar stays busy with neighborhood people who make this their "local." There are pizzas as well as hamburgers and those wonderful mushrooms in the front room, and excellent filet mignon, rib eye, and New York strip steaks in the back dining room. Your food tab can run anywhere from $4 to $16, depending on whether you're eating hamburger or steak (which is aged prime beef), and since business people come from all over the city to eat here, it's often jammed at regular eating times—try it at off-hours, or after 7 p.m., when people who work in the Quarter gather here to relax. Hours are 11 a.m. to 1 a.m. Monday through Friday, until 5 a.m. on Saturday and Sunday. Port of Call is open every day of the year except the Fourth of July, when the entire staff packs up and goes off on a picnic. *Note:* They also have a take-out service.

Should you tire of all that Créole and Cajun and French and Italian cooking and crave something in the line of Oriental food, don't despair. The **Asia Garden Restaurant**, 530 Bourbon St. (tel. 525-4149), is right in the heart of the Quarter in an Oriental garden atmosphere. There's all sorts of seafood cooked in Chinese style, and many authentic Mandarin, Szechuan, and Cantonese dishes. Polynesian drinks, cocktails, and wines are also available. Prices are moderate, in the $6 to $12 range, and there's service from 4:30 p.m. to midnight.

For lovers of Japanese cuisine, there's **Benihana of Tokyo**, 720 St. Louis St. (tel. 522-0425), where highly skilled Japanese chefs prepare steak, poultry, seafood, and vegetables right at your table. Prices are $9 to $18, the decor is charming, and dress is casual.

Best for Budget

"Budget" in the French Quarter can often mean "very, very good." That's due, I think, to two things: first of all, there are a good many favorite dishes here that aren't made of costly ingredients (red beans and rice, for example); and second, there are so many good cooks in this city who can make almost anything taste delicious. So whatever preconceived notions you bring with you about luncheonette-style eateries, be ready to revise them after trying one or two of the following.

If you're an oyster lover, there's nothing quite like standing at the oyster bar in the **Acme Oyster House**, 724 Iberville St. (tel. 523-8928), eating a dozen or so freshly shucked oysters on the half shell! (You can have them at table, but somehow they taste better at the bar.) If you can't quite go them raw, try the oyster loaf here—delicious. There's also a sandwich menu, and beer, of course, as the perfect accompaniment. This is a New Orleans institution and a fun place to eat—shuckers behind the bar are as much a treat as those lovely oysters. The Acme is open from 9 a.m. to "about 9 p.m.," and the cost of your meal will depend on your appetite (raw oysters cost $2.25 a half dozen, $4.50 a dozen, and the top price for anything else on the menu is $5 for shrimp—everything else is less!).

Of course, if you get a yen for oysters after 9 p.m., there's always **Felix,** 739 Iberville St. (tel. 522-4440), right across the street. It's also almost legendary among New Orleanians, and it stays open into the wee hours. In addition to raw oysters, there are plate specials for under $5, and their Créole cooking is quite good. It's a bit untidy, sometimes crowded and noisy, and almost always looks disorganized, but if you pass it by on those grounds you'll be missing a real eating experience. Prices are about the same as at the Acme, and hours are 11 a.m. to 2 a.m.

The **Coffee Pot,** 714 St. Peter St. (tel. 523-8215), has long been known for its breakfasts, which are served all day. And what a breakfast you can put together from the large, à la carte menu! Omelets come with just about anything you can think of—oysters, shrimp, chicken livers, red beans, ham and cheese, and there's even a "soul food" creation. Eggs Benedict, eggs créole, pancakes (strawberry, pecan, and sliced apple are just a few of the varieties), biscuits, and fresh fruit juices are all here. And this is probably the only place you'll find callas (traditional rice cakes served with grits and syrup) on the menu. I find it hard to pass them up any time of day.

For lunch or dinner, you might choose country steak, a Gulf Coast seafood platter, red beans and rice with smoked sausage, or any one of a dozen other offerings, at prices of $3.50 to $13. "Cousin " Pearl is the desert maker, and her bread pudding or fruit cobbler just can't be beat. True to its name, the Coffee Pot also offers some 20 varieties of coffee at $3 per cup (all are beefed up with alcoholic additives). They believe in the old Turkish proverb: "Coffee should be black as hell, strong as death, and sweet as love." One thing that makes the Coffee Pot so special is the help—Pearl (who waits tables when she's not making those luscious desserts) has been here some 25 years, and Delores has been here 13. Everyone in the place is friendly and helpful, making it a great favorite with locals. Hours are 8:30 a.m. to 10:30 p.m.

Just down the street from K-Paul's (see above) is another luncheonette "find," the **Tally-Ho,** 400 Chartres St., serving such good food at such reasonable prices that it too has become a favorite with locals. You can get a good breakfast (with meat) anytime for $2 and under, no lunches cost over $5, and there's a sandwich menu with prices of $1.90 to $3. There are daily plate specials (do try the red beans and rice or barbecued ribs) in that "under $5" group which could well be your major meal of the day. The Tally-Ho is open from midnight to 3:30 p.m., with a special omelet breakfast between midnight and 6 a.m. for only $3.75. And there's "take-out" for every item on the menu.

I first found **Molly's Irish Pub**, 732 Toulouse St., on a rainy day in the heart of the Quarter when I ducked in for an Irish coffee to ward off the chill and stayed to enjoy a platter of fried oysters, french fries, and salad for just $5.50. And I never had better anywhere else in the city. That says a lot for the kitchen here, especially since there is a very wide variety on the menu. It's open 24 hours a day and a great place to watch all sorts of New Orleans types, as well as tourists who find it as I did. Breakfast is served at any hour, making it a special favorite of nightowls who have a taste for bacon and eggs after a night on the town.

Jim Monaghan, who originated Molly's, now devotes full time to his three establishments over on Decatur Street across from the French Market. One of the prime movers in the upgrading of what was once a rundown, rather seedy part of the Quarter, Jim has brought his own brand of enthusiasm to this part of town. His warm personality is reflected by a staff which makes every visitor feel welcomed and, on a return visit, like a valued member of a special club. There's "drink and merriment" (to quote Jim) at **Bonaparte's Retreat**, 1007 Decatur, and the **Abbey**, a block down at 1123 Decatur, and very good eating at reasonable—no, budget—prices at **Molly's at the Market**, 1107 Decatur St. (tel. 581-9759). You'll find breakfast served all day (very good omelets), and lunch and dinner menus feature American, Italian, and Irish specialties, all for $6 and under. This is one of my favorite places to eat in the Quarter, and I find myself going a little out of the way just to drop in at any one of the three friendly places, even when it isn't mealtime. Molly's at the Market and Bonaparte's Retreat both open at 9 a.m., the Abbey at 6 p.m., and all three are open until 1:30 to 2 a.m. Molly's at the Market serves lunch from noon to 2 p.m. and dinner from 6 to 9 p.m.

Napoleon House, at the corner of Chartres and St. Louis Streets, is so named because at the time of the "Little Corporal's" death there was actually a plot ahatching in this 1797 National Landmark house to snatch him from his island exile and bring him to New Orleans. The third floor was added expressly for the purpose of providing him a home after the rescue. It wears its history well and with dignity: there's a limited menu of po-boys, Italian muffuletta sandwiches, and pastries ($2 to $6); and the jukebox plays only classical music. This is Dick Cavett's favorite New Orleans haunt, as well as a very popular spot with residents. Hours are 11 a.m. to 1 or 2 a.m.

Café Maspero, 601 Rue Decatur (tel. 523-6250), is open from 11 a.m. to midnight seven days a week and serves the largest portions I've run into—burgers, barbecue, steaks, etc.—as well as an impressive list of wines, beers, and cocktails, all at low, low prices. This is a lively spot, especially following a concert, opera, or the theater, when locals drop in in droves, and it's not unusual to see patrons lined up for tables. Be assured, however, that it's worth your time to wait—the quality is as good as the portions are large, and prices are in the $3 to $8 range.

The bright, charming **Honfleur Restaurant** in the Provincial Hotel, 1024 Chartres St. (tel. 581-4995), serves exceptional food at reasonable cost. Breakfast is especially good here, at prices that range from $1.75 to $6. Lunch specialties include Gulftail fried shrimp, southern fried chicken, and an open-face roast beef sandwich which is excellent. Prices run from $3 to $6. At dinner, choose from créole gumbo, shrimp, trout, or roast beef at prices from $4.50 to $8. The waitresses are among the friendliest in town, and Mrs. Evelyn Revertiga, the lovely manager, gives personal attention to every guest. It's open from 7 a.m. to 9 p.m. every day of the week.

Not for the fainthearted, but definitely for those who like good food at budget prices and plenty of it, **Buster Holmes,** 721 Burgundy St. (tel. 561-9375), is a ramshackle little pink building that's been a favorite with French Quarter residents for years. There are two rooms with tables and counter service. Red beans are the most famous dish here, but I lean toward the Créole dishes and some of the best fried seafood I've ever eaten (the fried chicken is great, too). Order gumbo, shrimp créole, créole sausage, or whatever—you won't be disappointed. The menu is a spoken one, and if you don't hear something you've looked forward to having, ask—many times it's there, just not listed when your waitress speaks her piece. Prices are in the $2 to $6 range, and hours are 6 a.m. to 6 p.m., seven days a week. There's also a *Buster Holmes Handmade Cooking* book available for $6.95 (you can order it at the same price plus $1 for postage).

A small, friendly neighborhood eatery in an off-the-beaten-track location, **Jackson's Place**, 1212 Royal St. (tel. 522-4468), has an excellent menu which changes daily. It's mainly Créole food like red beans and rice with sausage, jambalaya, and seafood gumbo that you'll find featured, and don't let the budget price range of $2 to $6 throw you off—everything I've tasted was superb (be sure to save room for the bread pudding, which is very special). With its brick floors, white and rose-trimmed walls, and bright artwork, this is a relaxing, homey spot. Hours are 7 a.m. to noon and 5 to 11 p.m., Tuesday through Sunday.

For Your Sweet Tooth

The tiny **La Marquise**, 625 Rue Chartres, serves pastries (French) on the premises, either in a crowded front room which also holds the display counter, or outside in a small but delightful patio. Maurice Delechelle is the master baker and guiding hand here, and I promise you, you've never had more delectable goodies. There are galettes bretonnes (butter cookies), pain chocolat (chocolate bread), cygne swan (an eclair in the shape of a swan filled with whipped cream), choux à la crème (creampuff), and mille feuilles (napoleon), as well as croissants, brioches, and a wide assortment of strudel and Danish pastries. Prices are minimal (some as low as 50¢), and you can buy coffee in paper cups if you decide to buy your sweet here and take it elsewhere. La Marquise is almost always crowded, and if the patio has no seats available, there's always Jackson Square just a few steps away for a dessert picnic. Hours are 8 a.m. to 5:30 p.m. on weekdays, 7:30 a.m. to 8:30 on Saturday and Sunday.

There's a larger La Marquise at 617 Ursulines St., so you can indulge that sweet tooth even when you're not in the Jackson Square vicinity.

Very Special

They call it **Michael's Coffee Bar**, 307 Exchange Alley, and it won't suit everyone. Tucked away on a small alleyway between Royal and Chartres Streets (enter from Bienville), it's small, only three or four tables, and there's no evidence here of frenetic New Orleans streetlife once you enter the cozy shop. But it's a find for those who treasure long episodes of quiet enjoyment in the company of regulars who come here for espresso or one

58 ARTHUR FROMMER'S NEW ORLEANS

of the other specialty varieties of coffee, 13 coffee drinks, five tea drinks, or a glass of wine. They also serve cola, soda, and tonic water, as well as fresh-squeezed citrus drinks. There are melt-in-the-mouth croissants or other crumbly fresh pastries, cheesecake, brownies, fresh baked bread, cake or pie, an excellent quiche, and Créole lunch specials. And all at prices which are shockingly low (55¢ to $5 for a lunch special). If you come for breakfast, there are eggs, waffles, biscuits, wheat or raisin toast, English muffins, and fresh fruits, individually priced at $1.25 and under. Best of all, it's a friendly, relaxed place to loiter a while, or as one patron said with a contented sigh, "Michael's is a good place to start the day in a good mood or to heal yourself at the end of a long, hard day." On Sunday you're on your own—it's closed. Other days, it's open from 8:30 a.m. to 5:30 p.m. Monday and Tuesday, until 10 p.m. Wednesday through Saturday. But be warned: come to Michael's only if you're prepared to settle in a while and appreciate their truly fine coffees (the owner is a coffee broker, so every cup reflects the best of any blend you order) and savor the freshness of their baked goods. In good weather, there's pleasant outdoor seating.

Chapter VI

DINING OUTSIDE THE QUARTER

GOOD EATING IN NEW ORLEANS is by no means confined to the French Quarter—you'll find it all over town. To make life easier for you as you move around the city, I'm listing restaurants in this chapter by area, however (it wouldn't do to be too organized!), not by price category. You'll find the most expensive listed first, then moderate prices, and budget places last. Area boundaries for this purpose are rather broad: "downtown" (remember, that's *downriver* from Canal Street) is outside the French Quarter, but on the same side of Canal Street; Central Business District is roughly the area upriver from Canal, extending to the elevated expressway (U.S. 90); "uptown" includes everything upriver from Canal and as far as Carrollton toward the lake, including the Garden District; "lake," of course, means the area along the shores of Lake Pontchartrain; and "out of town" means across the Mississippi River or Lake Pontchartrain. If all that sounds a little confusing, turn back to the map on page 10 and you'll get the general idea.

Because it can't be repeated too often, let me remind you again that price ranges quoted are those in effect *at press time*. Any differences you encounter will be due to our ever-present nemesis, inflation.

Downtown

Ever eaten in a church? Of course you have—church suppers, right? Well, it's an entirely different experience at **Christian's**, 3835 Iberville St. (tel. 482-4924). Started by a grandson of the Galatoire clan, this lovely restaurant serves a French and Créole cuisine, with lots of seafood specialties, some of it prepared with the most delicate of French sauces. Try the oysters Roland, quenelles, or the marvelous bouillabaisse. The little church building remains unaltered on the exterior, and inside it's been beautifully restored. Only about ten minutes from the French Quarter, it's open for lunch (11:30 a.m. to 2 p.m.) and dinner (5:30 to 10 p.m.), but closed Sunday, Monday, and certain holidays. Menus are à la carte, with a range of $7 to $13 at lunch, $9.50 to $20 at dinner, and there are specially priced children's plates.

The **Old Spaghetti Factory,** 330 St. Charles at Poydras (tel. 561-1068), is a fun place to eat, furnished with unusual antiques, Tiffany lamps, stained-glass windows, and even an old trolley! Prices are unbelievably low and portions generous for complete meals of spaghetti with a choice of seven quite good sauces. Lunch prices range from $4 to $6; at dinner, from $5 to $10; and there's a special child's plate for just $4—a great place to feed the whole family without breaking the budget. You can make the occasion even more memorable by sipping cocktails at the fabulous old brass-railed mahogany bar. Come during Happy Hour (4 to 7 p.m., Monday through Friday) and drinks cost less. Open 11:15 a.m. to 10 p.m. Sunday to Thursday, until 11 p.m. on Friday and Saturday.

Mention "Créole with Soul" in New Orleans, and every native will know you're referring to **Chez Hélène,** 1530 W. Robertson St. (tel. 947-9155). This small, unfancy restaurant is run by a great black chef, Austin Leslie, whose Aunt Hélène started things with the help of Austin's mother. Both ladies have since retired, but Austin learned his trade well from them. Fried chicken here is the sort that will turn the stoniest Yankee into a confirmed southerner—brown, crispy, and, in a word, perfect. Red beans and rice come with remarkable chaurice or hot sausage, and Austin's oysters Rockefeller rival those at you-know-where (where they originated). As one food critic noted, Chez Hélène proves beyond a shadow of a doubt that Créole cooking has always had Soul! Because this place is so popular, you'd better make reservations if you have a large party—if only one or two, it's fun just to come along and wait at the bar over a drink. Hours are 11 a.m. to midnight Tuesday to Thursday, to 1:30 a.m. on Friday and Saturday, to 6 p.m. on Monday, and to 10:30 p.m. on Sunday. As for prices, they're the same at lunch and dinner, and a meal will cost anywhere from $6 to $16.

Central Business District

Right at the riverfront, on the lobby level of the New Orleans Hilton, **Winston's,** 2 Poydras at the Mississippi River (tel. 561-0500, ext. 3250), is sheltered from the hotel hustle-bustle by pale wood trellises, lots of greenery, and a magnificent black lacquered screen from mainland China. Once inside, you're in an English country house dining room, where damask tablecloths are draped with an overcloth, Chippendale chairs are upholstered in dark green with a tea rose floral print, and tables are set with Villeroy and Bach china from Germany and hand-blown imported glassware. Fresh-cut flowers are everywhere in beautiful china vases. And as is entirely fitting in the midst of such elegance, each table is assigned a maid and butler to look after your every need. They'll advise you of the evening's fare, and whether you have the soufflé à la poire Williams, cadgery de saumon, or filet of redfish baked in seaweed, you may be sure it will be superb—the master chef here is an artist! Such perfection is, as you'd expect, pricey—$32 prix fixe, and wines are extra (the wine list is extensive and very good), but you'll leave knowing you've had your money's worth. Dinner is served nightly from 6 to 11 p.m. and reservations are an absolute must. *Tip:* If you arrive a little early, have a drink or two in the adjoining English Bar, where plush couches will set you up for the pampering to come.

As an important part of its Riverside addition, the Hilton has opened **Kabby's Seafood Restaurant** (tel. 561-0500), which looks out over the Mississippi through a 200-foot-wide, 14-foot-high window. It's a spectacular setting, and the decor in earth tones of green, beige, and brown is a charming blend of traditional and art deco styles. You enter through a New Orleans courtyard foyer which features a bubbling fountain, custom-designed lamp posts, and tropical plantings. The adjacent bar features a large stained-glass canopy, and live entertainment and dancing in the evening. At lunch, salads, sandwiches (oyster loaf, mufuletta, etc.), and other specialties run $8 to $15. At night, seafood is the thing to offer, and there's a sumptuous seafood combo that's a real feast and costs $29.95. Beef, chicken, and veal are also on the menu (at prices of $9 to $20), but remember that this *is* a seafood restaurant. Hours are 11:30 a.m. to 2:30 p.m. and 6 to 10:30 p.m. daily. Reservations are advised.

You'll find the **Bon Ton Café,** 401 Magazine St. (tel. 524-3386), absolutely mobbed at lunch with New Orleans business people and their guests, and at dinner you'll be seated *only* if you have reservations. Such popularity is largely due to its owner, Al Pierce. He grew up on the banks of Bayou Lafourche, learned Cajun cooking from his mother, came to New Orleans in 1936, bought the Bon Ton in 1953, and since then has been serving up seafood gumbo, crayfish bisque, jambalaya, crayfish omelet, and other Cajun dishes in a manner that would make his mother proud. This is a small, utterly charming place, and one not to be missed if you want to sample true Cajun cooking at its best (more subtle than Créole, making much use of shallots, parsley, bell peppers, and garlic). It's open from 11 a.m. to 2 p.m. for lunch ($6 to $12) and 5 to 9:30 p.m. for dinner ($14 to $19). The lunch menu is semi-à la carte, at dinner table d'hôte.

Back at the Hilton, the charmingly informal **Café Bromeliad**, 2 Poydras at the Mississippi River (tel. 561-0500), on the street level, serves a delicious breakfast, lunch, and dinner (buffet style on Friday and Saturday) at reasonable prices. Breakfast is from 7 to 9:30 a.m. (around $6.50), lunch from 11:30 a.m. to 2:30 p.m. ($8 and up), and dinner from 6 to 11 p.m. Sunday through Thursday (starting at $13). Children pay half price at all three. But take my advice and save your visit here for a Friday or Saturday night, when great food comes along with a decided air of festivity at no extra charge. On Friday from 6 to 11 p.m. there's the Cajun Seafood Buffet, with the Cajun Two—two lovely gentlemen straight from the bayou—strolling and strumming, a "boat" heaped high with cold boiled crayfish and shrimp, and a hot buffet of seafood dishes which look, smell, and taste divine (strong praise, I know, but I've a two-inch-expanded waistband to back it up!). Incidentally, there's an art to eating the cold crayfish (which look like tiny lobsters), and far be it from me to attempt to explain it on paper. Suffice it to say that the large bucket in the center of your table is for the part you *don't* eat—for further instructions, ask your waiter (they're all friendly, efficient, and don't mind at all sharing their expertise). On Saturday (same hours), it's Italian Festa time, with their own freshly made pizza, manicotti, osso buco, and veal parmigiana among the endless delights of the buffet and opera-singing waiters and waitresses to liven things up. Fun nights, both, and the cost, including coffee or tea (the beer is on you!), is $16. The Sunday Champagne Jazz Brunch in the café (11 a.m. to 3 p.m. and also a buffet) features all the traditional brunch favorites plus fresh, homemade pastries and, of course, ever-flowing champagne, at a cost of $16. I must confess that I seldom get so carried away by hotel eating spots, but my enthusiasm was more than confirmed when I noted that fully half, and maybe more, of the crowd at each of these events seemed to be local New Orleanians—and their judgment is not to be questioned!

You owe it to yourself to make at least one pilgrimage to **Mother's**, 401 Poydras St. (tel. 523-9656), which is within walking distance of the Superdome and major hotels. When you do, be sure and allow time to stand in line—bankers queue up with warehousemen, dockworkers, and just about everybody else from this part of town for *the* best po-boy sandwiches in New Orleans. Made on crisp french bread so fresh it's just cooled down from the oven, the po-boys here are real creations, many of them served with a rich thick gravy that may be leaky, but is so good you won't mind. Try the roast beef or ham. There are plate lunches too, such as the excellent gumbo, red beans, sweet-potato pie, and spaghetti pie. Mother's is always crowded, but don't let that throw you off—by the time you make your way through the line, there'll be room at a table. Hours are 6 a.m. (with one of the best breakfasts in the city) to 3 p.m. (to 2 p.m. on Saturday; closed Sunday and Monday), dress is casual, and your meal will be under $5.

If you're winding up a late evening in this part of town, there are two inexpensive 24-hour places worth a stop before heading home. **Bailey's**, in the Fairmont Hotel on University Place, is a cozy spot softly lit by Tiffany lamps and decorated with antiques. At any hour of the day you can order breakfast items like waffles, pancakes, or omelets, or New Orleans specialties like red beans and rice with hot sausage, or a seafood platter. There are also sandwiches and burgers, as well as a nice selection of po-boys. In the Hilton, 2 Poydras at the Mississippi River, **Le Croissant**, a 24-hour coffeeshop, serves light, moderately priced meals and snacks. It's on the lobby level, and a pleasant place to begin or end a day.

Uptown
(including the Garden District)

Since it opened in 1948, the **Caribbean Room** in the elegant Pontchartrain Hotel, 2031 St. Charles Ave. (tel. 524-0581), has won a list of culinary awards as long as your arm, and it really epitomizes New Orleans cuisine at its finest. The decor, like that of the rest of the hotel, is refined (almost understated) luxury. As for service—well, "impeccable" and "solicitous" come to mind. The French and Créole kitchen turns out specialties like shrimp saki and backfin crabmeat with a lovely creamy, rather tart house dressing (actually, it's a combination of two, mustard and French) that have made fans of a host of celebrities which include Artur Rubinstein, Gerald Ford, and Mary Martin. Lunch is served from 11:45 a.m. to 2 p.m. (semi-à la carte prices, $8 to $12), dinner from 6 to 10 p.m. (à la carte entrees from $18 to $25), and there's a Sunday Brûlot Brunch from 11:45 a.m. to 2 p.m. Best reserve for all.

The unusual, rather grand blue-and-white building at the corner of Washington Avenue and Coliseum Street was built as a restaurant in 1880 by Emile Commander and is now owned by members of the Brennan family of French Quarter fame. **Commander's Palace** (tel. 899-8221) is a consistent favorite of locals and visitors alike. The patio, fountains, lush tropical plantings, and soft colors are a perfect backdrop for mouthwatering Créole specialties. If you're a jazz buff, don't miss their famous Jazz Brunch (Saturday and Sunday, 11 a.m. to 2 p.m.), where Dixieland is played by jazz greats. Brunch prices start at $10, lunch runs from $7 to $12, and dinner from $20 to $25. Commander's, in addition to serving some of the best food in town, is a fun place and quite a social center—reservations are a must, sometimes days in advance.

For dining in the continental manner, you just can't equal the **Versailles**, 2100 St. Charles Ave. (tel. 524-2535). The lovely St. Charles Room looks out on tree-shaded St. Charles Avenue through glass walls; the warm, red-walled Marie Antoinette Room is lit with huge, cut-glass chandeliers; and the Trianon Room provides elegant seclusion. But what makes the Versailles really special is its food—specialties like bouillabaisse Marseillaise, escalope de veal Princess, and veal Financière are a gourmet's delight. They do their own baking, and the wine cellar is outstanding. Dinner hours are 6 to 10 p.m. every day except Sunday, when it's closed. Reservations are required. If you're driving, an added plus is free valet parking. Prices on the semi-à la carte menu are in the $15 to $25 range.

If you have New Orleans friends, chances are they'll take you at least once to **Pascal's Manale**, 1838 Napoleon Ave. (tel. 895-4877), for barbecued shrimp—if you don't have local friends, by all means go out on your own. It's crowded, noisy, and somewhat expensive, but you'll leave as much a fan as any native. Don't expect fancy decor or artificial "atmosphere"—the emphasis is on food and conviviality (Sunday nights are actually more like social gatherings than those of a commercial nature).

Manale's bills itself as an Italian-New Orleans steakhouse, but for my money, it's specialties like spaghettini Collins (with a butter sauce topped by chopped raw scallions), tiny buster crabs sauteed in butter and lemon, and snapper Catherine that account for its popularity (after, of course, those marvelous barbecued shrimp, a house creation). À la carte prices run from $7 to $12 at lunch and $10 to $18 at dinner, and hours are 11:45 a.m. to 10 p.m. Monday through Friday, from 4 p.m. on Saturday; it's closed on Sunday.

A short trolley ride from the Quarter, the **Delmonico Restaurant**, 1300 St. Charles Ave. (tel. 525-4937), was founded in 1895 by a gentleman who had been associated with the famous New York restaurant by the same name. It is essentially a comfortable, family-style eatery, with just a touch of elegance and one of the most varied menus in New Orleans. As a dedicated seafood lover, I favor the soft-shell crab Delmonico, but steaks are very good here, and they have a fresh vegetable salad that's a wonder. It's open daily from 11:30 a.m. to 9:30 p.m., and prices are in the $12 to $18 range.

Tom Pittari grew up in the Irish Channel section of New Orleans and developed a lifelong love for good food, a love reflected in the extensive menu at his establishment, **T. Pittari's**, 4200 S. Claiborne Ave. (tel. 891-2801). You'll find everything there from Maine lobsters (flown in daily) to Angus beef to Louisiana seafood to wild and domestic game birds. And the kitchen does well by all. If you think you know lobster, for instance, just try their lobster Kadobster—more than 13 ingredients are used to come up with a unique and delicious flavor. Maybe the success of the kitchen is due to Tom's adherence to an old Italian proverb that's been the restaurant's creed since it was founded back in 1895: "the eyes of the boss fatten the horse," loosely translated here as "if the owner keeps a close watch on his business, it will thrive." Whatever the explanation, the cooking is good, the service friendly, and the costs fairly moderate in this large (three dining rooms), popular spot. Hours are 11:45 a.m. to 10 p.m. (till 11 p.m. on Friday and Saturday), dinners are in the $12 to $18 range, and there's a lower priced children's menu.

There's no menu, no decor to speak of, and a wine list that one critic described as "rummaging through a refrigerator" at **Charlie's Steak House**, 4510 Dryades St. (tel. 895-9705). But there's a friendly, unpretentious atmosphere and good steaks cooked *exactly* to the doneness you specify and sizzling, plus some of the best fried onion rings you've ever tasted and a salad with a sharp, bleu cheese dressing. They catch their own shrimp for the cocktail appetizer and cut their own beef—both signs of excellence. An average dinner from the â la carte menu will run $11 to $18, and you're virtually guaranteed a fun evening. Hours are 10:30 a.m. to 11:30 p.m.

Another of the inexpensive, homey places so loved by people who live in New Orleans is **Casamento's**, 4330 Magazine St. (tel. 895-9761). The plain exterior holds a warm, friendly restaurant decorated in Spanish tiles and lots of plants. Almost always crowded (mostly with locals), Casamento's has an excellent oyster bar and some of the best seafood plates in town at unbelievably low prices. Their oyster loaf is especially good, but then, so are the fried soft-shell crabs and anything else you might order here. Incidentally, don't confuse the oyster *loaf* with the oyster sandwich—the loaf is made with a large loaf of white bread toasted and buttered and filled with fried oysters and large enough for two; the sandwich comes on regular toast. Hours here are 11:45 a.m. to 1:30 p.m. and 5:30 to 9 p.m. every day except Monday. Sad to say, Casamento's closes down from mid-June to mid-September. Average cost for a meal runs $8 to $15.

Petrossi's, 901 Louisiana Ave. (tel. 895-3404), serves a first-rate seafood gumbo, fried oysters, and boiled shrimp, as well as a heaping seafood platter at prices of $4 to $12. It's casual dress here, and if you come in a car there's free parking. Hours are 11 a.m. to 10 p.m. Wednesday through Saturday, until 9:30 p.m. on Sunday; closed Monday and Tuesday.

If you're out in the Riverbend area, don't bypass the **Camellia Grill**, 626 S. Carrollton Ave. (tel. 866-9573). It's right on the trolley line and serves a great variety of sandwiches, omelets, salads, and desserts at low-to-moderate prices. The hamburger is really special, sandwiches are stuffed to overflowing with corned beef, ham, or whatever, and omelets are enormous. This is one place you can count on having a filling meal at low cost, and although it's counter service and you may have a short wait for a seat, surprisingly, you'll be given a real linen napkin! That counter service is actually a bonus feature—it provides a frontrow contact with the friendly, entertaining waiters on the other side. Hours are 9 a.m. to 1:45 a.m. seven days a week, and you can walk away full for $4 to $8.

A young lady with whom I shared my Amtrak ride to New Orleans told me to be sure and stop in at **Ye Olde College Inn**, 3016 S. Carrollton Ave. (tel. 866-3683). You could, she told me, have marvelous red beans and rice, a good oyster loaf, or really good po-boys for prices under $6. She was right. Not only that, I found their fried chicken and many of the daily dinner plates to be well above par. The College Inn is rightly popular with locals, and it's open from 11 a.m. to midnight every day (to 2 a.m. on Friday and Saturday).

You'll find **Tyler's Beer Garden,** 5234 Magazine St. (tel. 891-4989), listed in the chapter on nightlife, but if you should find yourself in this rather offbeat section of town, you might like to know that they feature oysters on the half shell at 10¢ each, as well as a lively crowd of regulars, mostly of the younger set, who come for the live jazz music after nightfall and for conversation and oysters any time at all. It's open from about 11 a.m. until the wee hours. Incidentally, if you find the front door locked, go around to the side.

Metairie

You'd need a personal New Orleans friend to tell you about **Lido Gardens,** 4415 Airline Hwy. (tel. 834-8233). That's how I learned about the unpretentious roadside Italian restaurant which very quickly became one of my favorite places to eat. Run by the friendly Mongiat family, the place has a warm, homey decor sparked by red-checked tablecloths and a wishing well draped with wine bottles in the center of the dining room. Pasta dishes are outstanding here, and veal appears in a wide variety of traditional recipes (piccata, milanese, scalloppini, parmigiana, saltimboca, etc.), every one delicious. If you've never tried involtini (prosciutto and cheese rolled in veal and simmered in butter, wine, and rosemary), you'll be in for a real treat. Prices are in the moderate $7 to $15 range, and hours are 11 a.m. to 2 p.m. every day except Saturday for lunch; 5 to 9 p.m. for dinner Monday to Thursday, until 10 p.m. on Friday and Saturday. Closed Sunday.

Lake

Out by the lake, there's an authentic French bistro, nothing at all like the usual American version. **Crozier's Restaurant Français,** 7033 Read Lane (tel. 241-8220), is a small, unpretentious, but charming place which serves food that can only be described as superb. The tastefully simple decor boasts little decoration (but fresh flowers on every table), and you'll find no waitresses in fancy costumes here. What you will find are authentic French dishes: onion soup, escargots, coq au vin, escalope de veau, and lovely desserts. There's a limited (but very good) moderately priced wine list. Crozier's serves dinner only, 6 to 10 p.m., Monday through Saturday. Prices run $16 to $22. Reservations are a must because of its size and its popularity, and it's a bit on the dressy side (coats, ties, etc.).

Bruning's, 1870 Orpheum Ave., West End Park (tel. 282-9359), has been serving a classic New Orleans seafood menu since 1859, and on Friday and Sunday nights you may have to wait to be seated. There's a beautiful view of Lake Ponchartrain, and you'll dine over the water. The boiled seafood here is especially good, as is the seafood gumbo. A good buy, if you can't make up your mind, is the generous seafood platter. An average meal from the moderately priced menu will run approximately $10 to $15. Bruning's is open from 11 a.m. to 9:30 p.m. every day but Wednesday, and stays open until 10:30 p.m. on Friday and Saturday.

Out of Town

About 30 minutes' drive on U.S. 90 west of the city, in Waggaman, there's a plain plywood building with a shell front painted white that holds one of this area's best restaurants. **Mosca's** (tel. 436-9942) is well worth the drive. It was begun by Lisa Mosca in 1946, and since her death, son Johnny and daughter Mary have carried on her unique style of cooking that combines elements of Italian and local Créole cuisine. If an evening out of the city appeals to you, by all means make the trip and sample dishes you'll not find anywhere else. I can especially recommend the Italian crab salad (they use vinegar to flavor the crab and pickle the vegetables—delicious!), and Mosca's Italian oysters are a treat. Other specialties are quail with wild rice, squab and cornish hen, also with wild rice, and chicken cacciatore (you get the entire chicken). Everything is prepared to order, and you can wait as long as 40 minutes. A la carte prices run from $15 to $20, and they accept no credit cards or checks—and no reservations on weekends (they're absolutely essential other times). Mosca's closes on Sunday and Monday, is open 5:30 to 9:30 p.m. other evenings *usually,* but since they can vary, it's safer to call ahead, even on weekends when you can't reserve.

A more moderately priced, very popular restaurant across the river in Gretna is **Visko's,** 516 Gretna Blvd. (tel. 368-4899). It began as a small oyster and shrimp restaurant and has grown in both size and clientele. The fried dishes have always been, and still are, a drawing card, and the addition of steamed seafood has proved a happy one. You can put together a meal from the à la carte menu for $6 to $20 here any day but Sunday from 11 a.m. to 10 p.m. (to 11 p.m. on Friday and Saturday).

In the other direction, across the Lake Pontchartrain causeway in Lacombe (between Slidell and Mandeville) is another French restaurant that rates a rave. **La Provence**, Highway I-90, Lacombe, Mandeville-Slidell Road (tel. 626-7662), is a jewel of a place that could be bodily transported from the countryside of Louisiana to that of France and be perfectly at home. Founded by a Frenchman with the unlikely name of Chris Kerageorgiou (there's a Greek lurking somewhere in his ancestry, but he was born in Provence in France), the rustic country-inn atmosphere envelops you the minute you step inside. There's a great fireplace, waitresses dressed in Provençal dress (they're local ladies, friendly and efficient), and fragrances from the kitchen that tell you in advance you're in for a great meal. Chris and his Cajun wife Charlotte run things, and his creations combine classic French dishes with marvelous Greek, Créole, and south-of-France touches. If I had to pick a favorite, it would probably be poulet au fromage, which enhances chicken with vermouth, shallots, cream, and Swiss and bleu cheese. The duck à l'orange is positively magnificent, the rack of lamb superb, the pompano unique, and—well, you get the idea: I adore this place! Portions are large, and the wine list extensive (with a nice moderately priced selection as well as rare vintages), and La Provence is so popular you'd best reserve way in advance. An average meal from the à la carte menu will run $15 to $35, and dress is semi-casual (jacket optional). It's closed Monday and Tuesday, open for dinner 5 to 11 p.m. every other day except Sunday, when hours are 1 to 9 p.m. Lunch, served from 11:30 a.m. to 3 p.m. Wednesday, Thursday, and Friday, will run $6 to $10. This one's a "don't miss" if you have wheels.

Chapter VII

THINGS TO DO IN NEW ORLEANS

WE'LL BE TALKING ABOUT ENTERTAINMENT in this chapter, and in New Orleans, entertainment starts with jazz. It's everywhere—on the streets of the French Quarter, in jazz clubs all over the city, and in the heart and soul of everyone who lives here. Its counterpart, the blues, moan through the city in the soft, throaty notes of the clarinet. But there's more to New Orleans than just its heady nightlife. Its rich French heritage, strongly spiced by the Italians who've become such a part of its life, has left a real love of classical music and opera. Theater too plays a part in New Orleans entertainment. As for sports, well, just say "Superdome" and eyes light up. Horseracing has been important here too for years, and golf, tennis, and fishing are at your fingertips as well. We'll take a look at all of these and tell you where to find them.

Nightlife

When the sun goes down, New Orleans lights up. In the French Quarter, Bourbon Street turns into a ten-block-long street party; posh downtown hotel supper clubs start to swing; and uptown hideaways come to life with music. Jazz, that uniquely American contribution to the world's music, was born here. It grew out of the anger, fear, love, joy, pride, and backbreaking toil that made up the emotional lives of blacks in New Orleans from the days of slavery right up to the advent of "Storyville." Slaves, remembering the rhythms and chants of West Africa or the Caribbean, danced in Congo Square to the accompaniment of homemade instruments (a skin stretched across a piece of bamboo, reed flutes, banjos made of gourds, and clicking bones) as their white masters looked on, convinced the Sunday-

NEW ORLEANS NIGHTLIFE/ACTIVITIES 71

night revelry would be sufficient outlet for week-long frustrations and would squelch black magic voodoo rites. When Créole gentlemen fathered a large group of "free men of color" by their quadroon mistresses and sent them off to Europe to be educated, they brought back a knowledge of classical music and instruments which they promptly integrated with the black music of their native city. No longer confined to once-a-week happenings at Congo Square, the joyous, soul-lifting sounds moved out into the streets of the city to capture the attention of a white population already music oriented. "Spasm bands," made up of blacks using whatever instruments were available, played at street corners to audiences of foot-tapping whites.

When the restricted area around Basin Street opened up a world of highly competitive bordellos, saloons, and nightclubs, black musicians moved their vibrant, expressive music inside to provide entertainment for paying customers, and it wasn't long before it began showing up in the white man's world of college campuses, riverboats, and "respectable" nightclubs and restaurants. New Orleans-born masters of the art—like Louis Armstrong and "Jelly Roll" Morton—left New Orleans and moved upriver to St. Louis and Memphis, eventually carrying their music to Chicago, New York, and the West Coast. Others—"Papa" Celestin, Bunk Johnson, and Sweet Emma Barrett, to name just a few—stayed at home, keeping the free-spirited music alive at the scene of its birth. Today, jazz permeates the city, with black and white, newcomers and oldtimers, joining together to fill the air with its strains at all hours in the French Quarter and after dark outside the Quarter. And you'll still find uninhibited dancers performing in the streets outside jazz spots (sometimes passing the hat to lookers-on), jazz funerals for departed musicians (the trip to that final resting place accompanied by sorrowful dirges and "second liners" who shuffle and clap hands to a mournful beat, the return a joyful, swinging celebration of the deceased's "liberation"), and occasionally a street parade (even when it isn't Carnival), complete with brass band.

IN THE FRENCH QUARTER: Dear to the hearts of all jazz devotees (and I count myself among them) is **Preservation Hall**, 726 St. Peter St., where jazz is found in its purest form, uncluttered by such refinements as air conditioning, drinks, or even (unless you arrive very early) a place to sit down. The shabby old building offers only hot, foot-tapping, body-swaying music,

72 □ ARTHUR FROMMER'S NEW ORLEANS

played by whatever top professionals happen to be in town on a particular night and a solid core of oldtime greats who never left New Orleans. And nobody seems to mind the lack of those other refinements—indeed, the place is not only packed, its windows are filled with faces of those who stand on the sidewalk for hours just to listen.

Part of the fun is never knowing just who will be on the bandstand. This place holds a very special place in the hearts of jazzmen, and some of the greatest drop in to play when they're in town. Another part is the assurance that no matter who is sitting in, they'll all have as good a time as the audience. The atmosphere is that of an informal jazz session. Admission is an unbelievably low $2, and if you want to sit on one of the much-sought-after pillows right up front or the couple of rows of straightbacked chairs just behind them, be sure to get there a good 45 minutes before doors open at 8 p.m. Otherwise, you stand. The music goes on until 12:30 a.m., with long sets interrupted by ten-minute breaks and the crowd continually changing as parents take children home at bedtime (oh, yes, the kids *love* the hall) and sidewalk listeners move in to take vacant places. There's a marvelous collection of jazz records on sale, some of them hard-to-find oldies.

The Dukes of Dixieland have been making music in the New Orleans manner for a long time now, and jazz buffs know they're in for a treat when this group performs. Nowadays, they've settled in at **Duke's Place,** the rooftop lounge of the Monteleone Hotel, 214 Royal St. (tel. 581-1567). There's a sweeping view of the Mississippi, the French Quarter, and Canal Street from up here, and the music is always first-rate. The Dukes play for 9, 10:20, and 11:40 p.m. shows Monday through Saturday. No cover charge, but a one-time entertainment charge entitles you to two drinks and all three shows. It's a good idea to reserve.

Pat O'Brien's, at 718 St. Peter St., has been famous for as long as I can remember for its gigantic, rum-based Hurricane drink, served in 29-ounce hurricane-lamp-style glasses. But more than the drinks, the let-your-hair-down conviviality has earned it a special place among so many residents that it sometimes has a neighborhood air usually associated with much smaller places. There are three bars here—the main bar at the entrance and one of the loveliest patio bars in existence have no entertainment—but it's the large lounge just off the entrance that is the center of a Pat O'Brien's fun night. And the fun comes from several teams of female pianists alternating at twin pianos and an emcee who tells jokes (which can get pretty "blue" in the late hours). The girls must know every song ever written, and when they ask a patron "Where're you from?" quick as a wink they'll break into a number associated with the visitor's home state. Requests are shouted out and quickly honored, and singalongs develop all night long, sometimes led by a patron who's been invited up to the bandstand. About the only requests they shy away from are "Dixie" and "Yankee Doodle Dandy"—those postage-size tables were installed expressly to discourage enthusiastic Yankees and Rebels from using them as podiums from which to lead partisan cheering! There's no minimum and no cover (in fact, I once went in when things were so lively I never *did* get a drink, just had a terrific time enjoying the show and left unalcoholic, but happy). The main bar is open from 10 a.m. to 4 a.m., the patio from noon to 4 a.m., and the lounge from 8 p.m. to 4 a.m. (5 a.m. on Friday and Saturday).

Don't confuse the **Old Absinthe House** at 400 Bourbon St. (tel. 525-8108) with the Old Absinthe House at 240 Bourbon. That's right, they both have the same name, and what's more, they're both entitled to it! The one on the corner of Bourbon and Bienville Streets (that's 240) can claim the original *site,* while all the original *fixtures* are now to be found at 400, on the corner of Bourbon and Conti. That situation came about when federal agents padlocked the original (it was operating as a speakeasy) during the '20s, and some enterprising soul broke in, removed the bar, the register, 19th-century prints, ceiling fans, an antique French clock, and a handsome set of marble-based fountains once used to drip water into absinthe (which has been banned in the U.S. since 1918 because it's a narcotic). They all turned up soon afterward in the establishment on the next corner a block away, and New Orleans was blessed with two "original" Old Absinthe Houses! Anyway, it's the one at 400 Bourbon where you'll find rhythm and blues and progressive jazz—drinks only at the other. Beginning at 9 p.m. nightly, the music is continuous, sometimes with as many as three groups alternating, until all hours—there's no legal shutdown time in New Orleans, and it isn't unusual to find things still going strong here as dawn breaks. On weekends there's also daytime music. Don't look for Dixieland jazz—this is one of the few places in the Quarter you won't find it. There's a cover charge of $2 on Friday and Saturday nights (drinks are $2 and up).

I once heard a horse-and-carriage driver state unequivocally that the corner of St. Peter and Bourbon Streets was "the world's heaviest jazz corner." He may well be right, for jazz pours out of just about every door (and most are wide open) in this area. Not just any jazz, mind you, but *great* jazz, and it begins early in the day, doesn't stop until there's no one left to tap a toe. Almost anyplace along here will be a good spot to spend an evening, but if you're like most, you'll pop into several. The only charge is a one-drink minimum (and, of course, you aren't encouraged to spend the night at one place nursing that one drink). You might start at **Maison Bourbon**, 641 Bourbon St. (tel. 522-8818), which keeps its doors open to the sidewalk and employs three bands every day to play from 11 a.m. to 2 a.m. (or later). Right across the street, things are jumping at **Crazy Shirley's**, 640 Bourbon St. (tel. 581-0301), with Tommy Yetta and his New Orleans Dixieland Jazz Band alternating with visiting groups to keep the sound going. **& Mo' Jazz**, 614 Bourbon St. (tel. 522-7261), has Dixieland on tap from 8:30 p.m., as well as ballads, pop standards, and Big Band–era songs. At 339 Bourbon St., the **Famous Door** (tel. 523-9973) holds forth with Dixieland jazz from 7 p.m. to 3 a.m. and beyond.

Lulu White's Mahogany Hall, 309 Bourbon St. (tel. 525-5595), occupies what was once the much loved Paddock Lounge. The 200-year-old building has been restored to a replica of the original Lulu White's, a thriving bordello from 1897 to 1917. There's a huge mahogany bar, antiques, framed reprints of newspapers from that era, and a reproduction of the famous *Blue Book* of New Orleans bordellos. The bar opens at noon, and live jazz music begins at 8 p.m. and runs until 1 a.m., seven days a week. No cover charge; jumbo-size drinks are $3.75 during entertainment, less other hours. There's jazz (and dinner, if you choose) at the **Blue Angel**, 225 Bourbon St. (tel. 522-0301), from 9 p.m. to 2 a.m.

If rock 'n roll is more your thing—or if you just feel like a break from all that jazz—you can find it at the **Original Melius Bar**, 622 Conti St. (tel. 523-9292), after 9 p.m.

If you like your entertainment on the sexy side, but aren't quite game for Bourbon Street's strippers, the place to go is the **Chris Owens Club**, on the corner of Bourbon and St. Louis Streets (tel. 523-6400). This talented, and very beautiful, lady puts on a one-woman show of fun-filled jazz, popular, country & western, and blues music while (according to one devoted fan) revealing enough of her physical endowments to make strong men bay at the moon! Between shows, there's dancing on the elevated dance floor. The $11 door charge covers the show and one drink. Shows are at 10 p.m. and midnight, and reservations are a good idea.

Incidentally, those *other* sexy shows, where they often exhibit more skin than talent, can be found in the 300 and 400 blocks of Bourbon—and if you walk by slowly, you can take in more than just a peek, since doors are opened to the sidewalk frequently to lure in the paying public.

For a nightcap to the strains of top-notch piano music in one of the city's loveliest settings, stop by the **Esplanade Lounge** in the Royal Orleans, 621 St. Louis St. (tel. 529-5333).

Before leaving nightlife in the Quarter, there are two just-plain-bars I'd like to tell you about. Both are a bit out of the center of things, and both have a special appeal in this city full of good drinking spots. **Lafitte's Blacksmith Shop**, at 941 Bourbon St., dates back to 1772. Legend has it that the privateer brothers Pierre and Jean Lafitte used the smithy as a "blind" for their lucrative trade in contraband (and, some say, slaves they'd captured on the high seas). It had pretty much deteriorated by 1944, when a honeymooning visitor fell in love with it and devoted most of the rest of his life to making it a social center for artists, writers, entertainers, and journalists. All without changing one iota of the musty old interior—even today, you can see the original construction and "feel" what it must have been like when it was a privateers' hangout. Unfortunately, Tom Caplinger's penchant for treating good friends like Tennessee Williams, Lucius Beebe, and others to refreshments "on the house" was stronger than his business acumen, and he eventually lost the building. Friends say it broke his heart, but he rallied and a little later opened a new place down the block towards Canal Street called the **Café Lafitte in Exile** (the exile is his own, from that beloved blacksmith shop), which flourishes even after his death as an elite gay bar. All this is, of course, history, but I think it helps explain the comfortable, neighborhood air that still pervades the place. The interior is all exposed brick, wooden tables, and an air of authenticity. It's a good drop-in spot any time of day, but I especially enjoy relaxing in the dim, candlelit bar at the end of a festive night.

The younger set will find a friendly home at the **Cosimos Bar** on the corner of Burgundy and Governor Nichols Streets. Nothing fancy, and no special history here, just a favorite gathering place for a lively neighborhood crowd who welcome strangers and make them feel right at home. In fact, it's that sociability that sets the Cosimos apart.

76 ARTHUR FROMMER'S NEW ORLEANS

OUTSIDE THE QUARTER: Pete Fountain is one of those royal native sons who has never been able to sever hometown ties. For more than 20 years he held forth in his own Bourbon Street club, but these days you'll find him at the **New Orleans Hilton** at Poydras and the Mississippi River in a recreation of his former Quarter premises which seats more than twice the number that could be accommodated in the old club. The plush interior—gold chairs and banquettes, red velvet bar chairs, white iron-lace-railinged gallery—sets the mood for the popular nightspot. Pete is featured in one show a night, Tuesday through Saturday at 10 p.m. The club, on the hotel's third floor, is named simply **Pete Fountain's** (tel. 523-4374 or 561-0500), is closed Sunday and Monday, and you'll need reservations. The $20 cover charge includes one drink.

In a setting of sheer elegance, the **Fairmont Hotel's Blue Room,** on University Place (tel. 529-7111), features exciting big-name entertainers such as Tony Bennett, Ella Fitzgerald, Anthony Newley, Ben Vereen, Peggy Lee, or Carol Channing. This famous old room, all blue and gold and crystal chandeliers, has endured from the time the hotel's name was the Roosevelt and its bands were broadcast on late-night radio from coast to coast. It is, in many ways, the "grand old lady" of New Orleans nightspots, and I, for one, feel that no visit to the city is complete without at least one night here. No matter what star is appearing, there's the backup band of Bill Clifford, a reliable "big band" sound for listening and dancing between shows, and both atmosphere and service harken back to the days when a night out was a real occasion. A perfect Blue Room evening includes dinner, chosen from a menu that includes continental and Créole cuisine and an extensive wine list ($30 to $35 for dinner and show), but you can come for the show alone for a cover charge that may vary from $10 to $20, depending on the star attraction. Cocktails and dinner are available from 6:30 p.m., and show times (which vary occasionally) are usually 9 and 11 p.m. Reservations are essential, as are jackets.

The view is breathtaking any time of day, but especially so after dark, from the **Top of the Mart,** International Trade Mart Building, 2 Canal St. at the river, and it keeps changing as the large lounge makes a complete circle every 90 minutes. From up here, you'll see the bend in the Mississippi that gives New Orleans its "Crescent City" title, and the reflected lights of ships in the harbor reminds you that this is not just a fun town, but a very busy and important port as well. And, as you revolve, the

NEW ORLEANS NIGHTLIFE/ACTIVITIES 77

layout of the city unfolds all the way to Lake Pontchartrain. At night, there's a jazz band in attendance. No admission charge and no cover. Since no food is served (only drinks), they don't permit bringing along the kids. One tip to the ladies: Don't lay your purse on the windowsill when you're seated—*it* doesn't revolve, and you'll wind up either chasing it around the room or waiting in the hope that it'll come back around to you!

Another up-high spot with a glorious view (but one that stays still) is the **Rainforest,** atop the New Orleans Hilton, 2 Poydras at the Mississippi River (tel. 561-0500), which is as popular with residents as it is with out-of-towners. In daylight hours, the Rainforest is a sunny luncheon spot (see Chapter VI); at sundown, it's a perfect place for cocktails; but come 9 p.m., there's dance music and a spectacular light and sound show that simulates a thunderstorm (sound effects operate during the day, as well). The decor is that of a tropical paradise, with gnarled cypress trees, bamboo furnishings, and lots of greenery. No cover and no minimum here, just one of the most action-packed dance floors in town.

At the corner of Tchoupitoulas and Napoleon, **Tipitina's,** 501 Napoleon St. (tel. 899-9114), is a big old barn-like building within earshot of boat whistles on the Mississippi. It has been in turn a brothel, boxing club, and Dixieland jazz center. In its present incarnation, it's **Professor Longhair's Piano and Juice Bar,** founded to promote the professor's music and other locally rooted music. The range covers jazz, blues, reggae, rock and roll, and zydeco. Regional favorites like Clifton Chenier, the Radiators, the Neville Brothers, and the Meters are regulars, with appearances from time to time of such nationally known acts as Jr. Walker and the All Stars and Bo Diddley. Cover charges run from $2 to $10, and shows start at 9:30 p.m. on weekdays, 11 p.m. on weekends. For a late night of conviviality and dancing to some of the best music in town, Tip's is a winner.

Local artists also perform every night at **Tyler's Beer Garden,** 5234 Magazine St. (tel. 895-9146). There's no cover and no minimum—and delicious raw oysters that go for 15¢ apiece! Barbequed shrimp, boiled crabs, and boiled crawfish tails are also available. *Note:* You'll most likely find the front door locked in this informal, sometimes noisy, place, so just go around to the side door and settle in.

It's hard to know just how to describe the **Maple Leaf Bar,** 8316 Oak St. (tel. 866-9359). Located in the Carrollton section, it has, since its beginning in 1974, paired a neighborly "hang out" bar with such unlikely roommates as a deli, chess club, red bean kitchen, and a small laundromat. Always, there's been a jukebox offering an eclectic mix of musical styles, from classical to jazz to ragtime to Cajun, and there's a strong tradition of good conversation ranging from literary subjects (poetry readings every Sunday afternoon feature local and visiting poets and writers) to music to sports to almost any topic you choose. Come 10 p.m., however, the jukebox gives way to musical groups as diverse as Deacon John and his Rhythm & Blues Review, swing musician Gatemouth Brown, soul singer Johnny Adams, and Li'l Queenie and the Skin Twins, who dish out original rock-blues along with pop classics. Thursday nights and some weekends celebrate the lively music and dancing from southwest Louisiana's Cajun country, with standouts like the Bourre Cajun Band or the black Cajun zydeco renditions of Dopsie and his Cajun Twisters. The cover charge once the music starts can range from $2 to $5.

ON THE RIVER: A lovely night out in New Orleans is one on the water. The **Créole Queen** is a new paddlewheeler, built in the tradition of its forebears, which made its debut at the 1984 World's Fair and now offers superb Créole dinner and jazz cruises on Friday and Saturday nights. Departures are at 7 p.m., and you return to its dock at the Hilton around 9 p.m. There's a covered promenade deck and dance floors on all decks. Fare is $26 per person (which includes dinner), and there's continuous bar service. Schedules are subject to change, so call ahead to confirm days, times, etc.: 524-0814 (ticket booth) or 529-4567 (office).

From time to time the steamboat **Natchez** and riverboat **President** also offer moonlight cruises with music at fares of about $10, with optional dinner or snackbar service available at extra charges. Call 586-8777 to check sailings and fares at the time of your visit.

AFTER-DARK TOURS: If you're on your own and hesitant to set out alone for a taste of New Orleans nightlife, there are two excellent after-dark group tours available. Both will cost between $30 and $35, and include stops at more than one nightspot (usually three) for the show, dinner, and a nightcap at the Top of the Mart, the French Market, or somewhere similar. Both will furnish pickup and delivery service. For full details and reservations, contact **Gray Line of New Orleans** 1793 Julia St. (tel. 525-0138) or **Southern Tours**, 7801 Edinburgh St. (tel. 486-0604).

Theater, Opera, Concerts, Etc.

In spite of the fact that it's a little off the regular routes for touring Broadway shows, New Orleans does attract some very good national companies, and there's surprisingly good local theater. The city has a long-standing love affair with footlight entertainment—Le Petit Théâtre du Vieux Carré is one of the oldest playhouses in this country, light opera appeared as early as 1810, and grand opera was first sung here in 1837. Opera enjoyed its peak years during the Gay '90s and the early part of this century, and thrived until a fire destroyed the famous old French Opera House in 1919. It wasn't until 1943 that the New Orleans Opera House Association was formed to present several operas a season, with Metropolitan Opera stars in lead roles supported by talented local voices. Occasionally, the Met's touring company will also book performances here. If you're an opera buff and in town during one of the local offerings, don't pass it up—there's nothing amateurish about these productions. You'll likely find them (as well as concerts by top performers, symphony orchestras, ballets, and recitals by local and imported talent) in one of two buildings: the New Orleans Theatre for the Performing Arts or the New Orleans Municipal Auditorium (which also accommodates such general-audience shows as circuses, prize fights, ice shows, and the popular summer pops symphony concerts). The New Orleans Philharmonic Symphony Orchestra plays a subscription series of concerts during the fall-to-spring season, and the pops concerts on June and July weekends. Live theater got a big boost in early 1980 when the grand old Saenger Theatre was reopened after being rescued from demolition by a determined group of New Orleanians. There's a good dinner theater going strong, a small Toulouse Street playhouse, and sometimes good cabaret in bar or lounge settings. In short, you're unlikely to hit town when there *isn't* something worthwhile going on in the performing arts. You can get up-to-the-minute information on what's happening by calling the **Ticketmaster Entertainment Hotline**, 1500 Paydras St. (tel. 587-3999). They can also sell you tickets to current events.

80 □ ARTHUR FROMMER'S NEW ORLEANS

THEATERS: Since the **Saenger Theatre,** 143 N. Rampart St. (tel. 587-3200), is *the* theater news in New Orleans, let's start with it. First opened in 1927, it was regarded as one of the finest in the world, and it has now been completely restored in all its finery. The decor is Renaissance Florence, with Greek and Roman sculpture, fine marble statues, and glittering cut-glass chandeliers. The ceiling is alive with twinkling stars, with realistic (although man-made) clouds drifting by. It's a setting the likes of which are fast disappearing from the American theater scene, and New Orleans is to be congratulated on preserving such opulence. First-rate Broadway productions like *Evita* and *My Fair Lady* play here regularly. Check to see what's on when you're in town.

Le Petit Théâtre du Vieux Carré, 616 St. Peter St. (tel. 522-1054), is right in the heart of the French Quarter, and if you hear people talking about "The Little Theater," this is it. It's the oldest nonprofessional theater troupe in the country and periodically puts on plays which rival the professionals in excellence. Check when you're in New Orleans to see if the footlights are up, and if they are, *go!*

The **Toulouse Theatre,** 615 Toulouse St. (tel. 522-6484), has sent at least one home-grown production to New York's Off-Broadway scene (*One Mo' Time,* an authentic, rowdy history of New Orleans's Lyric Theatre in the '20s). The setting for stage shows, concerts, or occasional fine films that play here is sort of "comfortable 1920s elegance," and the theater is seldom dark. Incidentally, the adjacent Toulouse Jazz Café (open from 10 a.m.) is a delightful before- or after-performance stop, and they feature live jazz after 5 p.m.

The **Theatre of the Performing Arts,** 801 N. Rampart St. (tel. 522-0592), opened in early 1973 and has become the home of lavish touring musical shows, as well as concerts by cultural artists. Opera and ballet also appear here in season. It's a part of the New Orleans Cultural Center in Louis Armstrong Park.

The **Municipal Auditorium,** 1201 St. Peter St. (tel. 522-0592), is just across a flowered walkway from the Theatre of the Performing Arts in the Cultural Center and is used for just about every kind of entertainment, from the circus to touring theatrical companies to ballet and concerts. This is where most of those marvelous, elaborate Mardi Gras balls are held.

Other possibilities for theatrical performances (check when you're here, since none of these is open on a regular basis) include: **N.O.R.D. Theatre** (tel. 586-5275), for productions sponsored by the New Orleans Recreation Department; **Tulane University Theatre** (tel. 865-6204), which puts on student plays of very high caliber; and the **Superdome** (tel. 525-8573)—yes, that's right, the Superdome—which frequently hosts entertainment not even remotely connected with sports.

Sports

For the sports enthusiast, there simply is no off-season in New Orleans. If you're strictly a spectator, that palatial **Superdome** is the scene of all home games for the New Orleans Saints football team, University of New Orleans basketball, Tulane University football, and, of course, the Sugar Bowl on New Year's Day. The Superdome number for current information is 525-8573.

You can follow the horses out at the **Fair Grounds track**, 1761 Gentilly Blvd. (tel. 944-5515), or at **Jefferson Downs**, 1300 Sunset Blvd., Kenner (tel. 466-8521), just off I-10 via Williams Boulevard. Both have parimutuel betting and charge $2 for general admission, $4.50 to clubhouse; parking will run $1 to $2. Racing dates at the Fair Grounds are from the Friday before Thanksgiving until the end of March; at Jefferson Downs, from April 1 through the first week in September. Post time is 7:15 p.m., and there's racing Tuesday through Saturday.

Golfers can play year round on excellent courses. Just a few of the 18-hole locations open to visitors are: **City Park**, with four courses and a clubhouse at 1040 Filmore Ave. (tel. 283-4324); **Audobon Park Course**, 473 Walnut St. (tel. 861-9511); and **Pontchartrain Park Golf Course**, 6514 Congress Dr. (tel. 288-5342).

Tennis buffs will find courts in Audubon Park (tel. 861-2537) and City Park (tel. 482-2230 or 482-4888).

You can also **ride horseback** in both Audubon Park (tel. 861-2537) and City Park (tel. 482-2230 or 482-4888).

There's terrific **fishing** in the waters around New Orleans, and if you want to try your luck you can go after pompano, red snapper, bluefish, cobia, or channel bass in the coastal waters; crappie, bluegill, and largemouth bass from lakes and rivers; or set your sights on those gulf fighters, marlin, tarpon, and sailfish. Boat charters are easy to come by, and you can reserve by calling the **Fishing Boat Information Service** (tel. 282-8111) or **Barataria Charters**, in Barataria (tel. 504/689-2386).

Chapter VIII

SEEING FRENCH QUARTER SIGHTS

IN MANY RESPECTS the French Quarter *is* New Orleans, and many visitors never leave its confines. I think that's a mistake, and I'll tell you why in the next chapter. Be that as it may, *this* is where it all began, and in the 90 or so square blocks of the Quarter, there's more sightseeing excitement per square foot than many entire cities—or even states—can boast.

The narrow old streets are lined with ancient buildings (many of them a century and a half old) whose fronts are embellished with that distinctive lacy ironwork. Their carriage drives or alleyways are often guarded by more of the ironwork in the form of massive gates, and offer glimpses of backyard enchantment of some of the loveliest courtyards in the world. Secluded from street noises and nosy neighbors, the courtyards provide the beauty, relaxation, and privacy so dear to Créole souls, as well as very important ventilation for their homes. Of course, many of these venerable old buildings now serve as entertainment centers that often ring with merriment that is anything but restful; and many more house shops of every description. But above ground level, most also have apartments (many of them quite luxurious) in the time-honored custom of combining commercial ventures with living space. A diminishing few are still in the hands of original-owner families. Whatever their present use, almost every building in the Quarter could tell tales of romance and history within its walls which would enthrall the dullest soul.

Thanks to the Vieux Carré Commission, not even "progress" is allowed to intrude on a heritage which blends gaiety with

FRENCH QUARTER SIGHTS 83

graciousness, the rowdiness of Bourbon Street with quiet residential areas, and the "busyness" of commerce with a sense of leisure and goodwill. Progress is here, all right, with all its attendant benefits, but New Orleans *insists* that it conform to this special lifestyle, not the other way around. There's not even a traffic light within the whole of the French Quarter—they're relegated to fringe streets—and street lights are of the old gaslight style. Not to worry about those absent traffic lights—automobiles are banned from Royal and Bourbon Streets during a good part of the day, making them pedestrian malls, and the area around Jackson Square is a permanent haven for foot traffic, no vehicles allowed.

Laid out in an almost perfect square back in 1718 by a French royal engineer named Adrien de Pauger, the French Quarter is easy to get around. And even in these high-crime days, you're relatively safe wandering its streets during daylight hours. After dark, as in most metropolitan areas, it's best to exercise caution when walking alone outside the centers of activity—in New Orleans, that means Bourbon, Royal, and Chartres Streets and the streets which connect them (there's safety as well as fun in the numbers that throng those streets all night long).

Those driving into the French Quarter should know that all streets are one-way, and on weekdays during daylight hours, Royal and Bourbon Streets become pedestrian malls closed to automobiles between the 300 and 700 blocks.

It won't take you long to learn how streets run, especially if you have armed yourself with the excellent walking-tour map passed out by the **Tourist Commission,** 334 Royal St. (tel. 566-5011). In fact, no one should set out to explore this city—in- or outside the French Quarter—without first stopping by the commission. Both the walking and driving tours they suggest are circular in route, easy to follow, and so informative they're minicourses in New Orleans history and culture. They provide the best possible introduction to this grand old city.

There is so much to see in the French Quarter that the following can, at best, only be a very subjective list. One thing is certain: no matter how carefully you plan your time, you're bound to get back home and discover you've missed at least one sightseeing highlight. People who live here will tell you that the only thing to do is move down and settle in to a lifetime of exploration! Since you and I can't do that, I'll do my best to give you a rundown on the things I think shouldn't be missed. I've arranged them by streets, rather than in a suggested route, so

84 ARTHUR FROMMER'S NEW ORLEANS

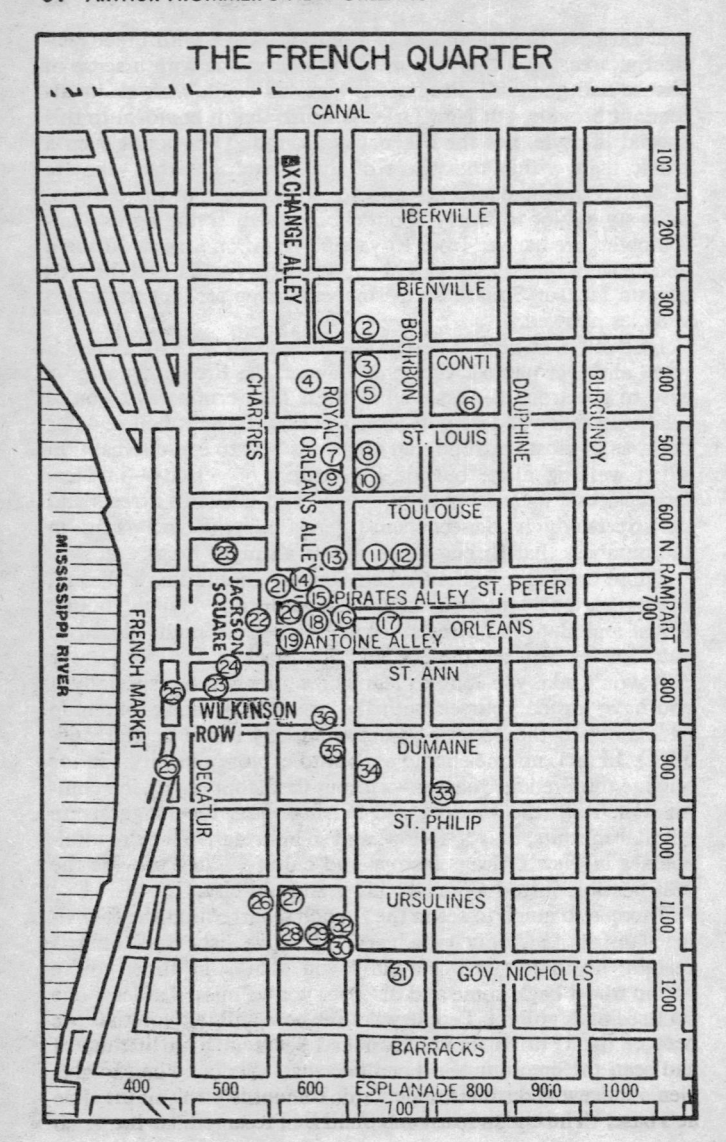

THE FRENCH QUARTER

FRENCH QUARTER SIGHTS 85

that no matter where you find yourself, you'll have an easy reference to what you're seeing. *(For a prescribed walking tour—on which I could not hope to improve—stick to the aforementioned Tourist Commission route.)* As I said, this is a very subjective list—by the time you leave for home, you'll have one of your own.

KEY TO THE NUMBERED REFERENCES ON THE FRENCH QUARTER MAP: 1. Old Bank of Louisiana; 2. Old Bank of the U.S.; 3. Old La. State Bank; 4. N.O. Court Building; 5. Casa Faurie; 6. The Hermann House; 7. Maison Seignouret; 8. Merieult House; 9. Casa de Comercio; 10. Court of Two Lions; 11. LeMonnier House; 12. Maison de Flechier; 13. Maison LeMonnier; 14. Spanish Arsenal; 15. Pirates Alley; 16. Cathedral Garden; 17. Salle d'Orleans (Orleans Ballroom); 18. Pere Antoine's Alley; 19. The Presbytere; 20. St. Louis Cathedral; 21. The Cabildo; 22. Jackson Square; 23. Pontalba Buildings; 24. 1850 House; 25. The French Market; 26. Old Ursulines Convent; 27. Beauregard House; 28. Soniat House; 29. Clay House; 30. LaLaurie House ("The Haunted House"); 31. Thierry House; 32. The Gallier House; 33. Lafitte's Blacksmith Shop; 34. The Cornstalk Fence; 35. Miltenberger Houses; 36. "Madame John's Legacy."

Jackson Square

Jackson Square lies at the very heart of the French Quarter, facing Decatur Street "riverside" and Chartres Street "lakeside," bounded on the "downriver" side by St. Ann Street, and by St. Peter Street "upriver." Since 1721 (when it was called Place d'Armes), it has served as a military parade ground; the flags fluttering from its flagpole have changed no fewer than seven times; it has witnessed ceremonies transferring the Louisiana Territory from French to U.S. control (perhaps the greatest real estate deal in history, since the land Pres. Thomas Jefferson bought from Napoleon for a mere $15 million was large enough to contain all or a part of 13 of our present states); there have been public hangings on its grounds; it has acquired its new name (in the 1850s, when New Orleans changed the name to honor its hero of the 1815 battle fought out at Chalmette Battleground) and seen the erection of a giant bronze statue of its namesake, Gen. Andrew Jackson. (Incidentally, that inscription on the statue's base, "The Union Must and Shall Be Preserved," is the work of a hated Union general, Ben Butler, during his occupation of the city during the Civil War, and his very *loose* interpretation of an Andrew Jackson remark made years before.) During all those years, it has been a focal point for New Orleanians' daily life, functioning as a sort of city courtyard, or patio. Today, you can enter through its lamp-topped iron gates for a brief respite from whatever your day's activities may be, or wander around the outside of its iron fence, making the sidewalk artists and their sketches and musicians and performers of all descriptions a part of those activities. (Look for Al Everette, the only silhouette artist "on the fence," and Charlie Ward, who has a studio at 508 Wilkinson and whose posters and prints are in many New Orleans shops.) It's a pleasant garden spot set aside as a pedestrian mall, with one side looking toward the Mississippi River and historic buildings lining all three of its remaining sides. The most famous, and *the* one most instantly recognizable New Orleans landmark, is the cathedral directly facing you if you view the square from the Decatur Street side.

The **St. Louis Cathedral** is across from the Chartres Street entrance to Jackson Square, and the one you see today is the third to stand in this spot. A hurricane destroyed the first, in 1723. Then, on Good Friday of 1788, the bells of its replacement were kept silent for religious reasons rather than ringing out the alarm for a fire which eventually went out of control and burned down over 850 buildings, and the cathedral was once again destroyed. Rebuilt in 1794, largely through the generosity of a Don Almonester who is buried beneath the marble at the base of its altar, it is of Spanish design, with a tower at each end and a higher central tower, and its construction is of brick covered over with stucco to protect the mortar from dampness. Inside, look for the six stained-glass windows showing scenes of Spanish domination in New Orleans—they were donated by the government of Spain in 1962. There's also a spectacular painting on the wall above and behind the main altar, showing Louis IX of France (the cathedral's patron saint) proclaiming the Seventh Crusade from the steps of Notre-Dame. You're welcome to poke around inside from 9 a.m. to 5 p.m. if, of course, services are not in progress.

On the uptown side of the cathedral, also facing Jackson Square, is the **Cabildo,** on the corner of Chartres and St. Peter Streets. It has been, in turn, a French police station and guardhouse, the statehouse of the Spanish governing body (the Very Illustrious Cabildo), New Orleans's City Hall, and the Louisiana

State Supreme Court. Today, it is owned by the Louisiana State Museum, and although its exhibits change fairly often, you can always view Napoleon's death mask (one of four in existence), made by the emperor's personal physician (who later lived in New Orleans and donated the mask to the city). There's an art gallery on the second floor (that's where the formal signing of the Louisiana Purchase took place), and the third floor is devoted to exhibitions of Mississippi River plantations and riverboats. Other exhibits show historic portraits, artifacts, and maps of French and Spanish colonial Louisiana in settings that reflect appropriate eras.

One further note: If you think those old Civil War cannon look pitifully small and ineffective by modern standards, you might like to know that in 1921, in a not-so-funny prank, one was loaded with powder, an iron ball rammed down its muzzle, and fired in the dead of night. That lethal missile traveled from the Cabildo's portico across the wide expanse of the Mississippi and some six blocks inland before landing in a house in Algiers, narrowly missing its occupants! The Cabildo is open every day except Monday, from 9 a.m. to 6 p.m., and admission is $2 for adults, $1 for students (under 12 free).

Incidentally, that's **Pirate's Alley** that runs between the Cabildo and the cathedral from Chartres Street to Royal Street. There's absolutely *no* evidence to support the story that pirates once transported their stolen goods along this pathway, but it holds onto the name with tenacity, despite its official tag of Orleans Alley. You'll usually find artists displaying their paintings here, as well as outside the railing of **St. Anthony's Garden,** directly in back of the cathedral (it is said that back in dueling days many a gentleman defended his honor in this little garden). The garden is named for a beloved Capuchin priest affectionately called Père Antoine, and the walkway between Chartres and Royal Streets on the downtown side of the cathedral is given the name of Père Antoine's Alley, in his honor.

On the downtown side of the cathedral, facing Chartres Street and Jackson Square, the **Presbytère** is very similar to the Cabildo and was originally intended to be used as a home for the cathedral priests. Ironically, it has never served that purpose, but the name still sticks. It was begun in 1794, but was not actually completed until 1813, when the government took it over. Since then it has been used as a courthouse, and since 1910 has been the property of the Louisiana State Museum. You'll be fascinated even before you go inside, for over to the extreme right of the colonnade, that cigar-shaped iron object is the first iron submarine ever built—by the Confederate Navy, no less! Named the *Pioneer* and built on the shores of Bayou St. John, the sub was launched in 1861, could travel all of four miles an hour, and made one trial run before being sunk in Lake Pontchartrain to keep it out of the hands of victorious Yankees. Do take a close look—it's a far cry from the atomic submarines of today. Inside, you'll find all sorts of historical exhibits, including antique toys, Newcomb pottery, Louisiana portraits, Audubon bird prints, and changing exhibition galleries. Hours are 10 a.m. to 6 p.m. Tuesday through Sunday. Adults pay $2; students over 12, $1; those under 12, free.

On both the St. Peter and St. Ann Streets sides of Jackson Square, those twin, four-story, red brick buildings are the **Pontalba Buildings,** with some of the most beautiful cast-iron balcony railings in the Quarter and a history that reflects the determination of a plucky New Orleans woman to compete with those upstart American "uptowners" and keep business concerns in the Quarter by providing elite-address shops and living quarters on the square. Indeed, these are said to be the first apartment buildings in the country—they were designed by Baroness Micaela Almonester Pontalba (she was the daughter of the Don Almonester responsible for rebuilding the cathedral) to accommodate shops on the ground level, with elegant living quarters (as well as servants' quarters) on the upper floors. They were begun in 1849 and built under her direct supervision; you can see her mark today in the entwined initials "A-P" in that lovely ironwork. The 16 row houses on St. Peter Street were completed in 1850, those on St. Ann Street in 1851. The luxury apartments have enormous rooms, high ceilings, and long windows which open onto the balconies. From the first, they have attracted prestige tenants (Jenny Lind was one of the first, and William Faulkner once lived here), and they are much sought-after even now, with a long waiting list. Those on St. Peter Street now belong to the city of New Orleans, and the State of Louisiana owns those on St. Ann Street.

The shops in both rows make marvelous browsing. When you're on the St. Peter Street side, stop by the **Puppetorium** at no. 514, where *The Legend of Jean Lafitte* is presented with 50 giant marionettes. It's open every day except Christmas and Mardi Gras (9:30 a.m. to 5:30 p.m.) for an admission of $2 for adults, $1 for children. The **Café Pontalba,** on the corner of Chartres and St. Peter, is a good spot to tarry for a light snack, a refreshing drink, or just people-watching. Over on the other side, the **1850 House,** 529 St. Ann St., is restored just as it might have been in that year, with Louisiana-French-Victorian furnishings that include a great tester canopied bed, authentic utensils, and toys of the period, and even servants' quarters up on the third floor. You can step back in history every day except Monday, 10 a.m. to 6 p.m., for a $2 charge for adults; students over 12, $1; under 12, free.

Decatur Street

Before the levees were built, Decatur Street was right on the riverfront. Over the years, however, the mighty Mississippi has deposited silt which gradually built up the land mass now housing wharves and warehouses. Starting at Canal Street, the entire 100 block on the lakeside is occupied by the massive **Custom House,** which was begun in 1848 and not completed until 1880. It's worth a few minutes to go up to its second floor to see the handsome "Marble Hall" in the very center of the building. Across the street toward the river stands the newly completed **Canal Place,** where you'll find branches of some of this country's leading fine stores.

Farther along, directly across from Jackson Square where St. Peter Street ends at Decatur, rises a big old six-story Romanesque Revival building. From 1891 until just a few years ago, this was the brewhouse of Jax beer, a regional brew still very popular in these parts. What you see from Decatur Street is the rear of the building, not too exciting. A group of enthusiastic, energetic native sons has, however, transformed the old landmark into an exciting food, entertainment, and shopping complex with a riverfront promenade to open up a long stretch of the Mississippi after years of its being obscured from pedestrian view. You could literally spend an entire day in the **Jackson Brewery.** Its first two levels hold specialty retail shops featuring local and imported foods, crafts, furniture, clothing, etc. But it's the third floor you're likely to head for time and again between explorations of the building: something they've dubbed the Jaxfest holds forth 12 hours a day, seven days a week, and I guarantee you won't go just once. In a rip-roaring celebration of New Orleans fine food, kiosks, booths, wine bars, international beer bars, and the like will be dishing up examples of the cooking that has made this city famous the world over. It's a place to sit down, relax, and indulge in good eating. For more of the same in somewhat fancier settings, you can dine in several restaurants on the fourth, fifth, and sixth levels, which are devoted to major dining establishments and entertainment.

Just past the Jackson Brewery, pretty riverside **Washington Artillery Park,** with its splashing fountain, has always been a "promenade" for New Orleanians, and now the elevated area has been renamed the **Moon Walk** (for Mayor "Moon" Landrieu). There are attractive plantings and benches from which to view the city's main industry, its busy port (second only to Amsterdam for tonnage handled each year). To your right, you can see the Greater New Orleans Bridge and the International Trade Mart skyscraper, as well as the Toulouse Street wharf, departure point for excursion steamboats.

Continuing "downriver," you're at the upper edge of the **Old French Market,** which runs for about six blocks along the Mississippi. By all means stop at the outdoor **Café du Monde** for café au lait and beignets to fortify you for serious sightseeing, to lift your spirits, or just on general principles (personally, I can never pass this place without at least one order's worth of people-watching). As for the market itself, there's been one here since Indian days (when Choctaws traded with the French), and the first building was constructed by the Spanish about 1791. Gradually, other buildings were added—a meat market, open-air vegetable stalls, spice stands, etc.—and three of the present buildings were put up in 1912. Since then, there have been two restorations, one by the WPA in 1937, and more recently a $2½-million effort in 1975 which has resulted in the old colonnaded buildings having their innards gussied up for all kinds of shops, candy and pralines bakeries. There are several good eateries in the market (see "Dining in the French Quarter," Chapter V), and there's still a Farmers' Market in the outdoor sheds back of the renovated buildings. Even if you're staying in a hotel room and are not in the market for fruits and vegetables, don't miss this section just for the lively conversation as vendors and customers continue the sort of trade that brought the French Market into being. Of course, there's good "take back home" shopping all through the market, and you'll hardly escape without a souvenir purchase or two. Back of the French Market, near Barracks Street, there's an open-air flea market every Saturday and Sunday that's one of the neatest free attractions in the city.

Across the street from the Old French Market, from Jackson Street all the way over to Esplanade, Decatur Street was, not too long ago, a seedy, rundown area of wild bars and cheap rooming houses. No more. There's an exciting Renaissance going on—all sorts of interesting shops (like Ye Olde Ship Store at 831 Decatur, Santa's Quarters at 1025-27 Decatur, and the Bombay Company at Ursuline and Decatur, 1 French Market Place); new eating places like Molly's at the Market (1107 Decatur) joining oldtimers like Tujagues (823 Decatur); and imaginative developments like the Marketplace (1015 Decatur) in an old warehouse filled with small shops, craft demonstrations, and some sort of entertainment—musicians, jugglers, magicians, or the like. That's just a smattering of what's there now, and Decatur Street is far from "finished"—it's already drawing a local clientele with a slightly bohemian flavor, and as more casual/smart bars open and nightlife assumes a relaxed "respectability," it will no doubt attract even larger crowds. At any rate, it's a fun street now, so allow enough time to stroll, browse, and perhaps bend an elbow or two. And as you pass 919 and 923 Decatur St., let your imagination conjure up the Café des Refugies and Hôtel de la Marine which were here in the 1700s and early 1800s, gathering places for pirates, smugglers, and European refugees (some of them outlaws), a far cry from today's scene!

Chartres Street

Pronounced "Charters," this street was named for a family of the French nobility. It runs along one end of Jackson Square and its most prominent buildings are those that face the square, described above. There are, however, several other points of interest on the street.

At the corner of St. Louis and Chartres is what was once a coffeehouse and exchange (where slaves once were bought and sold along with other "commodities"). The original Pierre Maspero's Exchange was a popular meeting place in 19th-century New Orleans, and when Gen. Andrew Jackson was in dire need of support (both men and supplies) for the defense of the city, it is said that he huddled here with the privateer Jean Lafitte to enlist his aid. He got it, and the Battle of New Orleans ended successfully for the Americans. Now, don't be surprised when you hear that these two plotted at other locations as well—apparently these two drank and schemed a lot, at several locations in the Quarter.

The **Napoleon House**, 500 Chartres St., was also the center of intrigue as far back as the late 1700s. There are actually *two* Napoleon Houses on Chartres Street, and both have interesting legends as to how they became associated with the "Little Corporal's" name. The house at 514 Chartres was, in 1815, the home of New Orleans's mayor, one Nicholas Girod. He was attending a play at the St. Philip Theatre when news came of Napoleon's escape from Elba and immediately took the stage to proclaim publicly that if the beloved emperor came to New Orleans (as everyone was certain he would—where else, after all, would he meet with such affection!), the mayor's residence would be placed entirely at his disposal. Napoleon, of course, never came, then or later. But during his later exile on St. Helena, a plot was hatched at *this* Napoleon House (500 Chartres St.) to rescue him from the island and bring him back to live here (indeed, the third floor was added expressly for that purpose). A ship was being outfitted with funds supplied by that same Nicholas Girod and manned by a crew recruited by Dominique You (one of Lafitte's pirate leaders) for the mission when news arrived of Napoleon's death from cancer. Today, you'll find a low-key bar (which serves sandwiches and snacks, see "Dining in the French Quarter," Chapter V) to the strains of classical music. The other Napoleon House (514 Chartres St.) was, during its long history, the shop and residence of a local druggist, Louis Dufilho.

Tradition says it was at the 538 Chartres St. site that wind from an open window blew a candle flame against flimsy curtains and set off a fire on Good Friday, March 21, 1788, which eventually wiped out more than 850 buildings. Because the cathedral bells were stilled in honor of the religious date, the fire was completely out of control before most of the townspeople even knew about it.

That fine old Spanish-style house at 617 Chartres St. was built in 1795 for Bartolomé Bosque. In the rear of the carriageway, there are three separate patios opening one into the other.

If your interests include art, there's an unusual gallery, the **Studio d'Artiste**, at 621 Chartres St. (tel. 523-6871). For the past 15 years or so it has been owned and operated by local artists, and customers deal directly with the artists. That often results in lower prices, since the middleman is eliminated, but more important, there is the stimulation of getting to know the creator of the work you purchase. There's a wide variety of styles and mediums: oil, acrylic, watercolor, batik, etchings, woodcuts, silkscreen, photography, pottery, and limited-edition prints, and paintings may be purchased either framed or unframed. The same group also operates the **Old Quarter Gallery** at 622 Royal St. (tel. 522-9752).

FRENCH QUARTER SIGHTS 93

The **Beauregard-Keyes House**, 1113 Chartres St., has more than one claim to fame. The "raised cottage" with its Doric columns and handsome twin staircases was built by a wealthy New Orleans auctioneer back in 1826 as a residence, and a world-famous chess champion, Paul Morphy, was born to his daughter in one of its rooms in 1837. Then, in the winter of 1866-1867, a defeated and financially broke Confederate, Gen. P. G. T. Beauregard, lived in a rented room here while he tried to find work. From the mid-1950s until 1970, it was the residence of Frances Parkinson Keyes, who wrote many novels about this region. One of them, *Madame Castel's Lodger*, is directly concerned with the general's stay in the house. *Dinner at Antoine's*, perhaps her most famous novel, was also written here. Mrs. Keyes left the house to a foundation, and the house, rear buildings, and garden are now open to the public. There's a $2.50 charge for adults, $1 for children over 13, and viewing hours are 10 a.m. to 4 p.m.

Across the street is the Archbishop Antoine Blanc Memorial, which includes the **Old Ursuline Convent**, 1114 Chartres St., completed in 1752, with the founder of the city, Sieur de Bienville, on hand for its opening. The Sisters of Ursula were, for years, the only teachers and nurses in New Orleans—they established the first school for Catholic girls, the first for blacks, the first for Indians, and set up the first orphanage in Louisiana. The nuns moved out of the convent in 1824 (they're in an uptown location these days), and in 1831 the state legislature met here. It now houses archives dating back to 1720. Especially noteworthy is the fact that this is the oldest building of record not only in New Orleans, but in the entire Mississippi Valley. Included in the complex is the beautifully restored old Chapel of the Archbishops erected in 1845 and still used as a house of worship. There are public tours on Wednesday at 1:30 and 3 p.m., with fees of $2.50 for adults, $1.50 for students, and $1 for children under 12. Special tours may be arranged by calling 561-0008.

Royal Street

Royal Street is perhaps best known for its concentration of antique shops. Not so well known is the fact that this is the street once traveled by the *Streetcar Named Desire*, a name made famous by New Orleans's adopted son, playwright Tennessee Williams. You'll find that streetcar parked at the Old Mint in the

400 block of Esplanade, but with or without streetcars, Royal Street is a sightseeing tour in itself.

In 1857, the four-story building at 127 Royal St. held a popular bar, the Gem, on the ground floor occupied these days by a doughnut shop and dry cleaners. The Gem was where many duels were arranged, as well as the meeting place for New Orleanians of all ilk, from governors to soldiers of fortune. But it was the meeting held in January of that year that proved so momentous for the city. You see, the heart of New Orleans revelry—Mardi Gras, itself—stood in danger of being abolished permanently because of so many attendant episodes of violence, and had not a small group formed a secret society (in the club rooms above the Gem) to restore order to the celebration, it might have perished in the very city with whose name it has since become synonymous. It was the Mistick Krewe of Comus that sprang to life that day, and it remains a Mardi Gras leader (see "The Festivals," Chapter X). Not much to see these days, but give the old building at least a token nod as you walk past in recognition of the very real part it played in keeping Mardi Gras on the New Orleans scene.

Three important banks once operated on corners of the Royal and Conti Streets intersection. The **Bank of Louisiana**, 334 Royal St., was erected in 1827. This handsome old building now houses the **New Orleans Tourist and Convention Commission**, and as I've said before, this should be the very *first* place you head for if you want to get the most out of your visit to the city. At 339 Royal, the old **Bank of the United States** was built in 1800—notice its fine hand-forged ironwork. The premises at 401 Royal was designed by Benjamin H. Latrobe, one of the architects of the Capitol in Washington, and opened in 1821 as home of the **Louisiana State Bank.**

The entire 400 block of Royal Street (on the river side) once held beautiful Spanish-style Créole town houses, all of which were demolished in 1907 in favor of the massive marble civil courts building, which was completed in 1910.

A dedicated missionary, Fr. Adrien Rouquette, was born at 413 Royal St. in 1813. Intensely interested in local Indians when no one else was, Father Rouquette not only ministered to the tribes across Lake Pontchartrain, but actually moved in with them and adopted their dress and many of their customs.

Brennan's Restaurant, at 417 Royal St. (of those well-known breakfasts, see "Dining in the French Quarter," Chapter V), is housed in a mansion built in 1801 for the maternal grandfather of Edgar Degas, the French painter. It later served as a bank (those initials in the balcony railings, "BL," were for Banque de la Louisiane) and the family home of chess champion Paul Morphy (he died in a second-floor bathroom in this house). It became a center of much entertaining, however, in the 1820s and 1830s, when its then owner, Martin Gordon, welcomed guests like Gen. Andrew Jackson to lavish banquets and balls. It seems fitting, somehow, that the tradition of gracious hospitality survives today in the famous restaurant.

Masonic Lodge meetings were held regularly in a drugstore at 437 Royal St. back in the early 1800s. But something more important to American culture also happened there, when the druggist, Antoine A. Peychard, served after-meeting drinks to lodge members in small egg cups, whose French name ("coquetier") was Americanized to "cocktail."

The **Brulatour Court** you'll hear mentioned from time to time in New Orleans is at 520 Royal St., a splendid home built in 1816 for wine merchant François Seignouret. WDSU-TV now lives here, but you're welcome to walk into the courtyard, and while you're there, notice the elaborate, fan-shaped ironwork on the right end of the third-floor balcony. Incidentally, the wine merchant is virtually revered today for the fine furniture he produced (with a graceful "S" worked into the ornamentation of every piece).

The **Merieult House,** at 533 Royal St., built in 1792, was one of the few French Quarter structures to escape that disastrous 1794 fire. The first owner's wife very nearly became mistress of a French castle when Napoleon offered one in exchange for her hair, which was flaming red in color (he wanted it for a wig to present to a Turkish sultan!). This dignified and beautiful New Orleans residence must have been quite enough for Madame Merieult, however, for she flatly refused the emperor. Nowadays, this is home to the **Historic New Orleans Collection** of artifacts, paintings, maps, and documents depicting Louisiana's colorful history from early explorers to the mid-nineteenth century, which are exhibited in some 11 galleries. The Historic New Orleans Collection is actually comprised of several buildings, including the Merieult House, a museum, gift shop, and a comprehensive research center for state and local history. The main exhibition area, free to the public (10 a.m. to 4:45 p.m. Tuesday to Saturday), presents changing displays on state history and culture. Guided tours are conducted for a $2 admission to both the Merieult House and the opulent "hidden house" of Gen. and

Mrs. L. Kemper Williams, who were wealthy, traveled collectors. Tours run from 10 a.m. to 3:15 p.m., Tuesday through Saturday; no children under 12 are admitted to the "hidden house"; and there are "touch tours" for the blind.

One of the best known landmarks in the Quarter is the **Court of the Two Sisters** at 615 Royal St. It was built in 1832 for a local bank president, on the site of the home of an earlier French governor in the 1700s. The two sisters were Emma and Bertha Camors (Bertha's husband owned the building), and from 1886 to 1906 they ran a variety store here. If you don't plan to have at least one meal in the restaurant now on the premises (see "Dining in the French Quarter," Chapter V), do stop by for a cool drink in the beautiful patio, which has a charming wishing well in the center.

The **Old Quarter Gallery**, 622 Royal St. (tel. 522-9752), is sister to Studio d'Artiste (see "Chartres Street," above) and always has an owner/artist in attendance.

Look for the **Loom Room** at 623 Royal St., where from 10 a.m. to 6 p.m. every day you can see exhibits of weaving and other American crafts, such as woodworking, glass, and pottery.

When you spot the **Old Town Praline Shop** at 627 Royal St., turn and walk through the carriage drive to see another of New Orleans's beautiful patios. This 1777 building is where Adelina Patti, the noted opera singer, came for a visit and stayed to become something of a local heroine in 1860. Only 17 at the time, Adelina saved the local opera company from financial ruin when she stepped in as a last-minute replacement for an ailing lead soprano in *Lucia di Lammermoor*—she was a tremendous hit and the season an assured success.

On the southeast corner of Royal and St. Peter Streets, **Le Monnier Mansion**, at 640 Royal St., once towered above every other French Quarter building as the city's first "skyscraper," all of three stories high when it was built in 1811! A fourth story was added in 1876 (perhaps to help it keep its skyline supremacy).

At this same intersection, the **LaBranch House**, 700 Royal St., is probably the most photographed building in the Quarter—and no wonder. Take a look at the lacy iron grillwork, with its delicate oak-leaf-and-acorn design, that fairly drips from all three floors. If you plan to preserve it on film, the best vantage point is diagonally across the street so that both street exposures will show in your picture.

The three houses at 900, 906, and 910 Royal St. are the **Mil-**

tenberger Mansions, built by a wealthy widow in 1838 for her three sons. Her great-granddaughter, Alice Heine, was born in 1910 and moved into the ranks of European royalty when she married first a duke, then the Prince of Monaco.

The house at 915 Royal St. is not the original building on this site, but there is a survivor of that earlier home—the unusual cast-iron fence in a pattern of cornstalks, complete with shucked ears, intertwined with morning glory vines and blossoms. It came by sea to New Orleans in 1834, when a Dr. Biamenti is said to have ordered it for his young midwestern bride who yearned for the waving cornfields of her home farmland.

The Italianate town house at 1132 Royal St. was built by James Gallier, Jr., a talented architect responsible for many of the fine old buildings in the French Quarter (including the grand French Opera House which burned in 1919). He built this as his own residence in 1860 and lived here until his death in 1868. Both the house and the courtyard (with colorful hibiscus and camellias) have been restored to their original appearance and are open to the public. Two adjoining buildings have also been added to house historical exhibits and a coffeeshop. Visitors can also see very instructive films on decorative plaster cornices and New Orleans ornamental ironwork. At the end of the tour, you'll be served complimentary light refreshments on the balcony. Plan to visit between 10 a.m. and 4:30 p.m. (actually, the last tour begins at 3:45 p.m.) Monday through Saturday. Admission is $2.50 for adults, $2 for senior citizens and students, $1 for ages 5 to 11, and under 5, free. There are special elevators to aid the handicapped.

Go by to see the **LaLaurie Home** at 1140 Royal St. in broad daylight—after dark, you might be disturbed by ghostly moans or the savage hissing of a whip, or even catch a glimpse of a small black child walking on the balcony. This is the Quarter's haunted house! Its story is a New Orleans tale of horror. It seems the very beautiful and socially prominent Delphine LaLaurie lived here and entertained lavishly, until one night in 1834 when fire broke out and neighbors crashed through a locked door to find seven starving slaves chained in painful positions, unable to move. The rescuers were appalled, and highly incensed. When the next day's newspapers suggested that the dazzling hostess might have set the fire herself, a mob assembled outside the house. Madame LaLaurie and her family escaped their neighbors' wrath, however, when they dashed out the carriage drive in a closed carriage and fled the city, eventually to Europe. The heartless woman did not return to New Orleans until several years later, when she died on the continent—and even then her body had to be buried in secrecy. This unhappy house has now been renovated and turned into luxury apartments—I wonder how its tenants sleep at night!

Bourbon Street

No, it's *not* named for the whiskey, but for the royal family of France. Still, sometimes you might wonder about that, especially when the sun goes down and Bourbon Street releases whatever inhibitions it might have during daylight hours to become one of the gayest "naughty ladies" anywhere. The nine or so blocks of bars, jazz clubs, strip joints, and restaurants (which vary from the sleaziest to the grandest) are alive with the sound of music, street dancers, and hundreds of visitors intent on just one thing—having a good time. It is, of course, lively enough during the day, but after dark there's no place else quite like it! Down toward Esplanade, things are a bit quieter, and it is very much like other streets in the Quarter—it's those *other* nine blocks that have made this street an instantly recognized name around the world.

Two blocks from Canal Street, the **Old Absinthe House**, at 238 Bourbon St., was built in 1806 by two Spaniards and is still owned by their descendants (although they live in Spain and have nothing to do with running the place). The drink for which it was named is outlawed in this country now, but with a little imagination you can sip a modern-day libation and visualize Andrew Jackson and the Lafitte brothers plotting the desperate defense of New Orleans in 1815. It's the custom here to put your calling card on the wall, and the hundreds and hundreds of browning cards form a covering not unlike tattered wallpaper. It was, of course, a speakeasy during Prohibition, and when federal officers closed it down in 1924, the interior was mysteriously stripped of its antique fixtures, including the long marble-topped bar and the old water dripper (used to drip water into absinthe), all of which just as mysteriously reappeared down the street at a corner establishment called, oddly enough, the Old Absinthe House Bar (400 Bourbon). It, too, follows the calling-card custom. If you can't keep all that straight, just remember that if you're in an "Old Absinthe House" that doesn't have entertainment, you're in the original *house*—and if you see that grand brass water dripper on a marble-topped bar, you're in the new home of the original bar and fixtures.

Give a nod to the **Landmark Bourbon Street**, 541 Bourbon St., in memory of the great old French Opera House that stood on this site from 1859 until it burned down in 1919. It was designed by Gallier, and was the first structure designed just for opera to be built in the United States.

The **Fortin House**, 624 Bourbon St., was built in 1834 by a doctor for his young bride. Walk back into the patio and you'll see how neighbors often built connecting doorways between their courtyards.

At the corner of Bourbon and St. Peter Streets (700 Bourbon St.) once stood the Bourbon House bar and restaurant, which was so beloved of writers and artists (Tennessee Williams was one who dropped in from time to time) that when it closed during the 1960s, they gave it a brass band funeral, and it lives on in the fond memory of many a native.

That little cottage-like building on the corner of Bourbon and St. Philip Streets is **Lafitte's Blacksmith Shop**, at 941 Bourbon St. For many years now it has been a bar (for the full story, see Chapter VII), but the legend is that Jean Lafitte and his pirates posed as blacksmiths here while using it as headquarters for selling goods they'd plundered on the high seas. It has survived (thanks to the loving care of owners in recent years) in its original condition, and you can still see the "brick between posts" construction. That simply means that bricks were used only to fill in a wooden frame (locally made bricks were too soft to be the primary building material). Step inside and the dusky interior will kindle your imagination—it's a tribute to its modern-day owners that they haven't let the age of chrome and plastic come anywhere near this old place.

Dauphine Street

The farther Dauphine Street (pronounce it "daw-*feen*") gets from Canal Street, the more attractive it becomes. You will, however, see buildings typical of the Quarter its entire length.

Look for the **Pierre Cottage**, 430 Dauphine St., another example of the brick-between-posts construction of the 1700s. Bricks for this house were made right in the courtyard, and the mortar was strengthened with shells from Lake Pontchartrain. It was built in 1780, only partially damaged in the great fire of 1788, and is one of the oldest cottages in the Quarter.

When John James Audubon was working on his 435-plate *Birds of America,* he did 167 of them in Louisiana. A good many were sketched upriver near St. Francisville, but he spent a year in the French Quarter (1821–1822) at 511 Dauphine St. The ornithologist and his family lived in the little cottage at a time when his fortunes were meager and times were hard.

No one has ever reported the presence of ghosts at the **LePrete Mansion,** 716 Dauphine St., but they may well be there. Like the LaLaurie house over on Royal Street, these walls could tell a tale of horror. It seems that back in 1792 there arrived in New Orleans a wealthy Turk, the brother of a sultan. That he was enormously wealthy was immediately apparent and his entourage included many servants, as well as a "family" of five beautiful young girls, and they all landed in the Crescent City in the *Youseff Bey,* a Turkish freighter which had evidently been hired for their exclusive passage. The rumor quickly spread that his wealth had been stolen from his brother and that the girls were also the sultan's "property," a part of his harem. Be that as it may, the Turk rented the LePrete house for the summer when its owner left to spend the season on his downriver plantation, and the palatial home very quickly became the scene of lavish entertainments with guest lists that included the cream of society. On one fateful night, however, shrieks were heard by neighbors, followed by complete silence the next morning, with no signs of activity. Eventually, neighbors entered the house and found the summer tenant's body lying in a pool of blood surrounded by those of the five young beauties. There was no sign of his servants. To this day, no one knows if they were responsible for the murders or if the freighter crew, with a late-found loyalty to the sultan, decided to return the ruler's stolen goods to win his favor (or, as seems more likely, they may have stolen the stolen gold and embarked on a career of piracy at sea). Another explanation put forth was that members of the sultan's court followed his brother to avenge the sultan and return the gold. Whoever was responsible, the murder victims have never returned to haunt the premises, which is now an apartment house.

Burgundy Street

In one of those New Orleans pronunciation quirks, this street is called "bur-*gundy,*" after the French Duke of Burgundy. It is primarily residential in nature and has more black residents than some other Quarter streets. It is interesting to stroll, if just to see another facet of the French Quarter's eclectic architecture. Houses are less elegant, but the small cottages are very much a part of the city's architectural mix. For years this street went by the inelegant name of Craps Street on the downriver side of Esplanade—real estate developer Bernard de Marigny christened it after his favorite game of chance!

It was primarily because of this street's large black (and poor white) population that the now-citywide-popular **Buster Holmes's Restaurant** at 721 Burgundy came into being. Serving large portions of red beans and rice, gumbo, and fried chicken for small change, the restaurant was literally the salvation of many of its neighbors. Today, New Orleanians make regular pilgrimages for the tasty food, which still is economy priced (see "Dining in the French Quarter," Chapter V).

Rampart Street

The mud ramparts which were early New Orleans's only protection ran along this street, then the city's outer boundary.

On the corner of Rampart and Conti Streets, **Our Lady of Guadaloupe Chapel / International Shrine of St. Jude**, 411 N. Rampart St., was put up in 1826 as a chapel convenient to the St. Louis Cemetery No. 1—funeral services were held here rather than in St. Louis Cathedral so as not to spread disease within the confines of the Quarter, and it became known as "The Burial Chapel." In intervening years, it has been renovated and it now houses an International Shrine of St. Jude (the saint of impossible causes who is often thanked publicly for favors in the "Personals" column of the *Times-Picayune*). Another saint is honored here by a statue next to the main altar. His name is St. Expedite, which legend says was given to the statue when it arrived at the church in a packing crate with no identification, but stamped "Expedite"!

The 700 block of Rampart Street faces what was once Congo Square, which then became Beauregard Square (for the Confederate general), and is now **Louis Armstrong Park** (for that beloved son, Satchmo). It is the site of the **Civic Cultural Center** (for more details, see Chapter IX, "Sightseeing Outside the Quarter").

Rampart Street is the last of the streets in the French Quarter that run from Canal Street to Esplanade. To examine those running from the Mississippi River to Rampart, let's start with those closest to Canal, the first of which is—

Iberville Street

Pronounced "*Eye*-bur-ville," this street is named, of course, for the French-Canadian explorer. Its main distinction (in my very subjective view) lies in the two marvelous oyster bars within a block of each other: the Acme, at 724 Iberville and Felix's, at no. 739. When an oyster appetite strikes during the day, I usually head for the Acme (along with the rest of New Orleans, it sometimes seems), and Felix's is a sort of oyster security blanket for a late-night yen, since it stays open until 2 a.m. As an aside: That old adage about eating oysters only during months which have an *R* in their names may have held true in the days before refrigeration when the hot months were *R*-less and seafood spoiled quickly, but nowadays you can enjoy them virtually any time of the year. For more complete information on these two oyster meccas, see Chapter V, "Dining in the French Quarter."

Bienville Street

This street too is lacking in scenic attractions (mostly commercial institutions of the more mundane sort), with one notable exception. **Arnaud's Restaurant,** 813 Bienville St., is an attraction in itself, as you'll see from my rave comments in Chapter V, "Dining in the French Quarter." The building is ancient, the food is magnificent, and the loving restoration of both by Archie Casbarian is enough to give Bienville Street a secure place in my affections. Go by to look, if not to eat, or have a drink in either of the two lovely old bars.

Conti Street

This is another street named for a family of the French nobility, and its New Orleans pronounciation is "*Con*-teye."

Between Chartres and Royal Streets, in the 600 block of Conti, there's a little alley called **Exchange Alley.** Back in the 1830s, it went all the way to St. Louis Street and the old St. Louis Hotel (where the Royal Orleans Hotel now stands), and the houses at the corner of Conti and Exchange were devoted to a practice much revered in New Orleans—dueling. These were the houses of the fencing masters, who specialized in assuring their clients of emerging victorious on the field of honor.

Farther up Conti, between Dauphine and Burgundy, you'll

find the **Musée Conti Wax Museum,** at 917 Conti St. (tel. 525-2605). New Orleans history is depicted here in marvelously lifelike tableaux of costumed wax figures in authentic settings using real antique furniture. Almost every scrap of history (carefully researched for authenticity) and many of the city's legends are represented—the time span is three centuries! There are 31 different scenes, so don't imagine that this is a "quickie." And at the very end of all that serious history, there's a strictly-for-fun haunted dungeon, with all the villains of literature shown going about their dastardly deeds. The whole family will love this place, which is open every day (except Christmas and Mardi Gras Day) at 10 a.m. The adult admission fee is $3.50; senior citizens pay $3; ages 13 to 17, $2.25; 6 to 12, $1.25; and those under 6 are admitted free with their parents.

St. Louis Street

It's too bad you and I have arrived in New Orleans too late to visit the old St. Louis Hotel—it must have been something to see! Of course, its replacement, the **Royal Orleans Hotel,** 621 St. Louis St., does its best to keep alive the old hostelry's traditions of grandeur (and even retains one of the original walls on the Chartres Street side of the building), but it takes some imagination to visualize the great building, with stores and business offices on the first floor and an auction block in the central rotunda. It was, without doubt, the grandest gathering spot in the Quarter in its earliest days (the mid-1800s), although it fared rather poorly after the turn of the century. Magnificent balls were held in the domed, marble-floored ballroom. Notables like Henry Clay, who made his only speech in the state here, were guests, as were carpetbagger legislators during Reconstruction years when the hotel served as the state capitol from 1874 to 1882. By 1915, it had deteriorated so badly (the English writer John Galsworthy was inspired to write "The Old Time Place" after finding a horse wandering around loose inside) that it was torn down during a campaign to rid the French Quarter of rats. (There was a near-panic at the time because of the danger of bubonic plague.) Despite a great public hue and cry, down it came.

The world-famous **Antoine's Restaurant** is at 713 St. Louis St., and has been at this location since 1870. The original Antoine (Alciatoire) operated a boarding house over on Royal Street which became so well known for its food that he moved into this

1850s building, which has been expanded to include five others to house 14 dining rooms. You'll find a complete description of the restaurant in Chapter V, "Dining in the French Quarter."

If you're a "states' righter" in these days of big government, take a good look at 720 St. Louis St.—Pierre Soulé, a prominent New Orleans attorney who spent his life fighting for "the cause" until his death in 1870, lived here.

At 820 St. Louis St., the **Hermann-Grima House** dates from 1831, when it was built by a wealthy merchant, Samuel Hermann. He sold it in 1844 to Felix Grima, a noted attorney, and these days it offers a look back into New Orleans's golden era, 1830 to 1860. The house has period furnishings and two courtyards. The original slave quarters are in the rear courtyard, and you can visit the old carriage house and stable (which still has stalls and feeders). From October through May on Thursday you can witness a demonstration of Créole cooking in the restored 1830s kitchen. The house is open Monday through Saturday from 10 a.m. to 3:30 p.m., and on Sunday from 1 to 4:30 p.m., for an admission fee of $3 for adults and $2 for senior citizens, students, and children 8 years and older.

Toulouse Street

You might call Toulouse a "bastard street," since it was named for an illegitimate offspring of France's Louis XIV. It is, however, a very legitimate part of French Quarter life.

An interesting, relative newcomer on the New Orleans theater scene is the **Toulouse Theater**, 615 Toulouse St. (see Chapter VII, "Things to Do in New Orleans"). If you can't take in the current production, its Jazz Café (open 10 a.m. until who-knows-when) makes a nice stopping-off point.

In the 700 block of this street, look for the **Court of the Two Lions**, at no. 710, which also has an entrance at 537 Royal St. Built in 1792, the house features a courtyard whose entrance is guarded by two lion statues. It is much photographed and has been used by at least one writer in works of fiction (it is the home of *The Crossing*'s heroine, whose author is a popular American writer of the early 1900s named Winston Churchill—*not* "Sir Winnie").

In the same block, you'll find the **Casa Hinard** at 723 Toulouse St., said to be one of the oldest in the Mississippi Valley. An old French map shows that it was here in the 1720s, although older records were destroyed in the 1788 fire and only those dating after 1797 remain. Since 1983, the ground floor has been occupied by Oaks Gallery, which features original designs in arts and crafts by local and national artists. The Casa Hinard Museum, filled with period antiques, is open for tours during June, July, and August.

The charming little **Hôtel Maison de Ville** at 727 Toulouse St. dates back to at least 1742 (its earlier records were also lost). It is outrageously expensive, but it won't cost a cent to walk back into its beautiful courtyard and take a peek at the slave quarters, now converted into guest accommodations.

St. Peter Street

St. Peter Street is one of Jackson Square's boundaries, and you'll find its 500 block described in that section of this chapter.

That rather grim building at 615 St. Peter St. was the site, in 1839, of the Spanish government's prison (or *calabozo*). The present building went up in 1803 as an arsenal, and it also became headquarters for a military organization known as the Louisiana Legion, an elite group of Louisiana "first family" sons, of both American and Créole descent. The insignia of crossed cannons above a mound of cannon balls, and the "LL" monogram of the legion are worked into the balcony railing (on the right-hand side) facing Pirates Alley. To see it, turn left off St. Peter and walk through the little alley (known as Cabildo Alley) to Pirates Alley and the rear of the arsenal. Union forces under the notorious General Butler moved in from 1862 to 1871. Since 1915, this building, known as the **Spanish Arsenal**, has been a part of the Louisiana State Museum, although it is not open to the public at present.

The Spanish-style building at 616 St. Peter St. houses **Le Petit Théâtre**, the oldest nonprofessional theater in the country. Construction on the house was begun in 1789, and it was severely damaged in the 1794 fire, but was restored shortly afterward. Since then, it has had such widely diverse tenants as cafés, bars, the first bishop of New Orleans, and since 1922, the Le Petit Théâtre group. Incidentally, the balconies were done by the same artisan who did the Cabildo ironwork, and they are survivors of the original building.

It was in a small apartment at 632 St. Peter St. that Tennessee Williams wrote his great play *A Streetcar Named Desire,* as that vehicle rumbled down nearby Royal Street. Later, he did much of the play's rewrite in the courtyard of the Maison de Ville, over on Toulouse Street.

The **Le Monnier House**, 714 St. Peter St., built in 1829 for a prominent physician by that name, was the home for several years during the 1860s of Antoine Alciatoire, who ran a boarding house here. His cooking became so popular with locals that he later gave up catering to "live-in" guests and moved into larger quarters on St. Louis Street to open the famous Antoine's Restaurant, which is run even today by his descendants.

You will know 718 St. Peter St. as **Pat O'Brien's**, a swinging, fun-filled nightstop (see Chapter VII), but it was known as the Maison de Flechier when it was first built in 1790 for a wealthy planter. Later, Louis Tabary put on popular plays here, and it is said that the first grand opera in America was performed within its walls. Sightseeing in New Orleans just wouldn't be complete without a look at the gorgeous courtyard, even if you pass on modern-day entertainment and liquid refreshment.

I highly recommend that you make your inspection of **Preservation Hall**, 726 St. Peter St., after 8 p.m., when its walls ring with some of the best jazz in the country (see Chapter VII). But a daytime stop will give you an intriguing glimpse through the big, ornate iron gate of a lush, tropical courtyard in back.

Orleans Street

Orleans Street begins at **St. Anthony's Garden**, back of the cathedral. Not only was this charming little garden a favorite dueling spot, but it is also the site of a marble monument put there by the French government in memory of 30 French marines who died doing volunteer nursing duty during a yellow fever epidemic.

Where the **Bourbon Orleans Hotel** now stands at 717 Orleans St., there once was a fine ballroom known as the Salle d'Orléans. Built in 1816, it hosted some of the grandest balls ever seen in New Orleans, including one in 1825 in honor of Lafayette. It also hosted balls whose "grandness" depends on your point of view. At the so-called quadroon balls, ambitious mothers would trot out their most beautiful mulatto daughters to be surveyed by the white gentry as possible mistresses (many of those duels in St. Anthony's Garden had their origins here as youngbloods quarreled over the lovelies!). Once chosen, the lucky (?) girl could look forward to being set up for life in one of the small cottages on and near Rampart Street, and any offspring would almost certainly be given a good education, which usually included some time at European schools. If you have any difficulty understanding or accepting this practice, keep in mind that along with the title "mistress" went that longed-for label "free."

Once in its history, the Orleans Ballroom was leased to the state legislature, when its own building had been destroyed by fire and it needed a temporary meeting place. Then, in 1881, the quadroon balls were perhaps avenged when Thomy Lafon, a "free man of color," bought the place and gave it to the black Sisters of the Holy Family as a convent. The ballroom became their chapel, and the sisters set up an orphanage on the premises. Over the ballroom door they placed a sign which read, "I have chosen rather to be an object in the house of the Lord than to dwell in the temple with sinners." Nowadays, you'll see the ballroom restored in the modern hotel.

St. Ann Street

There's a mid-19th-century town house at 825 St. Ann St. owned by the **New Orleans Spring Fiesta Association.** Furnished with lovely antiques of the Victorian era and many outstanding objets d'art from New Orleans's golden age of the 1800s, the house is open to the public for guided tours from 11 a.m. to 4 p.m., Monday and Thursday, for a $2 donation. It's a lovely peek backward in time. For Spring Fiesta information contact the Association at: 527 Dumaine St., New Orleans, LA 70116 (tel. 504/581-1367).

All those stories you will have heard about Marie Laveau, New Orleans's voodoo queen, happened at her home which stood at 1022 St. Ann. The house was torn down in 1903, but that act did little to erase Marie's memory or influence on "black magic" believers. When she lived here, her powers were much sought after, even by respectable Catholic families in the city. All and sundry looked for her to turn errant lovers and husbands into ardent, attentive slaves of those who purchased Marie's love potions and charms. And woe betide the object of her gris-gris ("gree-gree") if an enemy enlisted her help to cause sickness or death! A mixture of religion, Caribbean superstition, and African rituals, voodoo brought Marie a more-than-comfortable living and even a sort of "respectability." Still today, her grave is sought out (although there are two burial places which purport to be her final resting place) as a place to leave gifts of food and money (in 2¢ and 11¢ combinations, please!) to elicit good luck to the donor and bad luck to his or her enemies. I don't know if it works, but it might be worth a try—old Marie was credited with some mighty powerful stuff in her day!

Dumaine Street

Louis XIV's bastard son, the Duke of Maine, gave his name to this street, another example of New Orleans's nonconcern with the matter of legitimacy.

There are those who say that the house at 632 Dumaine St., known as **Madame John's Legacy,** is the oldest building on the Mississippi River. Others dispute that claim, saying that only a few parts of the original building survived the 1778 fire and were used in its reconstruction. Be that as it may, the house was erected in 1726, just eight years after the founding of New Orleans, and the reconstruction follows its design meticulously. Its original owner was a ship captain who died in the 1729 Natchez Massacre, after which the house passed to the captain of a smuggling ship, and it has had no fewer than 21 owners since. The present structure went up in 1789, right after that disastrous fire, and it's a fine example of a French "raised cottage." The above-ground basement is built of brick (to protect against floodwaters), and the upper story is of brick-between-posts construction, covered with boards laid horizontally. The hipped, dormered roof extends out over the veranda. Its name, incidentally, comes from a fictional quadroon who was bequeathed the house in "Tite Poulette," a Créole short story written by George Cable. It is now a part of the Louisiana State Museum complex, and you can visit it every day except Monday, from 10 a.m. to 6 p.m. (adults pay $2; students, $1; under 12, free).

There's another interesting little cottage at 707 Dumaine St.— interesting because of its roof. After the 1794 fire, all houses in the French Quarter were required by law to have flat tile roofs, and although most have since covered them with conventional roofs, this one is still in compliance with that long-ago ruling.

St. Philip Street

Although there's little of sightseeing interest today on this street, it was once peopled by those fleeing from the French Revolution or the slave uprisings in the Caribbean. Back then, there were cafés, bars, and even a theater (all long gone) in which they gathered to socialize and forget for a time the upheavals they had left behind.

FRENCH QUARTER SIGHTS 109

Ursulines Street

Named for the long-suffering nuns whose property it bounded, this street is supposedly the hatching ground for Texas independence. It is said that Stephen Austin met with a group of Freemasons in 1835 at 829-833 Ursulines St. to plan their strategy for the Texas War for Independence. Now, I can't vouch for that personally (and I haven't turned up any definitive research), but with New Orleans's record of encouraging military leaders and its history as a breeding ground for all sorts of plots, if they *did* meet here, they couldn't have picked a better place!

Governor Nicholls Street

This was originally called Hospital Street, and is probably where those Ursuline nuns did a good bit of nursing in the early days. It was renamed for a state governor of the Civil War era.

Henry Clay's brother, John, built 618-30 Gov. Nicholls St. for his wife in 1828, and in 1871 the two-story building was added at the rear of its garden. It was in this later building that Frances Xavier Cabrini (later sainted by the Catholic church) conducted a school.

The **Thierry House,** 721 Gov. Nicholls St., was built in 1814 and started an architectural trend that spread throughout the entire state. Designed by architect Henry Latrobe when he was just 19 years old, the house is in the Greek Revival style and features a classic portico.

Barracks Street

This street, as you might guess, was named for the military barracks that once stood here between Chartres and Royal Streets. The French garrison put them up in 1757, they were used by Spanish troops in 1769, and they perished in the 1788 fire.

It is said (and again I can neither confirm nor deny) that in the 1820s John James Audubon had a studio at 706 Barracks St. while working on his *Birds of America* series.

Just behind the French Market fruit stands, but on Barracks Street, there's an **open-air flea market** every Saturday and Sunday from 9 a.m. to sundown in fair weather. It's absolutely free, and a "don't miss." More than 100 artisans turn out to show their art, jewelry, and other handcrafts, and vendors offer books, clothes, and plants (actually, I couldn't begin to list all the things on sale), along with good New Orleans food specialties like red beans and rice, sausages, chicken, and gumbo. To quote one native, "It's the best street theater in town."

At the other end of the street, between Burgundy and Rampart, there's an interesting building known locally as the **Morro Castle**, 1001–1005 Barracks St. It's the first all-granite house in the city (the granite was shipped from Massachusetts), and was begun in 1832 by a Paul Pandelly, who promptly went broke and had to sell it before it was even finished.

Esplanade Avenue

This French Quarter boundary street, pronounced "es-pla-*nade*," served as the parade ground for the troops quartered on Barracks Street. It is a lovely, wide avenue lined by some of the grandest town houses built in the late 1800s. Sad to say, many of these proud homes no longer house just one family, but have become boarding houses, apartments, bars, cafés, and restaurants. One, the **Lamothe House**, at 621 Esplanade Ave., has held onto its former elegance while taking in paying guests, and is now one of the Quarter's leading guest homes.

The entire 400 block of Esplanade is occupied by the old **U.S. Mint**. This was once the site of Fort St. Charles, one of those built to protect New Orleans in 1792 (its troops also used Esplanade as a parade ground). It was here that Andrew Jackson reviewed the assortment of "troops" (comprised of pirates, volunteers, and a nucleus of trained soldiers) he would lead in the Battle of New Orleans. The mint was built in 1835, with three-foot-thick walls made of brick stuccoed over and a granite trim. The minting of coins commenced in 1838 (coin collectors greatly value those which show the "O" mintmark) and continued until 1862. In 1850, the mint was the scene of a glamorous ball given by its director for his daughter. When federal troops took over the city (and the mint) in the Civil War, one William Mumford staged his own rebellion by tearing down the American flag raised over the mint. He paid dearly for that act, when General Butler had him hanged from the middle of the mint's front porch as a public example. It was 1879 before coins again flowed from the mint, this time until 1910, and at its peak some $5 million poured forth each month. For a time after that it was used by the Veterans Administration, then as a federal prison. More recently, it has been acquired by the Louisiana State Museum, and it's currently being renovated. Plans call for the first floor to be devoted to small shops, an attractive addition to those

FRENCH QUARTER SIGHTS 111

up and down neighboring Decatur Street. At present there are two permanent exhibits, the **Jazz Museum** and the **Carnival Museum**. You'll find a complete and vivid record of the evolution of music first given life in New Orleans. There are pictures, musical instruments, and other artifacts connected with jazz greats (Louis Armstrong's first trumpet is here). Across the hall, there's a stunning array of Carnival mementoes, from ornate Mardi Gras costumes to a street scene complete with maskers and a parade float. Entrances to the Mint are on both Esplanade Avenue and Barracks Street, hours are 10 a.m. to 6 p.m., and there's an admission fee to the museums of $2. And if you've wondered what has become of that well-known "Streetcar Named Desire," it's parked out back of the mint—it too has been put in "mint condition" and opened for public visits.

Museums

Most of the following have been included in some detail in my street-by-street examination of the French Quarter. However, as a matter of convenience, I'm listing French Quarter museums here as well, with a brief description of each.

The **Cabildo**, 709 Chartres, on Jackson Square, is the site of Louisiana Purchase signing. Exhibits include a Mississippi River collection of steamboat-era artifacts, paintings, etc.; Napoleon's death mask; and early Louisiana settlement items. Open Tuesday to Sunday from 10 a.m. to 6 p.m.; $2 for adults, $1 for students; under 12, free.

Historic New Orleans Collection, 533 Royal St., is housed in two historic residences, with changing cultural and historical displays and a restored private home, plus a comprehensive research facility. Open Tuesday to Saturday from 10 a.m. to 4:45 p.m. The downstairs galleries are free; upstairs, $2 is the admission fee. There's also a "Touch Tour" for blind persons, and wheelchair accommodations.

Musée Conti Wax Museum, 917 Conti St., offers New Orleans history depicted by life-size wax figures with authentic costumes and settings, plus an added "Haunted Dungeon" illustrating well-known horror tales. Open from 10 a.m. daily (except Christmas and Mardi Gras Day). Admission: $3.50 adults; $3 over 62; $2.25 ages 13 to 17; $1.25 ages 6 to 12; under 6, free with parents.

Pontalba Apartments, 1850 House, at 523 St. Ann St., in the Lower Pontalba Buildings, are in a restored house of the period, authentically furnished from parlor to kitchen to slave quarters.

Open Tuesday to Sunday from 10 a.m. to 6 p.m.; $2 for adults, $1 for students; 12 and under, free.

The **Presbytère**, 751 Chartres St. on Jackson Square, was planned as housing for the clergy, but never used for that purpose. It holds exhibits of Newcomb pottery, Louisiana portraits, Audubon bird prints, and evolution of fashion from 1800 to present. Open Tuesday to Sunday from 10 a.m. to 6 p.m. Admission: $2 for adults, $1 for students; under 12, free.

The **Jazz Museum** and the **Carnival Museum** are in the Old Mint, 400 Esplanade Ave. A comprehensive collection of pictures, musical instruments, and other artifacts connected with jazz greats, and a large array of Carnival mementoes. Entrances to the Mint are on both Esplanade Avenue and Barracks Street, hours are 10 a.m. to 6 p.m., and there's an admission fee to the museums of $2.

Tours

As I've said earlier in this book, the very best way to see the French Quarter is on foot. And there's an excellent walking tour offered by the nonprofit volunteer group, **Friends of the Cabildo** (tel. 523-3939), which furnishes guides for a two-hour, on-foot exploration that will provide a good overview of this area. Leaving from in front of the Presbytère, 751 Chartres St., your guide will "show and tell" you about most of the Quarter's historic buildings' exteriors, and the interiors of two of the Louisiana State Museum properties. You're asked to pay a donation of $5 per adult, $2.50 for children from 13 to 20 (those 12 and under are free). Tours leave at 9:30 a.m. and 1:30 p.m. Tuesday through Saturday except holidays, and no reservations are necessary—just show up, donations in hand.

Show up, too, at the **Jean Lafitte National Historical Park Information Center**, 527 St. Ann St. (tel. 589-2636), at appointed times, and you'll be treated to free, interesting walking tours. A branch of the National Park Service, this organization conducts a 1½-hour walk through the Quarter emphasizing the historical, ethnic, and cultural diversity of the area. Called the "History of New Orleans" tour, it leaves at 10:30 and 11:30 a.m. and 2 p.m. For a two-hour tour of St. Louis Cemetery No. 1, reserve for their 1 p.m. "City of the Dead" walk, which includes a commentary on the historical development and social customs of the cemetery system in New Orleans. An intriguing "Odds and Ends" tour (which they say is alternately called "Everything But

FRENCH QUARTER SIGHTS 113

the Kitchen Sink") is a different 1¼-hour walk each day, leaving at 9:30 a.m. and sometimes exploring legends of the Quarter, haunts of Jean Lafitte, history of jazz, and many other subjects. You'll need reservations and streetcar fare (60¢) for their two-hour Garden District walking tour, which begins at 3 p.m. All tours originate at the 527 St. Ann St. center, they're run every day of the year except New Year's Day, Mardi Gras Day, and Christmas, and as I said, there's never a charge. Surely, one of New Orleans's best bargains! Call 589-2636 for reservations where required.

If you don't think your feet are up to all that walking, just head for Decatur Street at Jackson Square and hop aboard one of the **horse carriages** at the stand there. For $7 ($4 for children under 12), you'll not only view the Quarter in comfort, but will be treated to what is sure to be a highly individualistic narrative on its history from your guide. I've always thought this kind of tour should come under the heading of entertainment in New Orleans, since each driver has his own collection of stories about the landmarks, and if you took several different carriages, you'd get several different versions of New Orleans history.

Both **Gray Line**, 1793 Julia St. (tel. 525-0138), and **Southern Tours**, 7801 Edinburgh St. (tel. 486-0604), have tours of the entire city (including the French Quarter) in comfortable motor coaches for about $15—but take my word for it, the Quarter will demand a more in-depth examination than a view from a bus window! Take one of these excellent (and very informative) tours *only* after you've explored the Quarter in detail, or as a prelude to doing so.

Chapter IX

SIGHTSEEING OUTSIDE THE QUARTER

OUTSIDE THE BORDERS of the French Quarter lies "American" New Orleans. It came into being because of Créole snobbery. You see, those semi-aristocratic French Quarter natives had no use for the crass Americans who came flooding into the city in 1803 and the years that followed, and they presented a united and closed front to keep "their" New Orleans exclusive. Not to be outdone, the newcomers simply bought up land in what had been the old Gravier plantation upriver from Canal Street and set about building *their* New Orleans. With that celebrated Yankee enterprise, they very soon dominated the business scene, centered on Canal Street itself, and constructed mansions different from the traditional Quarter residences, but surrounded by beautiful gardens. In 1833, what we know now as the Garden District was incorporated as Lafayette City, and—thanks in large part to the New Orleans–Carrollton Railroad, which covered the route of today's St. Charles Avenue trolley—the Americans kept right on expanding until they reached the tiny resort town of Carrollton. It wasn't until 1852 that the various sections came together officially to become a united New Orleans.

Your sightseeing beyond the French Quarter will, because of all this, take on quite a different flavor—indeed, a mixture of flavors. You'll feel the pulse of the city's commerce; take a look at river activities which keep that pulse beating; stroll through parks more spacious than any that could be accommodated in the Quarter; drive or walk by those impressive "new" homes; get a firsthand view of the bayou/lake connection that explains why New Orleans was settled here in the first place; and run across a few places closely connected to French Quarter history. For example, just one street away from the Rampart Street boundary of the Quarter, you'll find—

SIGHTS OUTSIDE THE FRENCH QUARTER 115

Basin Street

You remember Basin Street, of course—the birthplace of jazz. But then there are those who will tell you that Storyville (the red-light district along Basin Street) only served as a place for jazz, which had been around a long time, to come in off the streets. Well, it did that, all right, with so many houses of ill-repute—ranging from the ornate "sporting palaces" with elaborate furnishings, musical entertainment, and a wide variety of "services," to the pitiful "cribs" of poorer women of the streets—that a directory (the famous "Blue Book") listed over 700 prostitutes in the district. And jazz flourished along with the ladies. "King" Oliver, "Jelly Roll" Morton, and Louis Armstrong are among the black musicians who got their start on Basin Street in the houses between Canal and Beauregard Square (which, ironically, is now named for "Satchmo"—but more about that later). Storyville operated with wide-open abandon from 1897, when Alderman Sidney Story proposed a plan for the concentration of illegal activities in this area, until the United States Navy (the secretary of the navy, that is, not the enlisted men) had it closed down in 1917.

What you'll find there today is a far cry from those rowdy days. A public housing project for low-income families now sprawls over the site, and by virtue of a series of statues depicting Latin American heroes, it is New Orleans's equivalent of the Avenue of the Americas in New York. Simón Bolívar presides over the Canal and Basin Streets intersection; Mexico's Benito Juarez comes next, with the inscription "Peace is based on the respect of the rights of others"; and Gen. Francisco Morazón, a hero of Central America whose likeness was given to the city by Honduras and San Salvador, is last in line at Basin and St. Louis Streets.

The first of New Orleans's "Cities of the Dead," St. Louis Cemetery No. 1, is in the 400 block of Basin Street. This is one of the places which may or may not hold the grave of voodoo queen Marie Laveau, and if you feel the need for a little help from her powerful magic, you can hunt for her tomb (she's purported to be in the one marked "Famille VVe Paris Née Laveau Ci-Git, Marie Philomé Glapion, décédée le 11 Juin 1897"), or take the guided tour for a small charge and ask the caretaker to point it out. Some say that even now a "gris-gris" (which is pronounced "gree-gree" and might be anything from a string around a bone to a doll stuck with a pin) left overnight there and then placed on the doorstep of the person you want

> **KEY TO THE NUMBERED REFERENCES ON THE "FRENCH QUARTER AND ENVIRONS" MAP:** 1. The Old U.S. Mint; 2. The Gauche House; 3. St. Louis Cemetery No. 1; 4. Our Lady of Guadeloupe Church; 5. Mayor Pitot House; 6. The Blanc House; 7. New Orleans Museum of Art; 8. City Park; 9. Dillard University; 10. Lakeshore Drive; 11. Southern Yacht Club; 12. Metairie Cemetery; 13. Notre Dame Seminary; 14. Old Carollton Courthouse; 15. St. Mary's Dominican College; 16. Audubon Park; 17. Tulane and Loyola Universities; 18. The Latter Memorial Library; 19. Academy of the Sacred Heart; 20. The Short House; 21. The Robinson House; 22. The Musson House; 23. The Morris House; 24. The Brevard House; 25. The Payne House; 26. The Johnson House; 27. Lee Circle; 28. Confederate Memorial Museum; 29. St. Patrick's Church; 30. Lafayette Square; 31. Gallier Hall; 32. Superdome; 33. Customs House; 34. Rivergate Exhibition Center; 35. International Trade Mart.

to influence will absorb some of that magic. For more about this cemetery and others, see the section on New Orleans burial grounds.

Between Basin Street and North Rampart Street (in the 700 block) is an area alive with history. It began as an Indian camp, but as the old walled village of New Orleans acquired more and more black slaves who held onto their secret voodoo ceremonies and wild native music in spite of everything their white masters could do to squelch them, the area across from Rampart Street was designated as Congo Square, to be used as a gathering spot for blacks on Sunday afternoons. It was hoped that this once-a-week opportunity to sing, dance, and generally let off steam would eliminate the voodoo rites at other times and locations. Unfortunately, not only did those secret rituals continue (and even attract prominent French residents), but Congo Square became the scene of wild, sensual dancing accompanied by beating drums, frequent fights precipitated by heightened emotions, and a source of fascination for as many as 2000 spectators who would congregate to watch the dancing until a 9 p.m. cannon boomed curfew for all slaves. After the Civil War, it was named for the locally loved Gen. P. G. T. Beauregard (he actually *started* that war by ordering the first shot on Fort Sumter), and in April of 1980 it was officially renamed **Louis Armstrong Park** in honor of the black man with a horn who carried the name of New Orleans with him all over the world.

SIGHTS OUTSIDE THE FRENCH QUARTER 117

FRENCH QUARTER AND ENVIRONS

Map courtesy of the New Orleans Tourist & Convention Commission

118 ARTHUR FROMMER'S NEW ORLEANS

Just behind the square, you'll see the **Municipal Auditorium** and the Theatre of the Performing Arts. There once was a canal (about where the auditorium is now) which linked New Orleans with Lake Pontchartrain back in 1796. A prison and an early charity hospital have also stood on these grounds.

New Orleans Burial Grounds

In the beginning, burials were made along the banks of the Mississippi, but when the little settlement of New Orleans began to grow, cemetery space was a necessity. But there was a problem—and a big one. The soggy ground was so damp that graves would fill with water even before coffins could be lowered. To solve that problem, above-ground tombs were constructed. The coffin would be put in place on the ground, walls of brick built around it, then the walls plastered and whitewashed. Entrances to the tombs were closed by marble tablets, and many were enclosed with iron fences. Some are even finished off with rounded roofs or topped with eaves, for all the world like tiny, windowless houses. Arranged along narrow paths (some of which have "street" names), it is easy to see why the cemeteries came to be called "Cities of the Dead." And these miniature cities have their "skyscrapers," as upper floors would be added as members of the same family passed away and were entombed right on top of the existing vault. Along the outer walls of the cemeteries, you'll see rows of wall vaults, or "ovens," which hold the remains of the city's poor. Incidentally, you may be perplexed by the long list of names listed for just one tomb—that's because, in a miracle of space engineering, New Orleanians use the same tomb over and over, simply removing the old remains after two years have passed and interring a fresh body in the vacated space!

St. Louis Cemetery No. 1, in the 400 block of Basin Street (see above), was the first, established in the 1740s; **St. Louis Cemetery No. 2** is a few blocks away down Conti Street on Claiborn Avenue (from Iberville to St. Louis Street), and if you see one of the unmarked "ovens" with red crosses on its concrete slab, that's the other place Marie Laveau may or may not be resting from her voodoo activities. It seems that no matter how many times the slab is painted over, the faithful keep coming back to mark the mark and ask her favors. **Lafayette No. 1 Cemetery** is in the Garden District bounded by Washington, Prytania, and Coliseum Streets. And perhaps the most beautiful of all, **Metairie Cemetery,** is at the intersection of Pontchartrain Boulevard and Metairie Road—and it wouldn't be here at all except for one New Orleanian's pique at being denied admission to the exclusive Metairie Jockey Club at the racetrack which once operated on these grounds! He was an American, and to strike back at those uppity Créoles who wouldn't let him in, he bought up the land, turned it into a burial ground, and swore that from then on, only the dead would gain admittance.

Before leaving this subject, there is one word of warning which must be added—a sad commentary on these modern days. Because there have been several muggings in St. Louis Cemeteries No. 1 and No. 2 (the oldest), it is best not to walk in them alone. Either go with a party or tour or take the guided tour at No. 1 so as to have the company of the caretaker. Even better, join the two-hour tour that leaves 527 St. Ann St. (tel. 589-2636) everyday at 1 p.m. to walk through this cemetery—no charge.

Canal Street and the Central Business District

There's just no street more central to the life of New Orleans than Canal—just for starters, the location of *everything* is described in reference to its relation to Canal Street. It took its name from a very shallow ditch that was dug along this border of the French Quarter in its early days. Given the rather grand name of "canal," it was never large enough to be used for navigational purposes. Down at the foot of the street, right on the Mississippi River, you'll find the free ferry to Algiers. It's a lovely way to view the city and the harbor, whether you're on foot or behind the wheel of your car, and takes about 25 minutes each way, so be sure to allow sufficient time. As you pass Canal Street's street lights, be sure to dawdle for a close look. Lights on the tall posts are arranged in the French fleur-de-lis pattern, and each post has four bronze plaques imbedded in its base, one for each government that hoisted its flag over the city: French Domination, 1718–1769; Spanish Domination, 1769–1803; Confederate Domination, 1861–1865; United States Domination, 1803–1861 and 1865 to date. Looking at the broad, neon-blighted street these days, you'd never guess it was once residential. It is here, in what is now called the Central Business District (roughly bounded by Canal toward the lake to Loyola Avenue and upriver to the elevated Pontchartrain Expressway—Bus. I-90—and the Mississippi River to the west), that you'll find several of the newest hotels, downtown department stores, all manner of clothing stores, drugstores, dime stores, movie houses, restaurants, and all the other bits and pieces that make up a major city's leading commercial thoroughfare. Only at Mardi Gras does Canal put aside business for pleasure, and then it becomes a veritable sea of humanity intent on revelry, its tide ebbing and flowing to follow floats that drift down the street as each krewe parades.

Down at the river, the **International Trade Mart**, 2 Canal St., is the center of New Orleans's maritime industry, as well as the home of most international consulates. On the 31st floor, there's an observation deck, that looks out over the city and a harbor scene which might include naval vessels (from submarines to aircraft carriers), cruise ships (those that simply ply excursions in local waters and those that leave here for far-away ports), and freighters flying flags from around the world. For a stunning ride up, use the outside elevator—more timid souls can opt for the one inside. The observation deck, called Viewpoint, is open every day except Christmas and Easter from 9 a.m. to 5 p.m. This is truly an incomparable view! Also included in admission price are two exciting slide shows about the city, a colorful international flag and map display, and individual recorded cassette tours of the observation deck. There are high-power telescopes to zoom in on your favorite site for only 25¢. Adults pay $2; children 6 to 12, $1; under 6, free. For more relaxed viewing, go on up to the 33rd floor revolving cocktail lounge (see Chapter VII).

A stone's throw away is the **Rivergate Exhibition Center**, at 4 Canal St., a $13½-million building constructed to encourage and aid New Orleans's booming convention activity. Its huge main hall (132,500 square feet) is seldom without a trade show of one sort or another, and the kitchen can serve as many as 10,000 hungry conventioneers at one sitting. Come Mardi Gras time, however, it—like the rest of the city—puts business aside. That massive floor space is used by a Carnival krewe for its ball, and even parades its giant floats right through the Rivergate.

Big as it is, the Rivergate looks almost puny when compared to the colossal **Superdome**, located in the 1500 block of Poydras Street. Tall as a 27-story building, with a seating capacity of 76,000, the windowless structure has a computerized climate-control system that uses over 9000 *tons* of equipment. It is the largest building in the world in diameter (680 feet), and its grounds cover some 13 acres. Inside, no posts obstruct the view for spectator sports like football, baseball, and basketball, and movable partitions and seats give it the flexibility to form the best configuration for almost any event. Most people think of the

Superdome as a sports center only, but this great big flying saucer of a building plays host to conventions, trade shows, and large theatrical and musical productions as well. The giant-screen television system suspended from the roof (in a six-sided gondola that weighs 75 tons) cost $1.3 million to build, and looks for all the world like the product of a futuristic imagination. Guided tours are run daily at regular intervals from 9 a.m. to 4 p.m. at a cost of $4.50 for adults, $2 for ages 5 to 12. For tour information, call 587-3645.

That complex of five modern buildings you see surrounding the plaza on Loyola Avenue between Poydras Street and Tulane Avenue is the **Civic Center.** The 11-story City Hall is the most imposing—the others are the State Supreme Court, Civil Courts Building, State Office Building, and the Main Public Library (which many natives consider a modern monstrosity because of its cubistic architecture).

The huge granite building which fills the block of Canal Street bounded by Decatur and North Peters is the historic **Customs House.** Its construction, begun in 1847, was interrupted by the Civil War, among other things, and it wasn't actually completed until the 1880s. Under renovation at this writing, the Customs House will be a sightseer's delight when it is again open to the public (check when you're there). Its gigantic Marble Hall, 128 by 84 feet, rises to a height of 58 feet and has life-size bas-reliefs of two city heroes, Bienville and Andrew Jackson. The ceiling, a great white and gold iron frame holding large ground-glass plates, is supported by 14 white marble columns—it's absolutely breathtaking to walk into the sunlit hall from the dusky corridors. One part of the unfinished building was used to hold Confederate prisoners during the reign of Union General Butler.

Uptown and the Garden District

If you don't have time for an in-depth exploration of uptown —and, indeed, even if you do—one thing you shouldn't miss during any visit to New Orleans is the hour-and-a-half **trolley ride** out St. Charles Avenue and back. The streetcars were "modernized" in the '20s, and as late as 1948 you could take the trip "around the belt" for only 7¢. These days, you'll pay 60¢ each way—one of the best buys in town! The streetcar passes through or on the edges of the most interesting parts of New Orleans's "American" section, and for the most complete sightseeing, climb aboard at Canal and Carondolet Streets. This is a fine way to reach the Garden District, Loyola and Tulane Universities, Audubon Park, or the Riverbend shopping area without the hassle of driving, and you can spend a lovely, meandering day riding the streetcar in spurts from one to another. Don't worry about lunch—there are loads of good restaurants (see Chapter VI, "Dining Outside the Quarter"), and an even better idea is to pick up a box lunch at your hotel or favorite restaurant and picnic in the park. Make your day as long as you please—the streetcars run around the clock. There's a description of what you'll see along the way in Chapter II, but you might like a general guide for the architecture you'll be viewing: if it has cupolas, gingerbread trim, and turrets, it's Victorian; those above-ground basements, covered porches, and iron-railed galleries are of the Louisiana "raised cottage" genre.

To walk around the Garden District, get off the streetcar at Jackson Street (be sure to wear comfortable shoes so weary feet won't cut short your tour). The lavish formal gardens surrounding the lovely "town" mansions (the pride of wealthy planters who many times spent part of every year on their plantations), along St. Charles Avenue and the numbered streets that cross it, gave this district its name. If you could peep inside these large homes of colonnaded galleries and ironwork balconies (and you can at certain times of the year—see Chapter X, "The Festivals"), you'd see a decor of ornate moldings, mahogany bannisters, mantels of rosewood or Italian marble, winding staircases, crystal chandeliers, and priceless antiques.

The "uptown" Americans were determined to equal, if not outdo, those snooty Créoles in the French Quarter, and they certainly came close! Many of their descendants still live in these houses, although some have been sold to wealthy new owners who maintain them with loving care. Alas, some have yielded to "progress" in the form of apartments or commercial ventures. Space limitations will not, of course, permit a description of every home worthy of note, but I'll do my best to point out those of special interest. As in the Quarter, I'll simply arrange them by streets and leave you to determine your own route through this beautiful section. I'll start with St. Charles Avenue and its parallel streets, then list the streets that cross it, beginning with Jackson Avenue.

ST. CHARLES AVENUE: The famed James Gallier, Jr., was one of the architects of 2265 St. Charles. It was built in 1856, and the side wing was added later.

When the cottage at 2336 St. Charles was built in the 1840s, the avenue was a dirt road known as Nayades, nothing like the broad street you see today.

At 2919 St. Charles, the **Christ Church Cathedral** is one of the oldest Protestant churches in the Mississippi Valley. This is the fourth building on the site, and it suffered the loss of its steeple in a 1915 hurricane.

The house at 2926 St. Charles was built in 1882, with a gallery for every room and an early air-conditioning system—a 12-inch space between inner and outer walls. Don't be confused by the number 710 above its front door—it's left over from an outdated numbering system.

PRYTANIA STREET (parallel to St. Charles): There's a central hall 67 by 12 feet in the house at 2127 Prytania. Dating from 1857, it has been fully restored.

The Victorian villa-style home at 2221 Prytania was built in 1850, and you'll notice that the architect, Henry Howard, added Greek Revival touches—another example of New Orleans's tolerance for mixing whatever styles appealed to the fancy of the builder.

The unpretentious "raised cottage" at 2340 Prytania is probably the oldest residence in the Garden District. It was built in 1820 by Thomas Toby, a wealthy merchant who came to New Orleans from Philadelphia and brought many of the materials for this house from there. He had the house built for his overseer, but decided to live there himself. The unlucky Mr. Toby lost most of his fortune later, when he helped finance the Texas War for Independence. The structure saw some changes in an 1855 remodeling.

Wealthy sugar planter Bradish Johnson built the elegant town house at 2343 Prytania, and it cost him $100,000 even back in 1870. It was probably designed by the Paris-trained architect James Freret, and before a deadly hurricane in 1815 the magnolias out front were said to be the largest in the country. Since 1929 the house has been a prominent private girls' school (the Louise S. McGehee School), and its cafeteria is in the old stables, its gym in the carriage house. Some wings have been added, as well.

The house at 2507 Prytania is built on a truly grand scale—

every room is 22 feet square except for the hall (which measures 11 by 44 feet) and the ballroom (22 by 44 feet). It was erected in 1850, and in 1870 the ballroom was paneled and a motif of Louisiana birds added to its decor.

The 1857 mansion with a lovely marble entryway at 2521 Prytania houses Our Mother of Perpetual Help Chapel.

At 2605 Prytania, there's a Gothic "cottage" dating back to 1850.

COLISEUM STREET (parallel to St. Charles): There's something reminiscent of a Swiss chalet in the 1870 house at 2627 Coliseum. Maybe that's because of its rather unique use of wooden gingerbread and cast ironwork.

A New Orleans "developer," architect William Freret (brother of James), built the houses from 2700 to 2726 Coliseum in 1861. They were identical in design, and he meant them to turn a tidy profit, but the Civil War came along and his money-making scheme was gone with the wind, leaving these houses with a local nickname of "Freret's Folly."

CHESTNUT STREET (parallel to St. Charles): Notice the "raised cottage" at 2838 Chestnut—it was built sometime between 1840 and 1850, and during the Civil War an "enemy" (Union) general lived here.

MAGAZINE STREET (parallel to St. Charles and the river boundary of the Garden District): Most of Magazine Street is now commercial, and it can furnish a fascinating day's ramble all by itself, with antiques and "classy junque" on display in many of the stores. However, in this look at the Garden District, go by 2319 Magazine to see the home architect John Turpin built for himself. He was a Londoner who went into partnership with New Orleanian James Gallier, and the house was built in 1853.

JACKSON AVENUE (crosses St. Charles): At 1329 Jackson, the Trinity Episcopal Church dates back to 1851, and its architecture might be described as "Victorian Gothic."

Notice the Ionic columns, cast-iron railings, and gardens of the mid-1800s house at 1410 Jackson.

SIGHTS OUTSIDE THE FRENCH QUARTER 125

PHILIP STREET (crosses St. Charles): The all-wood residence at 1220 Philip was built in the 1850s. A subsequent owner was the wealthy sugarcane and molasses dealer whose nephew, Isaac Delgado, donated his art collection to start the Museum of Art—Isaac spent most of his growing-up years in this house.

The beautiful gardens at 1238 Philip brought citywide fame to its owner, John Rodenberg. It was constructed in 1853 and has the two-story columned gallery typical of houses in this district.

Don't call the elegant home at 1433 Philip a "mansion"—in New Orleans, it's a "raised cottage," never mind those stately columns and the fancy ironwork. It dates to the late 1850s.

FIRST STREET (crosses St. Charles): A close friend of Confederate President Jefferson Davis, Judge Charles Erasmus Fenner used slave labor to build 1134 First St. After the Civil War, Jefferson often visited here for long periods of time, and even wrote *The Rise and Fall of the Confederate Government* while a guest. This is where his daughter made her debut to society. When the aging president of the Confederacy fell ill at his plantation home, Beauvoir, in Biloxi on Mississippi's Gulf Coast, friends brought him to Judge Fenner's home, and he died in a ground-floor room in this house in December of 1889. It's no wonder that Davis loved to visit the 1850s house—just take a look at the gardens and summerhouse, a beautiful, restful retreat. The judge's descendants retained ownership of the house until 1935, and its new owners have continued its upkeep in the old style.

The house at 1236 First St. was constructed in 1847 by one John Gayle for his young bride. Its interior features elaborate plaster medallions on ceilings and black marble mantelpieces.

Can you believe that the elegant Greek Revival house at 1239 First St. was built for a total cost of $13,000? Of course, that was in 1857, but still.... The interior woodwork is especially notable. The hexagonal wing off to one side was an afterthought, added in 1869. Notice the beautiful ironwork embellished with a rose pattern.

The 1331 First St. house, built in 1869, is noteworthy primarily because of its three cast-iron galleries. During its restoration in recent years, a ceiling mural painted on canvas was uncovered.

SECOND STREET (crosses St. Charles): This is not the original site of the 1845 house at 1427 Second St. It was moved to the city location from Mrs. Jane Fawcett's nearby plantation, and it didn't gain the decorative ironwork until the 1930s.

THIRD STREET (crosses St. Charles): In-laws of Edgar Degas, the French impressionist painter, built the Italian villa-style home at 1331 Third in the 1850s. In 1884, its elaborate stables out back and the cast-iron galleries were added, to make it one of the most outstanding in the Garden District.

The largest home in the district was built in 1865 at 1415 Third St. by a wealthy tobacco merchant from Virginia, Walter Robinson. The elaborate structure cost Mr. Robinson a whopping $80,000 even then (can you imagine its present-day value?). The luxurious interior boasts a marvelous winding staircase, and there's an interesting carved wooden eagle, fished from the river after a violent storm, adorning the dining room chimneypiece.

The little carriage house at 1417 Third belonged originally to the large house around the corner on Prytania. It was built in 1853, with walls 13 inches thick.

FOURTH STREET (crosses St. Charles): Louis Herman, a New Orleans cotton broker, started building from the back at 1241 Fourth. The kitchen and slave quarters went up in 1844, then when the "big house" was added up front at a later date, the two were connected.

If your French Quarter sightseeing included the Cornstalk House on Royal Street, you'll see a twin to that fence at 1448 Fourth. This house was built in 1859 for a Col. Robert Short of Kentucky. Its double parlors measure a spacious 43 by 26 feet, and the cast-iron fence with the motif of cornstalks entwined with morning glories was cast in Philadelphia.

WASHINGTON AVENUE (crosses St. Charles): It's no longer there, but there once was a gymnasium at the corner of Washington and Prytania, and that's where "Gentleman" Jim Corbett trained for his match with John L. Sullivan. It also held the first Turkish bath in the city.

From Prytania to Coliseum, on Washington, you'll find one of the interesting "Cities of the Dead," Lafayette No. 1 Cemetery (see "New Orleans Burial Grounds," above). This one was laid out in 1833, and yellow fever victims had it almost completely filled by 1852. The little wooden mortuary first served as a Catholic church at another location—it dates from 1844.

SIGHTS OUTSIDE THE FRENCH QUARTER 127

SIXTH STREET (crosses St. Charles): When Newcomb College was in this district, the building at 1240 Sixth was its Music School. Other buildings were torn down when the school moved out.

SEVENTH STREET (crosses St. Charles): The two houses at 1221 and 1215 Seventh were twins when they were built as wedding gifts for two sisters. As you can see, they've taken on individual personalities as modifications were made over the years.

The house at 1506 Seventh still has the original cornices and chandeliers. It dates from the 1850s.

EIGHTH STREET (crosses St. Charles): Writer George Washington Cable lived in the 1874 house at 1313 Eighth. Mark Twain and Joel Chandler Harris (author of the Uncle Remus stories) were entertained in the house, which was built off the ground to prevent flood damage and (it was hoped) yellow fever. The poet Joaquin Miller was a resident during the 1884–1885 Cotton Exposition.

HARMONY STREET (crosses St. Charles): The "raised cottage" at 1328 Harmony, with its wide central hall and galleries at both front and back, is typical of the 1860s, when it was built.

LOUISIANA AVENUE (crosses St. Charles, and a boundary street for the Garden District): There's another "raised cottage" of the 1860s at 1424 Louisiana. This one has double chimneys and brick gable ends.

CHARLES AVENUE (beyond the Garden District): Moving out of the Garden District, along St. Charles Avenue, take note of the lovely home at 5005 St. Charles. The exclusive Orleans Club (a private social and cultural women's club) now occupies the premises, but it was built in 1868 by a Colonel Lewis as a wedding gift for his daughter. It is sometimes used for debut teas and wedding receptions (but no rice-throwing allowed—might damage those beautiful floors!)

The 1907 mansion at 5100 St. Charles Ave. was at one time the home of silent-screen star Marguerite Clark. In later years, the house was given to the New Orleans Public Library by a prominent family as a memorial to the son they lost in World

War II, and its official name now is the **Milton H. Latter Memorial Library.** It's worth a stop just to see the painted ceiling and the paneling.

Loyola University occupies the 6300 block of St. Charles Avenue on the site of a preparatory school, Loyola Academy, which stood there from 1904 until 1911, when the university was established. The campus covers some 14 acres, and its brick-front main buildings form three sides of a square facing the avenue. Behind them, the modern Dana Center student union is a popular gathering spot, and its cafeteria and snackbar are open to visitors. Loyola, incidentally, is the largest Catholic university in the South.

Right next door, in the 6400 block of St. Charles, is the older **Tulane University.** It dates back as far as 1834, when the Medical College of Louisiana was founded. The University of Louisiana, begun in 1847, was merged with the Medical School, and when Paul Tulane left a bequest of $1 million to the combined schools, they changed the name in gratitude to their benefactor. That generous gift financed what is now one of this country's leading medical and law schools. (The medical school has since moved to a downtown campus on Tulane Avenue.) An interesting facet of the legal education offered here is its emphasis on the Code Napoléon, a rather peculiar system of law practiced in this country only in Louisiana. Other specialties such as engineering, architecture, art, social sciences, and the oldest college of commerce in the country add to the university's prestige. It is on the 93-acre campus that the Sugar Bowl used to be played every New Year's Day, but that was before the Superdome came along. Also on the campus is the Harriet Sophie Newcomb Memorial College for Women, which was founded in 1886 and was located in the Garden District until it moved here in 1918. Nowadays, it is an undergraduate college of Tulane. The university's Howard Tilton Memorial Library has an unusually fine collection of rare books, documents, and early New Orleans data. You're welcome to stop in at the University Center for a snack during your tour of the campus. And in case you're wondering about that shady oval with a gatehouse guarding its entrance, that's **Audubon Place,** one of the last privately owned streets in the city (it's been called "millionaire's row," and when you look at the mansions that line the little street, you'll know why). The gatehouse, which is occupied around the clock, is older than any of the homes it guards. The white house out front is where Tulane's president lives.

Across the street from both Loyola and Tulane, **Audubon Park** sprawls over 340 acres, reaching from St. Charles Avenue all the way to the Mississippi River. This tract of land once belonged to Bienville, the founder of New Orleans, and later was part of the Étienne de Bore plantation, where sugar was granulated for the first time in 1794. The city purchased it in 1871, and on that section which is now a golf course the World's Industrial and Cotton Centennial Exposition was held in 1884–1885. In spite of having what was then the largest building in the world (33 acres under one roof!) as its main exhibition hall, the exposition was such a financial disaster that everything except a Horticultural Hall had to be sold off (the Horticultural Hall fell victim to a hurricane a little later). After that, serious work was begun to make this into a park. The huge trees with black bark you see here are live oaks, and some go back to the days when this was a plantation. They're evergreens and shed only once a year, in early spring. Their spreading limbs turn walkways into covered alleys, and there are winding lagoons, fountains, and statuary, as well as a very nice zoo. Look for the bronze statue of John James Audubon, for whom the park was named—it's in a grove of trees (as is altogether fitting) and the naturalist is shown with notebook and pencil in hand, as he no doubt was most of the time during his sojourn in Louisiana (perhaps on this very land). Scattered about are gazebos, shelters, and playground areas—and that funny-looking mound over near the river is called "Monkey Hill," constructed so that the children of the city could see what a hill looked like in this flat land! Especially nice is the pavilion on the riverbank that is one of the most pleasant places from which to view the Mighty Mississippi.

Now, as far as I'm concerned, the trees and wandering paths and general atmosphere of peace and quiet are quite enough for any park. But if you're looking for recreation facilities, you'll find those here, too. There's a golf course (18 holes) in the front half, picnic facilities, tennis courts, a swimming pool, horseback riding, and bike rentals. The zoo, aquarium, sea lion pool, and a small amusement park are toward the back of the park.

The ornate white wooden building at 7214 St. Charles Ave. is the main building for St. Mary's Dominican College. It was built in 1872, but the school goes back to the 1860s. It was founded by Dominican nuns who came to New Orleans from Ireland and started a school for girls.

When you reach the end of St. Charles Avenue (it's where the streetcar turns onto Carrollton Avenue), the green hill over by the river is the levee—if the water happens to be high enough, you'll see the tops of ships as they pass by.

Right here too is where you'll find the **Riverbend** area, and even if you don't spend a cent, you might want to wander about a bit. The place is literally crowded with shops, but they're located in charming old houses, and they hold everything from arts and crafts to elegant clothing to paintings and sculptures to fine jewelry to antiques to eating places. To reach it, turn at Burthe, then left on Dublin Street.

Back at St. Charles Avenue's end, you've reached what was once an independent town, **Carrollton**. When Gen. William Carrollton's troops camped here in 1812, a tiny settlement sprang up. When a railroad came along to connect it to New Orleans (along the same route covered by today's streetcars), a depot was built and New Orleanians began flocking out of the city on weekends to this "country" town. Before long a resort hotel went up, beautiful gardens were laid out, and there was even horse racing for the town sports. Gradually, the wilderness between New Orleans and Carrollton gave way to those Garden District mansions and other developments, and in 1874 the resort town was annexed to the city. The depot and hotel went down when the river changed its course and the levee was built.

At 719 S. Carrollton Ave., that antebellum building is now the Benjamin Franklin public high school, but it was originally built as Carrollton's courthouse.

Along this section of Carrollton Avenue, you'll see yet another architectural style much used in New Orleans, the "shotgun house." Only one room wide, the little houses would permit a bullet fired through the front door to go right out the back, passing through every room in the house.

The Irish Channel

The area between the Garden District (Magazine Street) and the river is known locally as the Irish Channel. No one really knows why—it's true that a good many Irish immigrants settled here, but so did Germans, and for some reason it was never known as the German Channel. Whatever the reason for its name, it is an interesting, although somewhat seedy, section of town these days. It houses many of New Orleans's poor today, just as it did in the early days when Irish men and women lived a day-to-day existence along these streets. An illuminating sidelight to the city's history is the fact that between 1820 and 1860 the more than 100,000 Irish newcomers were considered more "expendable" than costly slaves, and were killed off by the dozens in dangerous construction work and any other manual labor that might endanger health and well-being. In spite of that, however, there was a toughness and lively spirit that gave the Irish Channel a distinctive neighborhood flavor, and although it is mostly populated by blacks and Spanish Americans nowadays, there is still a sort of "street camaraderie" character alive here.

At the corner of Camp and Prytania Streets, you'll see a statue to one Irish immigrant, Margaret Haughery, who toiled in a bakery and dairy and devoted every spare free minute to the care of orphans. When she died, she left her hard-won earnings all to charity. The Carrara marble statue, whose inscription is simply "Margaret," was unveiled in 1884, one of the first dedicated to a woman anywhere in the country. Appropriately, there's a day nursery that dates back to 1850 on the edge of the small park that holds Margaret's monument.

Remember Sir Henry Morton Stanley, of "Dr. Livingstone, I presume" fame? Well, long before he set out for darkest Africa in 1871 on his rescue mission, he came to New Orleans from Wales and was taken under the wing of an American merchant named Stanley, whose name the young John Rowlands took as his own. He grew up in the house at 904 Orange St., and his signature can still be seen cut into a windowpane of the little room that was his, just off the kitchen.

The Irish built **St. Alphonsus Church** at 2029 Constance St. in 1855, and the gallery and columns will remind you rather vaguely of St. Louis Cathedral in the French Quarter. A beloved Redemptorist priest, Fr. Francis Xavier Seeles, is buried in the church. He is credited with the working of many miracles, and if you visit the church, you're likely to see letters of petition on his tomb.

At the foot of Jackson Avenue, the second of New Orleans's free ferries will take you across the Mississippi—this one lands at the little town of Gretna.

Camp Street

There are two sightseeing attractions on Camp Street (which got its name when there was a slave camp here). **St. Patrick's Church,** at 724 Camp St., was founded in a tiny wooden building to serve Irish Catholics in the parish. When the present building was begun in 1838, the new edifice was constructed around the old one, which was then dismantled inside the new building. The distinguished architect, James Gallier, Sr., designed much of the interior, including the altar. It opened in 1840, proudly proclaimed as the "American" Catholics' answer to the St. Louis Cathedral in the French Quarter (where, according to the Americans, God spoke only in French).

At 929 Camp St., the **Confederate Museum** was established in 1889, close enough to the end of the Civil War for many donations to be in better condition than is sometimes true of museum items. There are battle flags, weapons, personal effects of Confederate president Jefferson Davis (including his evening clothes), part of Robert E. Lee's silver camp service, and many portraits of Confederate military and civilian personalities. A series of detailed pictures traces Louisiana's history from secession through Reconstruction. There's a $1.50 charge for adults, 50¢ for students, 25¢ for children under 12. Hours are 10 a.m. to 4 p.m., Monday through Saturday.

Dryades Street

Because you wouldn't be human if you didn't wonder about that gilded dome so prominent against the skyline (especially as you drive on the elevated expressway), I'm including the **Church of St. John the Baptist,** at 1139 Dryades St. It was built by the Irish in 1871, but its most noteworthy features (except for the exceptional brickwork of the exterior) are the Stations of the Cross and Sacristy murals which were painted during and after World War II by a Belgian artist, Dom Gregory Dewit, as well as the beautiful stained-glass windows crafted by artists in Munich. Now, aren't you glad you know?

The Bayou, Another Park, and the Lake

Bayou St. John was one of the most important reasons New Orleans is where it is today. When Sieur de Bienville was commissioned to establish a settlement that would protect the mouth of the Mississippi River for the French crown against British expansion, he recognized the strategic importance of the "backdoor" access to the Gulf of Mexico provided by the bayou's linkage to Lake Pontchartrain. Boats could enter the lake from the gulf, then follow the bayou to within easy portage distance of the Mississippi mouth. The Indian tribes hereabouts had used this route for years, and Bienville was quick to see its advantages.

The path from city to bayou back in those early days is today's

SIGHTS OUTSIDE THE FRENCH QUARTER

Bayou Road, an extension of Governor Nicholls Street in the French Quarter. The modern-day Gentilly Boulevard, which crosses the bayou, was another Indian trail—it led around the lake and on to settlements in Florida after a relatively short boat trip.

As the new town grew and prospered, planters moved out along the shores of the bayou, and in the early 1800s a canal was dug to connect the waterway with the city. It reached a basin at the edge of Congo Square. The lake itself became a popular recreation area, with fine restaurants and dance halls (as well as meeting places for voodoo practitioners, who held secret ceremonies along its shores). Gradually, the city reached out beyond the French Quarter and enveloped it all—farmlands, plantation homes, and resorts. So on your exploration of this part of New Orleans, you'll see traces of that development. The canal is gone, filled in long ago, and the bayou itself is no longer navigable (even if it were, bridges were built too low to permit the passage of boats of any size), but residents still prize their waterfront sites, and rowboats and sailboats make use of its surface.

The simplest way to reach the Bayou St. John from the French Quarter is to drive straight out Esplanade Avenue about 20 blocks. Just before you reach the bayou, you'll pass St. Louis Cemetery No. 3 (it's just past Leda Street), which holds many prominent New Orleanians—among them are Thomy Lafon, the black philanthropist who bought the old Orleans Ballroom as an orphanage for black children and thus put an end to its infamous "quadroon balls," and Fr. Adrien Rouquette, who lived and worked among the Choctaw Indians. Just past the cemetery, Esplanade reaches Moss Street, and a left turn will put you on that street, which runs along the banks of Bayou St. John.

MOSS STREET: The **Pitot House** at 1440 Moss St. is perhaps the most notable of several built along this side of the bayou in the 1780s and early 1800s. It dates from 1799, when it was built for an aristocratic family named Ducayet, and it originally stood where the nearby modern Catholic school is now. In 1810, it became the home of James Pitot, New Orleans's second mayor, and it is now known by his name. A typical West Indies–style plantation house, it has wide galleries on three sides and large columns supporting the second floor. There's a beautiful collection of Federal period antiques inside, and you can tour the interior Wednesday through Saturday from 10 a.m. to 3 p.m. for a $3 fee for adults, $1 for children. Call 482-0312 for tour information.

The Greek Revival plantation house at 1342 Moss was built about 1834 and now serves as a school.

At 1300 Moss St., you'll see an old plantation home built about 1784 in the West Indies style, with above-ground living quarters, sloping roof, and wide gallery. The land grant for a farm here dates from 1708, and because legend says that goods traveling on the bayou were sometimes checked here, the house has come to be known as the Old Spanish Custom House.

You'll have to return to Esplanade to cross the bridge (turn left on Esplanade) to the entrance to—

CITY PARK: Right at the entrance is yet another statue of Gen. P. G. T. Beauregard, who ordered the first shot fired on Fort Sumter to open the Civil War and who New Orleanians fondly call the "Great Créole." The park was once part of the Louis Allard plantation, and its extensive, beautifully landscaped grounds hold four golf courses, picnic tables, a restaurant, lagoons for boating, tennis courts, horses for hire for the lovely trails, bicycle rentals, a bandstand, miniature train, and an amusement area with carnival rides for children. **Children's Storyland** is free (open every day except Friday from 10 a.m. to 5 p.m.) and an enchanted place for youngsters, where larger-than-life, papier-mâché figures of such Mother Goose characters as Jack and the Beanstalk and Humpty Dumpty will delight even their parents. It's right across from the tennis courts on Victory Drive.

The huge old oaks in City Park looked down on a favorite pastime in New Orleans during the 1700s—dueling. To the proud Créoles, nothing—not even death—was to be feared so much as the loss of honor, and when a dispute ended with a heated "under the oaks at sunrise," it was here, under what came to be called the **Dueling Oaks,** that the rendezvous was kept. The practice persisted into the early 1800s (there were, in fact, ten fought on just one Sunday morning in 1837), but duels changed very much in character after "Americans" arrived on the scene. You see, Créoles observed a very formal and strict dueling etiquette, using the meetings to demonstrate their expertise with rapiers, broadswords, or pistols (fists were never used among gentlemen), and only seldom was it that either party was actually killed. With the Americans, however, came a whole new concept

—duels became a fight to the death, with such "rude" weapons as rifles, shotguns, clubs, and even axes. After the Civil War, when Reconstruction made life almost unbearable for Créole and American New Orleanians alike, the two factions united in overcoming their common problems and dueling died out. It had always been forbidden by both church and law (a fact heretofore completely ignored), and after the war there was a stricter enforcement of the laws—perhaps because there was less to enforce. One of the mighty oaks became known about then as the "Suicide Oak" because of its popularity as the setting for that action. Another, McDonogh Oak, is believed to be over 600 years old, and its 142-foot branch spread served as a shady canopy as recently as 1958, when the City Park superintendent held a breakfast for 526 visitors under the tree.

You'll find the **New Orleans Museum of Art** on LeLong Avenue in City Park in a building that is itself a work of art. The neoclassic, columned main building is a beauty, inside and out. Its Delgado Great Hall on the first floor leads to a branched staircase at the back which rises to a mezzanine overlooking the Hall. Beautiful! Notice, too, the bronze statue of Hercules as an archer just outside the entrance. The original building, which is about 70 years old, has been expanded by the addition of three wings, and the art inside does justice to its housing. There's a lovely portrait of Estelle Musson, a relative of the French impressionist painter Edgar Degas, who painted this likeness on one of his visits to the city. Twenty-two sections of the Kress Renaissance collection, pre-Columbian art, and bronzes by Rodin live happily with contemporary, 20th-century art, and galleries are arranged to show the logical progression of the history of art. The museum is open from 10 a.m. to 5 p.m. Tuesday through Sunday, and is closed on Monday. There's a $3.50 admission fee for adults, $2 for children.

Leaving City Park by the Esplanade entrance, cross the bridge again and turn left on Wisner Boulevard to drive out to—

LAKE PONTCHARTRAIN: As you drive along Wisner, along this bank of Bayou St. John, you'll pass some of New Orleans's grandest modern homes, a sharp contrast to those over on Moss Street. Stay on Wisner Boulevard to Robert E. Lee Boulevard, turn right and drive to Elysian Fields Avenue, and then turn left. That's **Louisiana State University's New Orleans campus** on your left (its main campus is in Baton Rouge).

Turn left onto the broad concrete highway that is Lakeshore Drive. It runs for 5½ miles along the lake, and in summer the parkway alongside its seawall is usually swarming with swimmers and picnickers. On the other side are more luxurious, ultramodern residences.

Lake Pontchartrain itself is some 40 miles long and 25 miles wide. Indians once lived along its shores on both sides, and it was a major waterway long before white men were seen in this hemisphere. You can drive across it over the Greater New Orleans Causeway, the 23¾-mile-long bridge, the longest in the world.

When you cross the mouth of Bayou St. John, you'll be where the old Spanish Fort was built in 1770. Its remains now nestle among those elegant modern homes. In the early 1800s there was a lighthouse here, and in the 1820s a railroad brought New Orleanians out to a hotel, casino, bandstand, bathing houses, and restaurants that made this a popular resort area.

Look for the Mardi Gras fountain on your left. Bronze plaques around its base are inscribed with the names of Mardi Gras krewes, and if you time your visit out to the lake so you'll be there at sundown, you'll see the fountain beautifully lit in Mardi Gras colors of purple (for justice), green (for faith), and gold (for power).

Down at the end of Lakeshore Drive, you'll come to the old white Coast Guard lighthouse, and you'll know you've reached **West End.** This is an interesting little park that's home for several yacht clubs, a marina, and restaurants, many of which have been here for years and look just like lakeside restaurants should (not too fancy—more interested in the view out over the water and good eating than in "decorator-style" interiors). This old fishing community has, over the years, become the main pleasure-boating center of New Orleans, and the Southern Yacht Club here was established in 1840, the second oldest in the country. After the railroad began bringing pleasure-seekers here from the city in the 1870s, showboats and floating circuses would often pull up and dock for waterside performances. West End is an excellent place to stop for a bite to eat, if indeed it isn't your destination when you set out for the lakeside with a fresh seafood dinner in mind.

To reach **Buckstown,** which lines the banks of a narrow canal behind the restaurants on the western side of West End park, turn to the left on Lakeshore Drive at the Coast Guard station, then turn right on Lake Avenue (it's the first street you come to). Buckstown is another small fishing community which still retains its oldtime atmosphere. There are also many good seafood restaurants here.

Longue Vue

Just off of Metairie Road, at 7 Bamboo Rd., you'll find the lovely, eight-acre Longue Vue estate, one of the most beautiful garden settings in this area. The mansion is built in the classical tradition. Like the great country houses of England, there is a close rapport between indoors and outdoors, with vistas of formal terraces and pastoral woods. Some parts of the enchanting gardens were inspired by those of the Generalife in Granada, Spain, and besides the colorful flowering plants, there are formal boxwood arrangements, fountains, and a colonnaded loggia. Highlights are the Canal Garden, Walled Garden, Wild Garden (which features native iris), and Spanish Court with pebbled walkways, changing horticultural displays, and statuary. You can visit Longue Vue Tuesday through Friday from 10 a.m. to 4:30 p.m., and from 1 to 5 p.m. on Saturday and Sunday (it's closed holidays). To visit the gardens only, adults pay $2; students and children, $1. Admission to both house and gardens is $5 and $3, respectively.

Other Points of Interest

JACKSON BARRACKS: At 6400 St. Claude Ave. (that's an extension of Rampart Street downriver from the French Quarter), there's a series of fine old brick buildings with white columns. They were built in 1834–1835 for troops who were stationed at the river forts. Some say Andrew Jackson, who never quite trusted New Orleans Créoles, planned the barracks to be as secure against attack from the city as from outside forces. The Barracks now serve as headquarters for the Louisiana National Guard, and there's a marvelous military museum in the old powder magazine. It's open from 7:30 a.m. to 4 p.m. Monday through Friday; closed Saturday and Sunday. There's no admission charge, but it's best to call 271-6262, ext. 242, before you go to confirm that the Barracks and museum are open.

About a mile away, you'll come to another site connected with Andrew Jackson.

CHALMETTE NATIONAL HISTORICAL PARK: To reach the park, continue on St. Claude Avenue until it becomes St. Bernard Highway. The park will be on your right. On these grounds, a horrendous battle was waged on January 14, 1815. Ironically, the battle should never have been fought at all, since the War of 1812 had by then been concluded by a treaty signed two weeks before in Ghent, Belgium—word had simply never reached Congress, the commander of the British forces, or Andrew Jackson, who stood with American forces to defend New Orleans and the mouth of the Mississippi River.

The British, having defeated Napoleon in Europe earlier in 1814, had turned their full military might against the United States. Campaigns on Lake Champlain and the Chesapeake Bay had failed, however (in spite of their attack on Washington and the burning of the White House), and control of the Mississippi River became vitally important. In December of 1814, under General Packenham, brother-in-law of the Duke of Wellington (Napoleon's nemesis at Waterloo), the British had massed a huge invasion force just off the waters of Ship Island in the Gulf of Mexico, with its chief aim the capture of New Orleans. Gen. Andrew Jackson, then in command of American forces in Louisiana (which meant mostly militiamen from the hills of Tennessee and Kentucky), hurried to the city to set up some sort of defense. With few trained troops of his own, he set about gathering volunteers, and the crew he assembled was, if not motley, certainly diverse. There were Créoles, Irish and German immigrants, "uptown" Americans, slaves, a few "free men of color," and even Indians. So compelling was Jackson's appeal to New Orleanians that even the privateer Jean Lafitte joined in the defense effort, not only supplying troops from his pirate band, but also furnishing great quantities of weaponry and ammunition. (This is when Lafitte and Jackson held all those meetings in all those cafés and bars in New Orleans.) The British managed to come up the river by way of Bayou Bienvenu to within nine miles of the city. Jackson, with the help of his colorful collection of recruits, built earthworks along the river on the grounds of the Chalmette plantation and kept the British forces stalled for several days. General Packenham, faced with a serious morale deterioration among his men, ordered a head-on land attack, much to the dismay of his junior officers. Jackson's men, behind their rampart, let loose with rifles, cannons, pistols, and other assorted weapons, and effectively mowed down the redcoats as they approached in tight, orderly lines of march. It was over in little or no time, with more than 2000 British casualties littering the battleground. The British flotilla continued to fire on forts downriver, and General Packenham's men were encamped close by for another ten days before the general ordered them back aboard their ships and sailed for home. The bloody battle, so costly to the British, left only 13 American dead—as I said, however, the whole thing would never have happened had word of the Peace Treaty of Ghent reached this side of the Atlantic in time. The battle did, however, succeed in bringing New Orleanians together more than they had ever been, and in making Andrew Jackson a hero forever in this city.

You can visit the battleground and see markers which will let you follow the course of the battle in detail. In the Beauregard plantation house on the grounds, you will find a film presentation and interesting exhibits. There is also a National Cemetery here, which was established in 1864 and holds only two American veterans of the Battle of New Orleans, but some 14,000 Union soldiers who fell in the Civil War. For a really terrific view of the Mississippi River, climb the levee in back of the Beauregard House. There's no charge to visit the park, which is open from 8 a.m. to 5 p.m. daily.

Museums Outside the Quarter

Here's a quick-reference list of the museums outside the French Quarter already discussed in detail:

The **Louisiana Maritime Museum**, 130 Carondelet St., offers a treasure trove of nautical charts, ship models, paintings, old steamboat furnishings, and many other items relating to New Orleans's long association with river traffic. Open 10 a.m. to 4 p.m. Tuesday through Saturday. Admission: $2 for adults, $1 for ages 2 to 12; under 2, free. Maximum of $5 for family groups.

The **Pitot House**, 1440 Moss St., is a typical West Indies–style plantation home built in 1799, restored and furnished in Federal period antiques. Open Wednesday through Saturday from 10 a.m. to 3 p.m. Admission: $3 for adults, $1 for children.

The **New Orleans Museum of Art**, LeLong Avenue in City Park, is in a neoclassical building housing pre-Columbian, Renaissance, and contemporary art exhibited to show the history of art development. Closed Monday, open 10 a.m. to 5 p.m. Tuesday through Sunday. Admission: $3 for adults, $1.50 for children.

Jackson Barracks, 6400 St. Claude Ave., is a plantation-style, columned military barracks built in the 1830s. The powder magazine has a museum of military items. Open Tuesday through Sunday, 9 a.m. to 4 p.m.; no admission charge.

Chalmette National Historical Park, St. Bernard Highway, is the battlefield where the Battle of New Orleans was fought in 1815. Beauregard plantation house has film presentation and exhibits. There's also a National Cemetery dating from 1864. Open 8 a.m. to 5 p.m. daily. Free.

Tours

Once you leave the confines of the French Quarter, sightseeing tours can save a lot of time, to say nothing of wear and tear on the nerves, especially if you're the one behind the wheel. Buses will pick you up at your hotel and deliver you back there, and guides can be depended on for complete, accurate information (as well as occasional entertainment by way of amusing anecdotes and legends about the city). Another marvelous way to view the city is from the riverboats that cruise the harbor and a little stretch of the Mississippi River. Docks are at the foot of Toulouse and Canal Streets, and there's ample parking space for the car while you sit back and relax on the water. Reservations are required for all these tours, and I would remind you once more that the prices quoted here are those in effect *at press time,* and are subject to change.

BUS TOURS: The **Gray Line,** 1793 Julia St. (tel. 525-0138), has a complete city tour which begins in the French Quarter, with an informative narration on many historic buildings in the Quarter, as well as the Créole cottages and elegant mansions along Esplanade Avenue. From Esplanade, the tour travels to City Park, then on to Lake Pontchartrain. One of the old cemeteries is a stop, and then it's back to the Garden District for a look at those antebellum mansions. Before delivering you back to your hotel, the tour will show you the Superdome, the New Orleans River Bridge, and the old Custom House. It's a three-hour trip, with departures at 9 a.m. and 1 p.m., and the fare is $15 per person.

For $23 per person (and 5½ hours of your time), Gray Line will include a two-hour cruise on the paddlewheeler *Natchez.* You'll have lunch on board (cost *not* included in the tour price) as you take in the sights and sounds of the harbor. This tour has an 11 a.m. departure time. They will pick you up at your hotel; reservations are necessary for both tours.

SIGHTS OUTSIDE THE FRENCH QUARTER

Southern Tours, 7801 Edinburgh St. (tel. 486-0604), has a bus tour that covers 50 miles within the city. You'll visit old marketplaces, the riverfront and busy wharves, the French Quarter, City Park (they'll show you those dueling oaks), the Museum of Art (from the outside), Lake Pontchartrain, the Garden District and other uptown landmarks, and the Central Business District sights which include the Civic Center and the Superdome. The tour costs $15 per person, and departure times are 9 a.m. and 2 p.m. with pickup and delivery at your hotel.

For tours of the city conducted in Spanish and Portuguese, call **Latin Tours,** 348 Barrone St. (tel. 524-1157 or 524-8983). They provide a very complete sightseeing service. The fare is $15 per person.

RIVERBOAT CRUISES: The steamboat **Natchez,** 2340 International Trade Mart (tel. 586-8777 or 524-9787), a marvelous three-deck sternwheeler docked at the Toulouse Street wharf across from Jackson Square, offers three two-hour harbor cruises daily, at 11:30 a.m., 2:30 p.m., and 6:30 p.m. Narration is by professional guides, and there's a snackbar, cocktail bars, and gift shop aboard. Adult fare is $9.50; children pay $4.75; and those under 6 are free. Call to confirm sailing times.

The sternwheeler **Cotton Blossom** offers a real departure in the cruise world—the exciting Zoo Cruise. Passengers travel the Mississippi by sternwheeler, tour the busy port, and dock to visit the Audubon Zoological Gardens, one of the finest zoos in the world. There are three round trips from the Canal Street dock daily, beginning at 9 a.m. Adult fare is $9.50; ages 3 to 15, $4.75; under 3, free—and all include zoo admissions. Call 587-0740 or 586-8777 for exact sailing times and reservations.

New Orleans's newest paddlewheeler, the **Créole Queen,** departs from the Poydras Street Wharf adjacent to the Hilton Hotel at noon and 2, 4, and 6 p.m. for 1½-hour narrated excursions of the port and points downriver. There's a covered promenade deck, and the inner lounges are air-conditioned and heated. Snackbar and cocktail service are available on all cruises. Fare is $8.50 per person. To confirm sailing times and current fares, call 529-4567 or 524-0814.

There are longer cruises (they'll take the better part of a day) which make excursions into the bayou country and visit plantations along the river (see Chapter XII).

Chapter X

THE FESTIVALS

NEW ORLEANS *MEANS* "FESTIVAL"—and if you don't believe it, try this simple little "free association" test. What's the first thing that comes to mind when someone says "New Orleans"? Mardi Gras—right? Well, that's the biggie, of course, but it's only *one* of this lively city's celebrations. There's something about the frame of mind here that just won't tolerate inhibitions —whether there's a declared celebration in progress or not! Personally, I always feel I'm celebrating something every day I'm in the "City That Care Forgot." Actually, I don't really believe that care forgot New Orleans (there are plenty of problems to be faced and solved)—it's just that New Orleanians seem to look it in the face, shrug their shoulders, and work it out with a grin and a wink. They simply refuse to be grim about it!

As for officially designated festival days, a Calendar of Events issued by the Tourist Commission lists no fewer than 26 spread over the year that are observed either in the city proper or in its neighboring parishes. There's the Sugar Bowl spectacular, of course; a festival of jazz and food; a celebration of spring when ladies don the costumes of long ago and shepherd an admiring public through gorgeous old mansions; there's a food festival just to celebrate the fine art of eating as it's practiced around here; there's an oyster festival, a catfish festival, and numerous crayfish festivals (which sometimes feature a crayfish race) to celebrate the generous waters of the area; there's a two-week extravaganza built around Bastille Day (the French themselves probably lack the enthusiasm that's shown here for that day!); and . . . well, you get the idea. If there's any possible reason to celebrate, New Orleans throws a party.

I can't, of course, cover them all in these pages. I'll tell you about some of the most interesting, and if you take my advice, you'll write ahead to the **Greater New Orleans Tourist and Convention Commission**, 334 Royal St., New Orleans, LA

70130, for a current Calendar of Events to see what's going to be doing when you plan your visit. If, however, you don't see anything spectacular listed, not to worry—you'll feel festive from the moment you arrive.

Mardi Gras

This is the granddaddy of all New Orleans festivals, and it's been here in one form or another as long as the city itself. Volumes could be written about its history, and almost any native you encounter will have his or her own store of Mardi Gras tales. What follows here is a thumbnail sketch of its background and a quick rundown on present-day krewes, parades, and balls.

To begin with, the name "Mardi Gras" means "Fat Tuesday" in French, and that's a very appropriate name, since it is always celebrated on the Tuesday before Ash Wednesday—the idea being that you have a sort of obligation to eat, drink, and be as merry as you possibly can before the Lenten season of fasting and repentance sets in. The name "Carnival" is Latin in origin (from *carnis-vale*, meaning "farewell to flesh") and refers to the period from January 6 to Mardi Gras Day (in New Orleans, the Carnival season is officially opened by the Krewe of Twelfth Night Revelers ball, the only one which has a fixed date).

Where did the custom start? Nobody knows for certain, but some historians see a relationship to ancient tribal rites connected with the coming of spring. And a glorious, sin-filled, pagan orgy which highlighted mid-February for ancient Romans may have been an early ancestor of today's Mardi Gras. The Christian church did its best to stamp out such wild goings-on, but about all it succeeded in doing was to insist on a strict period of fasting and praying for forgiveness to follow the festive season. The point is that while New Orleans can properly claim Mardi Gras for its own in the United States, its spirit of revelry belongs to the history of the world. So, when the first Frenchmen arrived at the mouth of the Mississippi, what could be more natural than their bringing Mardi Gras along with them.

When Iberville, the French explorer, and his group of colonizers camped along the Mississippi in 1699, he didn't bother with keeping records, other than to note that the date was March 3. We don't know for sure, therefore, what that day's activities were in the little camp. What we *do* know is that March 3 was the day before Ash Wednesday in that year, and that Iberville named the spot, some 12 miles north of the river's mouth, "Point du Mardi Gras." Seems likely that with a centuries-long tradition of French Mardi Gras celebration behind him, Iberville celebrated the day in some fashion, however primitive.

It wasn't long after New Orleans was established in 1718 that the French were at it again, although their Mardi Gras consisted largely of private masked balls and parties, with street dancing limited to the poor (but lighthearted) elements of the population. When the Spanish governors took up residence, they slapped a ban on such doings, and the Americans who began arriving in 1803 continued it. It wasn't until 1823 that French Quarter Créoles persuaded the city fathers to permit the masquerade balls once more, and by 1827 it was legal to wear masks in the streets on the great day. When those street maskers started marching in processions that might—by a *big* stretch of the imagination—be called parades, is uncertain, but in 1837 the *Daily Picayune* published for the first time an account of a Mardi Gras parade.

For the next few years things began to get out of hand, with so much wildness in the streets that it seemed inevitable the city government would have to do something to quell the disorderliness. The future of Mardi Gras in New Orleans was very much in doubt, as newspapers and citizens aroused by street violence called for a permanent end to the festival. It took six new residents of the city, who had formerly lived in Mobile, Alabama, to turn things around. Determined to save Mardi Gras and restore some semblance of order and dignity to its observance, they met with 13 friends in what was known as "the club room" over the Gem bar at 127 Royal St. What came out of that meeting was a secret society, the Mistick Krewe of Comus, dedicated to preserving the institution of Carnival. They actually coined the "krewe" appellation, and they planned the first formal, torch-lit parade that was the pattern for all that have followed. Still adhered to, as well, is the practice of building each krewe's parade around a central theme, as did the Krewe of Comus in that first parade. It was from the Comus krewe too that New Orleanians took the practice of forming secret societies, ending parades with private fancy balls, always preceded by an elaborate tableau.

The Civil War put a temporary halt to things, but Comus was parading again by 1866. In 1870, a krewe known as the Twelfth Night Revelers was founded and added two new policies that still endure: they began the throwing of trinkets to onlookers (the first thrower was dressed as Santa Claus), and they were the first to have an official "Queen" reign over their ball. A royal visit in 1872 contributed something more to New Orleans Mardi Gras traditions. The Grand Duke of Russia, Alexis Alexandrovitch Romanoff, followed his lady love, a musical comedy star named Lydia Thompson, from New York when she came here to star in *Bluebeard*. The city went all out to welcome him, and when it was learned that his favorite song was her favorite burlesque tune, "If Ever I Cease to Love You," every band in the Rex parade was asked to play it—that sprightly melody is now the official song of Mardi Gras. Incidentally, the prestigious Krewe of Rex was born that year when a group of citizens banded together to raise money for an impressive welcome ceremony for the duke. The royal colors (purple for justice, green for faith, and gold for power) were also adopted as the festival's official colors.

Mardi Gras, despite its avowal of a "pleasure only" basis, has served a social purpose at least once in New Orleans. During Reconstruction days following the Civil War, public unrest forced the cancellation of the festival in 1875, but in 1877 the Krewe of Momus used as its parade theme "Hades, a Dream of Momus," which held the Grant administration up to such ridicule that the entire country's attention was focused on the deplorable conditions in the South.

Today's traditional ending of Mardi Gras had its beginning in 1882, when Rex and his queen called on the Court of Comus at that krewe's ball. The Krewe of Rex also began throwing medallions instead of trinkets in 1884, and the doubloons which came many years later are an outgrowth of that substitution. The doubloons, usually of aluminum or anodized gold, show the krewe's coat of arms on one side and the parade theme of the year on the other—a marvelous, permanent souvenir of Mardi Gras if you're lucky enough to catch one. You can also purchase them at some New Orleans stores, but somehow it just isn't the same. They have become highly prized, so hold onto any you may acquire—some serious collector may someday offer a good price for it. The best way to come by one is to stand in the crowd and yell "Throw me something, mister" along with everyone else as the floats pass by. If your luck holds out, your pleas will be heard, and if your catch is good, you'll get it before someone else snatches it from the air.

New Orleans blacks entered the Mardi Gras scene through a fun-filled back door. In 1909, a black man named William Storey mocked the elaborately garbed Rex by prancing after his float wearing a lard can for a crown. Storey was promptly dubbed "King Zulu." By 1916, his followers had grown so in numbers that they formed the Zulu Social Aid & Pleasure Club, and for years they observed Mardi Gras by wandering all over town, from one barroom to another which would extend hospitality to King Zulu. These days, they get the day off to a start when His Majesty arrives by boat on the river at 7 a.m. (at the foot of Canal Street) and follows a set parade route through the city's streets on proper floats instead of the banged-up trucks and wagons used in their early years. They're worth getting up early to see just for their grass skirts and sometimes outrageous makeup and masks. Besides the monarch's colorful raiment, there's a "Provident Prince" and a "Big Shot of Africa" all decked out in the-Good-Lord-only-knows-what to look for. The most notable King Zulu was probably Louis Armstrong, in 1949, and in 1980 his good friend Woody Herman realized a longtime dream when he donned blackface and was crowned king of the Zulus.

Other early-morning Mardi Gras groups not to be missed are the nine "walking clubs," with names like Jefferson City Buzzards, the Pete Fountain Half Fast, and Peggy Landry's Silk Stocking Strutters. To quote my good friend Arthur Hardy (author of an excellent Mardi Gras guidebook I'll tell you about later on), these clubs are "sometimes mistakenly named 'marching clubs'—actually, they *never* march; some do walk, but more than a few stumble!" You can catch these "marchers," who as much as the krewe parades embody the spirit of the day, anywhere along their St. Charles Avenue route (between Poydras and Washington).

What can you expect to see and take part in if you come to New Orleans for Mardi Gras? Well, first of all you must remember that this is, primarily, a party New Orleans throws for itself —those spectacular balls are private, attended only by members and their invited guests. Attendance is by invitation, not by ticket, except, that is, for the Bacchus supper dance (and even those tickets are usually hard to come by). If you should be invited to a krewe ball, there are a few things you should know. You'll be a spectator, not a participant, and unless you're a lady and have been issued a "call-out" card, you'll be seated in a separate section to view the tableau after the previous year's queen and her court have been escorted to seats of honor and masked and costumed krewe members have taken their reserved, up-front seats. Members, who guard their secrecy not only during Mardi Gras but all year, are always in costume and masked

—for guests, it's white tie and tails if the invitation reads *de rigueur*, tuxedos if only "formal." Lady guests, of course, are always in formal gowns. Those lucky "call-out" ladies will be seated separately from other guests (even their escorts) until the dancing begins and they've been called out by the krewe member who sent them the card. After a turn around the floor, they'll be given a krewe favor (a souvenir representative of that year's ball theme) and returned to their patiently waiting escorts. As members of the krewe and their ladies continue dancing, the current "royal court" will repair to the queen's supper, where friends and guests will be entertained the rest of the night—and morning.

One of the nicest things about New Orleans's private party is that the whole world is happily invited to come and look. And that results in a whole new cadre of not-so-private entertainments. If you think this town's restaurants and nightclubs and bars and jazz clubs are pretty special most of the time, you should see them during Carnival! You can, in fact, more or less form your own informal "krewe" of friends and have a ball that might be as much fun as those private ones, just by making the rounds in a group.

Whatever else you do or don't do, you surely won't miss seeing a Mardi Gras parade. If, that is, you come during the final 11 days of Carnival. You'll know one's coming when you hear the scream of motorcycle sirens and a herd of motorized police come into view. They'll be followed by men on horseback (sometimes mounted police, sometimes krewe members) who clear the edges of the streets for the approaching floats. It's the king's float first in line, with His Majesty enthroned and waving to the mass of cheering humanity with his scepter. Then will come a float with a banner proclaiming the theme of the parade. After that, each float will illustrate some facet of the theme. And it's a grand sight—the papier-mâché lions or elephants or flowers or fanciful creatures or whatever are sometimes enormous (there are people in New Orleans who work all year designing and building Mardi Gras floats), and there's much use of silver and gold tinsel that sparkles in the sunlight or the light of torches. Those torches, or *flambeaux*, are carried by dancing blacks dressed in hoods and white smocks. Each float has masked krewe members who wave and throw doubloons and souvenirs. And in some of the parades, the floats keep coming until you think there's no end to them—Bacchus, for instance, had 23 in 1982 and Rex had 25! Each krewe has its designated time and parade route (which makes a current Mardi Gras guidebook invaluable) and most follow some part of St. Charles Avenue, sometimes a portion of Jackson Street as well, and Canal Street, and end up at the Municipal Auditorium, where all parades disband except the renegade Bacchus with its Rivergate terminus. Since there are more than 50 parading krewes, and only 11 days in which to do the parading, the streets are seldom empty, day or night, during this period. And the rollicking, costumed crowd filling the streets is as much something to see as the parades themselves. Every conceivable manner of costume appears, and maskers made bold by their temporary anonymity carry on in the most outrageous, hilarious manner you can imagine. A great good humor envelops the whole scene, and I absolutely *defy* anyone to look on with disapproval!

On the last day of Carnival, Mardi Gras, the walking clubs are out at the crack of dawn, then King Zulu arrives around 9 a.m., the Rex parade is mid-morning, and Comus closes the day with its evening parade (about 6:30 p.m.). The high point of this final day is probably when Rex, the only Mardi Gras king whose identity is disclosed, arrives on his majestic float. It is a very high honor to be chosen Rex, and the selection always comes from among prominent men in the city, most well past the first blush of youth. Rex's queen, on the other hand, is always one of the current year's pack of young debutantes. While that may make for a pretty ill-matched royal couple, there've never been any reports of incompatibility between the rulers-for-a-day. The choosing of Rex and his queen is done in the strictest secrecy, adding to the excitement that attends his first public appearance in the parade.

Another thing that's nice about Carnival in New Orleans is the fact that it doesn't cost the city one red cent except the cost of extra police for the parades and that of cleaning up the streets after Fat Tuesday. This is truly a private celebration, planned, executed, and paid for by New Orleanians themselves—and I'll wager that if not one of us dropped in for the festivities, the celebration would change not one iota!

Now, for the practicalities—you'd like to be there for Mardi Gras, so the details have to be attended to. First of all, you can't really just drop in. If you do, you may find yourself sleeping in Jackson Square or on a sidewalk somewhere. Rooms are booked solid in the city itself and in the nearby suburbs, so *make your plans well ahead and book a room as soon as they are finalized.* It is no exaggeration to say that you should plan one year to go the next, and make your reservation right then. Prices are usually a little higher during Mardi Gras, and most hotels and guest houses impose minimum-stay requirements.

One way to eliminate many of the hassles for space during Mardi Gras is to book one of the several packaged tours. Amtrak, for example, sometimes offers hotel space and some extras during Carnival, so you should check with your local Amtrak tour desk. **Abbott Tours**, 840 North Rampart St., New Orleans, LA 70116 (tel. 504/827-5920), has Festival Tours which include a minimum of four nights, an invitation to one of the tableau balls, a cocktail supper following the ball, and a city tour. In 1984, costs ranged from $305 to $533 per person (double occupancy), depending on your choice of hotel. Transportation to and from the city is not included in that price. Abbott Tours may be booked through most travel agents.

You will surely want to join the maskers with your own costume, and while it's best to plan ahead and come prepared, there are several shops in town that specialize in Mardi Gras costumes and masks (see "Shopping" in Chapter XI). One of the most reasonable is **Garland's Mardi Gras Center**, 831 Chartres St. (tel. 524-4384). If you come early enough, they can custom-make a costume to your own design; if not, they are well stocked with new and used costumes, wigs, masks, hats, and makeup.

When you arrive, remember that while all those crowds add to the general merriment, they also make it more difficult to get in and out of restaurants in a hurry. And your progress from one part of town to another will be slowed down considerably. The point is, be sure that you come in a relaxed frame of mind, with enough mental flexibility for the delays to be a source of enjoyment (after all, who knows *what* you may see while waiting) and not irritation.

You'll enjoy Mardi Gras more, too, if you've done a little homework before you come. Write the **Greater New Orleans Tourist and Convention Commission**, 334 Royal St., New Orleans, LA 70130, asking for their current Mardi Gras information. And I can't think of any one more valuable bit of preparation than the handy little *New Orleans Mardi Gras Guide* published by Arthur Hardy (P.O. Box 8058, New Orleans, LA 70182). He'll send you a copy postpaid if you send along $2.95—if you arrive without one, they'll be in most bookstores and on newsstands in the city. It contains a complete history of the festival, a rundown on each krewe, parade times and routes, and a lot of other miscellaneous information that will make Mardi Gras even more fun.

Just one more thing should be said: Mardi Gras will be February 19 in 1985, February 11 in 1986—you can figure out the date for subsequent years, since it always falls exactly 46 days before Easter.

CAJUN MARDI GRAS: For a really unique Mardi Gras experience, drive out to "Cajun Country." Lafayette, a booming but charming town in the very heart of French Acadiana, celebrates Carnival in a manner quite different from the New Orleans fête—a manner that reflects the heritage and spirit of those hard-working, fun-loving Cajuns. (For their full story, see Chapter XII, "Side Trips.") There are four full days of parades leading up to Mardi Gras, with all sorts of attendant activities designed to *"laissez les bons temps rouler"* ("let the good times roll," an absolute creed around these parts during Carnival). This is, in fact, second in size only to New Orleans's Mardi Gras, and there's one *big* difference—the Cajuns open their final pageant and ball to the general public! That's right, you can don your costume and mask and join right in.

Instead of Rex and his queen, in Lafayette festivities are ruled by King Gabriel and Queen Evangeline. They are the fictional hero and heroine of Longfellow's epic poem *Evangeline* which was based on real-life Acadian lovers who were separated during the British expulsion of Acadians from Nova Scotia just after the French and Indian War, and their story is still very much alive here among descendants of those who shared their wanderings. On Monday night before Mardi Gras, Queen Evangeline is honored by the parading Krewe of Bonaparte. The King's Parade, held the following morning, honors King Gabriel and opens a full day of merriment. Lafayette's black community stages the Parade of King Toussaint L'Ouverture and Queen Suzanne Simonne about noon, just after the King's Parade. And following *that,* the Krewe of Lafayette invites everyone to get into the act as its parade winds through the streets. You can trot along with those on foot or ride in the vehicle of your choice (and some very imaginative modes of transportation turn up every year). If you're still up to it when this parade comes to an end in late afternoon, you'll hie yourself off to the hotel to get ready for the Mardi Gras climax, a brilliantly beautiful, exciting formal ball presided over by the king and queen and their royal court. Every-

NEW ORLEANS EVENTS   151

thing stops promptly at midnight, of course, as Cajuns and visitors alike depart to observe the solemnity of Lent with the fondly remembered glow of Mardi Gras to take them through to Easter.

Out in the Cajun countryside that surrounds Lafayette, there's yet another form of Mardi Gras celebration, and I'll guarantee you won't find another like it anywhere else in the world. It's very much tied to the rural lifestyle of these displaced people who have created a rich culture out of personal disaster. And since Cajuns firmly believe that nothing is ever quite as much fun alone as it is when shared, you're entirely welcome to come along. The rural celebration goes like this: Bands of masked men dressed in patchwork costumes and peaked hats (*capishons*) set off on Mardi Gras morning on horseback, led by their *capitaine*. They ride from farm to farm, asking at each "Will you receive the Mardi Gras?" (*"Voulez-vous reçevoir le Mardi Gras?"*) and dismounting as the invariable "yes" comes in reply. Then each farmyard becomes a miniature festival, as they "make monkeyshines" (*faire le macaque*) with song and dance, much drinking of beer, and other antics loosely labled as "entertainment" for the farm family. As payment for their show, they demand—and get—"a fat little chicken to make a big gumbo."

When each band has visited its allotted farmyards, they head back to town, where everyone else has already begun the general festivities. There'll be dancing in the streets, rowdy card games, storytelling, and the like until the wee hours, and you may be sure all those "fat little chickens" go into the "gumbo gros" pot to make a "big gumbo." It's a real "down home" sort of festival, where you can let your hair all the way down. And if you've never heard Cajun music (sort of like American country, but with a difference) or eaten gumbo cooked by real Cajuns, you're in for a treat.

You can write ahead for full particulars on both these Mardi Gras celebrations to: **Lafayette Parish Convention and Visitors Commission,** P.O. Box 52066, O.C.S., Lafayette, LA 70505.

Other Festivals

JAZZ AND HERITAGE FESTIVAL: By the time mid-April rolls around, Easter has passed, the Mardi Gras is a fond memory of this year and grand expectation for next, and New Orleanians turn to another festival celebration. Actually, the Jazz and Heritage Festival combines two fêtes, as its name implies. From one weekend to another (one of the last weeks in April or first in

May), musicians, mimes, artists, craftsmen, and cooks head out to the Fairgrounds Racetrack on the weekends and settle into hotel ballrooms, jazz joints, the Municipal Auditorium, and even on board the riverboat *President* on weeknights to put on a never-ending show of what New Orleans is all about. Over 3000 performers turn up—and that's not counting the street bands! Famous-name jazz players are drawn like a magnet, and they very happily share the ten stages out at the Fairgrounds with lesser known Cajun groups who stomp out rhythm and blues, and the voices blended in sweet harmony over at the gospel music tent. You can find your favorite and stand in front of the stage all day long, or make the rounds, coming back to favorites or to see what new group has taken over. Remember, this is a New Orleans festival—completely unstructured with the emphasis on pure enjoyment. That's out at the Fairgrounds; on weeknights, street bands are everywhere, and if you can't find a performance of *your* kind of music going on somewhere, well, it just must not exist. If Dixieland happens to be your preference, you'll be in heaven!

As for the "heritage" part of the festival, local craftsmen and imported artisans are there en masse with their wares (you can also see some demonstrations of just how they work), and that top-priority heritage, good food, is present in such abundance you'll be tempted to stuff yourself way beyond the limits set by our modern health freaks. Red beans and rice, jambalaya, gumbo, crayfish, sweet-potato pie, oysters, fried chicken, andouille, boudin, po-boys, crabs, shrimp—that, believe it or not, is only a partial list of what's available! And there's plenty of cold beer to wash it down. There's just nothing quite like munching fried chicken from the Second Mount Triumph Missionary Baptist Church booth in an outdoor setting where the air is filled with strains of Dixieland, ragtime, reggae, and the blues. There are well over 30 booths, and it's a safe bet you'll want at least to sample each one, so come hungry.

You can find out about current dates, artists who will be there and where they'll be performing in concert during the week, and background information by sending a stamped, self-addressed envelop to the Jazz and Heritage Festival, P.O. Box 2530, New Orleans, LA 70176 (tel. 504/522-4786).

SPRING FIESTA: One of the best times of the year to visit New Orleans is during the 19-day-long Spring Fiesta. It's been going on since 1937, and this is the one time you can get to see the inside of some of those lovely old homes. Those ordinarily closed to the public throw open their doors, and hostesses clad in antebellum dress will escort you through the premises, with all sorts of information and anecdotes about each house or historic building that you might otherwise never know. In the French Quarter, there are balcony concerts by sopranos rendering numbers sung here in the past by Jenny Lind and Adelina Patti. Out River Road, there are plantation home tours; in the Quarter, candlelight tours of patios; and as a highlight, the gala "Night in Old New Orleans" parade features carriages bearing passengers dressed as prominent figures in the city's history and some of the best marching bands in town. Spring Fiesta always opens the first Friday after Easter (1985 dates are April 12-30), and for full details, reservations, and a schedule of the modest admission fees for some of the homes, you can write: Spring Fiesta Association, 527 Dumaine St., New Orleans, LA 70116 (tel. 504/581-1367).

FOOD FESTIVAL: Yes, there *is* food in every conceivable form at the Jazz and Heritage Festival in April. But by late June (sometimes early July), it's time to celebrate the local cuisine all over again, with a festival all its own. This time it's held in the Rivergate Convention Center, and literally dozens of chefs set up food-tasting booths for everything from spicy Créole dishes to exotic Oriental treats to Cajun specialties to seafood in creative forms. There are also magnificent food presentations, so artistically done it seems a shame they're made to be eaten. As one reviewer commented, the Food Festival adds up to "an epicure's dream, a dieter's nightmare." The whole affair is climaxed by a superb gourmet dinner. For exact dates and full details, write: New Orleans Food Festival, P.O. Box 2410, New Orleans, LA 70116.

FESTIVALS ACADIENS: This is a "Cajun Country" celebration —or, rather, *seven* celebrations—all held during the third week of September in Lafayette. These festivals, lumped under the heading Festivals Acadiens, pay tribute to the culture and heritage of Cajun families who have been here nearly 200 years after the British expelled them from their Nova Scotia homeland. The festive week includes: the Bayou Food Festival; the Cajun Music Festival; Louisiana Native Crafts Festival; Acadiana Fair and

Trade Show; RSVP Senior Fair and Craft Show; the Art Center for Southwestern Louisiana Festival; and the Acadian Village and Gardens Festival.

At the **Bayou Food Festival,** you'll be able to taste the cuisine of more than 30 top Cajun restaurants, in one location. Specialties like stuffed crabs, crayfish étouffée, oysters Bienville, shrimp créole, oysters Rockefeller, shrimp de la Teche, and catfish en brochette, jambalaya, chicken and sausage gumbo, smothered quail and hot boudin are everyday eating for Cajuns, and this is a rare opportunity to try them all. It works like this: for about $6, you're given an admission ticket plus a book of coupons to be redeemed for food—a bargain in anyone's book! And if you're wondering about the quality of Lafayette's restaurant food, let me tell you that it sells more restaurant food per capita than any other American city.

The **Cajun Music Festival** (*L'Hommage à la Musique Acadienne*) got its start in 1974, when some Cajun musicians were engaged to play briefly for visiting French newspaper editors. In spite of its being a rainy night, some 12,000 Cajun residents showed up to listen in! Well, the walls rang for three solid hours with old French songs, waltzes, two-steps, Cajun rock rhythms, and the special music some have dubbed "Cajun Country." And even after all that, nobody wanted to go home. Since then it has become an annual affair, and over 50,000 visitors are usually on hand. Because of the crowds, the festival is now held outdoors in Girard Park, where fans can listen in grassy comfort. Performed almost entirely in French, the music includes both traditional and modern Cajun styles (and one form, known as zydeco, combines the blues of the blacks with more traditional Cajun sounds). The music starts early and ends late, and there's no charge to come to the park and listen. Sales from food and beverage stands all go toward a fund to build a Cajun Music Preservation Hall.

You'll see native Louisiana craftsmen demonstrating their expertise at the **Louisiana Native Crafts Festival.** All crafts must have been practiced prior to or during the early 1900s, and all materials used must be native to Louisiana. Meeting these criteria are such arts as woodcarving of all types (with an emphasis, it seemed to me, on duck decoys), soap making, pirogue (pronounced *pee*-rogue—it's a Cajun canoe made from a dugout cypress log) making, chair caning, doll making, palmetto weaving, Indian weaving, quilting, spinning, dyeing, pottery making, jewelry making, and probably a few more I've missed.

And the elders who have passed these crafts down to many of the younger Cajuns you'll see at the Native Crafts Festival have their day in the sun at the **RSVP Senior Fair and Craft Show** (the RSVP stands for Retired Senior Volunteer Program). They're all over 60, and it's a rare treat to meet them and see their homemade articles and listen to them talk of the old days.

The **Acadiana Fair and Trade Show** is put on by Lafayette merchants and businessmen, and there's an indoor display of their goods and services, plus an outdoor carnival with rides, a midway, and games. It's sponsored by the Lafayette Junior Chamber of Commerce, and the Jaycees also provide free shuttle bus service for the public from one festival to another.

At the **Art Center for Southwestern Louisiana** (a big, colonial Louisiana plantation-style house), the festival features films, lectures, musical events, and one-act plays, as well as a fine permanent collection of sketches, drawings, paintings, and sculpture by Cajuns, which capture the very essence of their unique culture. The house itself could almost qualify as an "exhibit," with its cypress-paneled library, brick flooring sealed with hot beeswax, and hand-carved wood moldings and fireplace facades. It was built entirely by local craftsmen.

You can visit the **Acadian Village Gardens** any time of the year, but during Festivals Acadiens, they serve as the setting for special musical and theatrical performances. And what a setting it is! If you have any interest at all in Acadiana's history, you'll find this little village a trip back in time. Homes and buildings here are not models or even reconstructions of originals—they're all original old Acadian homes which have been found, restored where needed, and moved to the village to create (or, as the Cajuns say, "reassemble") a typical 1800s village. It's a tranquil, charming spot centered around a bayou and surrounded by the Around-the-World Tropical Gardens. More than 40 flowerbeds of annuals and perennials, as well as a wealth of tropical plants, embroider the intricate weaving of streams, islands, brick walks, and foot bridges.

For exact dates and full details on Festivals Acadiens, write: **Lafayette Parish Convention and Visitors Commission**, P.O. Box 52066 O.C.S., Lafayette, LA 70505 (tel. 318/232-3737).

ANNUAL SUGAR BOWL SPORTS SPECTACULAR: Beginning just after Christmas, when there's a general letdown until New Year's Day almost everywhere else, New Orleans is putting on a sort of sports festival. There's a college basketball tournament, a junior and collegiate tennis tournament, a yachting regatta, national intramural flag-football tournament, a road race, and all kinds of side events. Of course, the *big* event comes on January 1, when two of the country's top college football teams meet in the Sugar Bowl classic.

If you plan to be here for the sports-filled week, plan *way* ahead—rooms are simply not to be found if you wait until the last minute.

FOR FROG FANCIERS: To prove my point that just about anything is cause for celebration in New Orleans and its environs, let me tell you about the **Rayne Frog Festival.** It's held in Cajun Country, just a few miles west of Lafayette. Now, the Cajuns can hold their own when it comes to drumming up festivals—a harvest, a new season, a special tradition, a special talent, or just the job of being alive—and in this case, they simply turn to the lowly frog as an excuse for a *fais-dodo* (dance) and a waltz contest. Not to forget the reason for it all, things get underway with frog races and frog-jumping contests—and if you arrive without *your* frog, there's a "Rent-a-Frog" service! To wind things up, there's a lively frog-eating contest. The Rayne Frog Festival is held in September, and if it's not exactly your cup of tea, just glance over the list of other festivals scheduled—I told you, this is festival country!

Chapter XI

SHOPPING IN NEW ORLEANS

LIKE EVERYTHING ELSE IN NEW ORLEANS, shopping is fun. I say that as a dedicated nonshopper, one who keeps the mail-order houses in business. Still, the shops are so different, so intriguing, that I'm in and out of them all along the streets. There's *everything* in New Orleans, and if you can't find something, you can find someone to make it for you! The place is loaded with craftsmen and artisans in every material conceivable: cast iron, wood, leather, fabric, brass, plastic, and precious metals. You can even have one of those marvelous oldtime overhead fans shipped back home.

Antique shops are really special here, many with patios and gardens that actually seem to enhance their goods. Some are located in old French Quarter homes, giving another dimension to browsing. And the emphasis that was always placed on fine home furnishings in New Orleans has left a residue of some of the loveliest antiques I've ever viewed. Many came from Europe in the early days; others were crafted right here in the city by cabinetmakers internationally known for their exquisite pieces. And for the nautically minded, there are shops which specialize in marine antiques, wonderful mementoes of long-ago voyages and the ships that made them.

Because its port is the landing place for goods from all over the world, New Orleans fills its shops with a rich variety of imported items, from home furnishings to kitchen utensils to pottery to designer clothes to whatever else you can name. Art galleries too display the works of leading world artists as well as those closer to home. The creation of fine jewelry is a much-practiced art, and a visit to some of the jewelers is akin to an art gallery visit.

You'll notice, of course, the abundance of gift shops—post-

158 □ ARTHUR FROMMER'S NEW ORLEANS

cards, sunglasses, and T-shirts displayed outside won't let you miss them. Well, don't dismiss them all as cheap souvenir places. Some of my most blissful browsing has come as a surprise when I entered such a place to buy postcards and found an interior stocked with imaginative imported gift items. (Which is not to say that that's true of all of these little shops, but it pays to look.)

The following listing is far from complete, but if you don't see a particular category which is of special interest to you, be assured you'll more than likely find it when you arrive in New Orleans. For convenience, I'll show the major shopping centers first, then the leading department stores, followed by shops grouped by category. Happy shopping!

Shopping Centers

CANAL STREET: This is where shopping first expanded outside the French Quarter when American merchants began arriving in 1803. Today, you'll find just about every kind of commercial enterprise there is on Canal Street. The leading department stores are all here (with branches in some of the other centers); there are small, exclusive boutiques, leather goods stores, less expensive clothing chains, camera shops, jewelers, and several fast-food chains. You'll find branches of such fine stores as Saks Fifth Avenue and Brooks Brothers in the new Canal Place complex at the corner of Canal and Decatur.

THE FRENCH MARKET: On Decatur Street across from Jackson Square, right at the riverside boundary of the Quarter, this has been a marketplace since Indians traded here. Now, there's happy browsing or shopping, with candy shops (one that offers Créole recipes and cookware and the spices that go with them), a toy shop, an exclusive women's dress shop, and other fascinating boutiques. And, of course, in between shopping there's the delightful Café du Monde for café au lait and beignets while you indulge in a little people-watching.

THE MARKETPLACE: At 1015 Decatur St., just across from the French Market, the Marketplace almost counts as a sightseeing attraction, with its unique combination of old-world charm and the most modern merchandise. Located inside an old warehouse (this was one of the first Decatur Street upgrading projects), it is composed of small shops lining a brick road. Shops specialize in such items as brass and copper, quilts, soaps, baskets, music boxes, blended coffees and teas, and clocks, and there's a New York Deli looking right at home here in the South. Truly a delightful place to shop, it's open seven days a week, from 10 a.m. to 5:45 p.m., and there is sometimes a craft demonstration, street musicians, or some other form of entertainment going on inside the Marketplace.

RIVERBEND: Riverbend is in the Dublin Park area. To reach it, go all the way out St. Charles Avenue (the streetcar ride is by far the best way to get there), turn right onto Carrollton Avenue to Burthe (you can get off the trolley here). Walk one block to your left on Burthe, then turn left on Dublin. This is a lovely old residential area whose houses have been turned into charming boutiques, art and craft galleries, and shops that sell everything from tennis togs to antiques.

UPTOWN SQUARE: At 200 Broadway, this unique new shopping center consists of a maze of one- and two-story buildings interspersed with pleasant plazas and fountains. It's a central place to find fine fashions (Holmes Department Store has a large branch here), family clothing, housewares, distinctive gifts, toys, plants, books, and wines. There's also an upstairs, cafeteria-style restaurant with balcony seating if you wish.

WILKINSON ROW: Just one block from Jackson Square, toward Canal Street, between Chartres and Decatur Streets, what was once a row of old warehouses has been transformed into charming shops, offering anything from antiques to designer clothes to painting and sculpture to very special gifts.

Department Stores

MAISON BLANCHE: The store at 901 Canal St. has been world famous for quality and luxury goods as long as I can remember. There are branches at: Clearview Shopping Center (tel. 888-7200); Lake Forest Plaza (tel. 241-8121); and Westside Shopping Center, Gretna (tel. 362-5300). There's a special service for Spanish-speaking customers (ask for Centro de las Americas), and most stay open until 9 p.m.

D. H. HOLMES COMPANY, LTD.: At 819 Canal St. (tel. 561-6611), this is another longtime New Orleans favorite. Many local business people also frequent its excellent restaurant and cafeteria, which serve very good food at very reasonable prices. Hours are Monday through Saturday, 10 a.m. to 5:40 p.m. (to 7 p.m. on Thursday). Suburban stores (which are open until 9:30 p.m. daily) are located at: Lakeside Shopping Center, Metairie (tel. 834-2424); Oakwood Shopping Center, Gretna (tel. 362-4800); Lake Forest Plaza (tel. 241-7711); and Uptown Square (tel. 861-8141)

KRAUSS CO., LTD.: At the intersection of Canal and Basin Streets, at 1201 Canal St. (tel. 523-3311), this is a large, medium-priced department store that sells everything from home furnishings to cosmetics. They have an outstanding fabric and drapery selection. Hours are 10 a.m. to 5:45 p.m. Monday through Saturday, till 7 p.m. on Thursday.

Shopping by Categories

ANTIQUES: Boyer Antiques–Dolls & Buttons, 241 Chartres and 404 Chartres St. (tel. 522-4513). In addition to the usual assortment of antiques, you'll find an enchanting collection of old dolls and doll furniture. Hours are 9:30 a.m. to 5 p.m. daily.

Endangered Species, 604 Conti St. (tel. 568-9855). This unusual shop features ethnic jewelry, tribal arts, and ivory artifacts personally selected by the owner on travels through Africa, Asia, and the Middle East. The marvelous collection includes Hindu temple carvings and wildlife trophies. Open Monday through Saturday, 9:30 a.m. to 5:30 p.m.

Le Petit Soldier Shop, 528 Royal St. (tel. 523-7741). If you've ever wanted to play "toy soldier," don't go near this intriguing shop—you'll never leave if you do! There are miniature soldiers and miniature military antiques, and full-size antique helmets, swords, books, and prints. You can come in a private and go out a general. Hours are 10 a.m. to 5 p.m. Monday through Saturday.

Magazine Arcade, 3017 Magazine St. (tel. 899-9144). This part of Magazine Street is right on the edge of the Garden District, and this is a fascinating arcade of antique shops—there are art prints, jewelry, antique furniture, music boxes, stained glass, and so on. You just must allow plenty of time to see it all.

A short ride from Canal Street on the Magazine Street bus, it's open from 10 a.m. to 4 p.m., Monday through Saturday.

ART GALLERIES: Davis Gallery, 3964 Magazine St. (tel. 897-0780 or 897-0248), features West Africa's tribal art, with periodic exhibits of pre-Columbian and Oceanic artifacts. Give them a call to check on current showings. Hours are 10 a.m. to 5 p.m. Monday through Friday, to 3 p.m. on Saturday.

Dixon & Dixon Art Gallery, 315 Chartres St. (tel. 524-0282), is housed in another beautiful restored mansion in the Quarter, with a lovely courtyard open to customers. The art is 18th- and 19th-century original oils. Come by from 10 a.m. to 6 p.m. Monday through Saturday.

Hanson Galleries, 229 Royal St. (tel. 566-0816). It's contemporary art here, with such masters as Dali, Alvar, Boulanger, LeRoy Neiman, and Vasarely. Also acrylics of Bijan Bahar and the innovative metal sculpture of Thom Wheeler. Hours are 10 a.m. to 5 p.m. seven days a week.

Lorenzo Bergen Galleries, 730 Royal St. (tel. 523-7882), specializes in posters and limited-edition graphics. This is the place to shop for those New Orleans posters you want to carry home (although the extensive collection is not limited in subject). Lorenzo is an artist, Margarita is his sister, and both are knowledgeable and friendly. Hours are 10 a.m. to 7 p.m. daily.

Old Quarter Gallery, 622 Royal St. (tel. 522-9752), is one of the artist-owned and operated galleries described in Chapter VIII. A different artist is in the gallery every day to discuss a wide variety of subjects (wildlife, florals, portraits, etc.), styles (abstract to traditional to realism), and media (oil, acrylic, watercolor, batik, etchings, woodcuts, photography, and limited-edition prints). The gallery offers fine art at reasonable prices; hours are 10:30 a.m. to 5 p.m. daily.

Nahan Galleries, 540 Royal St. (tel. 524-8696), specializes in signed graphics by Miró, and Calder (among others), and oils and watercolors by contemporary artists. They are also agents and publishers for Theo Tobiasse, Max Papart, and others. Open 9:30 a.m. to 5:30 p.m. seven days a week.

The **Oaks Gallery,** 723 Toulouse St. (tel. 522-8119), specializes in originally designed handcrafted ceramics, stained glass, baskets, and quilts by regional and national artisans, displayed in the "gentleman's office" of Casa Hinard, a lovely Spanish-style French Quarter home. Hours are 10 a.m. to 6 p.m. daily.

Sports Art, 617 Bienville St. at Exchange Alley (tel. 525-2467 or 525-3846). This attractive store, the largest sporting and wildlife gallery in the South, represents wildlife artists from all over the country. Signatures on their paintings and prints include David Maass, Harry Adamson, Maynard Reece, and David Hagerbaumer, to name a few. They also have sportsmen's clocks, glasses, jewelry, hand-carved wooden decoys, and a fine line of old and new books. They're open daily from 10 a.m. to 5 p.m.

Studio d'Artiste, 621 Chartres St. (tel. 523-6871), is a sister operation to the Old Quarter Gallery (see above), with the same types of art, artists on hand daily, hours, etc.

ARTS AND CRAFTS: Arius Tile Company, 504 St. Peter St. (tel. 529-1665), is a perfect place to find that "just right" New Orleans memento to take home. Beautiful hand-painted art tiles—use them for trivets, kitchen counters, murals, table tops, bars, or just plain decoration. There are more than 200 designs, and if you have something special in mind (a slogan or company logo, for instance), they'll custom-make your own design. Hours are 10 a.m. to 5 p.m. daily, and they have a catalog available.

Loom Room Studio, 623 Royal St. (tel. 522-7101). This is a fun browsing spot, but you probably won't leave without at least one of their marvelous hand-woven products. The Loom Room specializes in American crafts such as wood, glass, pottery, and jewelry. It's open every day from 10 a.m. to 5 p.m.

Out of the Woods, 812 Royal St. (tel. 522-1211). If you love beautiful wood and the things fine craftsmen can do with it, this is the place to go. In addition to handmade toys (including a handsome rocking horse), kitchen utensils, and other utilitarian objects, there are art objects, jewelry, boxes, clocks, some furniture, and wall hangings. The shop is open every day from 10 a.m. to 5:30 p.m.

Weavers Workshop Ltd., 716 Dublin St. (tel. 866-0820). Hand-woven items made by local weavers are on sale in this Riverbend shop, along with anything and everything you might need if you practice the craft yourself or want to try it. Looms, yarns (including unusual ones like llama and alpaca), hard-to-find weaving accessories, a variety of gift items, and books on fiber arts offer stimulating shopping. Come in Tuesday through Saturday from 10 a.m. to 4 p.m.

Sandro, Inc., 633 Toulouse St. (tel. 524-9926), displays wonderful specimens of Mexican handicrafts and art, silver jewelry, onyx gifts, ponchos, and Aztec and Mayan items. There's a Spanish-speaking sales force on hand. Open Monday through Saturday from 10 a.m. to 6 p.m., and from 2 to 6 p.m. on Sunday.

BOOKS: You'll find a wealth of interesting, well-stocked bookstores in the French Quarter—indeed, scattered all around town. These are just two, which I happen to like very much:

Beckham's Bookshop, 228 Decatur St. (tel. 522-9875). There are two entire floors of old editions and some rare, secondhand books that will tie up your whole afternoon or morning if you don't tear yourself away. The owners also operate **Librairie Bookshop,** at 829 Royal, and **Old Books,** at 811 Royal (both of which you'll surely have found if you're a book lover). Hours are 10 a.m. to 6 p.m. every day of the week.

Doubleday Bookstore, 633 Canal St. (tel. 522-6536). In addition to the broad range of general-interest books you'd expect to find in a Doubleday bookshop, there are interesting books on New Orleans and Louisiana, as well as records (including a large selection of New Orleans jazz), and discounted books. Open 10 a.m. to 6 p.m. Monday to Saturday.

CAMERAS: **Alfredo's Cameras,** 928 Gravier St. Suppose you left home in a hurry and arrive in New Orleans without your camera. Tragedy? Not necessarily. Just get yourself over to Alfredo's, where they have everything you could possibly need, plus a lot of accessories you probably didn't know you needed. If you did bring along the trusted old Brownie and it chooses this time to break down, Alfredo's will repair it. They also have 24-hour processing on most film. You'll find the doors open from 8:30 a.m. to 5:30 p.m. Monday through Friday, 9 a.m. to 1 p.m. on Saturday.

CANDIES AND PRALINES: Once you taste New Orleans pralines, you're likely to become addicted, and you'll surely want to take some home. If your bags are already full, most shops will mail them for you.

Aunt Sally's Praline Shops, Inc., 810–827 Decatur St. in the French Market (tel. 524-5107). You can watch skilled workers cook the original Créole pecan pralines here right before your eyes in a 150-year-old process. You'll know they're fresh. The large store also has Créole cookbooks on sale, along with a fascinating array of china, glassware, jewelry, and souvenirs. And they'll ship any of your purchases, which can lighten the load going home considerably. Hours are 8 a.m. to 6 p.m. every day.

Laura's Original Praline and Fudge Shoppe, 115 Royal St. (tel. 525-3880). There are seven varieties of pralines on sale here, plus hand-dipped chocolates, rum-flavored pecans, Vieux Carré Foods, and their great praline sauce. Take home a feast, or have it shipped. And drop in almost anytime—they're open from 9 a.m. to 10:30 p.m. every day of the week.

Old Town Praline Shop, 627 Royal St. Mrs. Louise Glynn has operated this shop (it's in the Adelina Patti house, and that gorgeous courtyard is open for a stroll) for the past 42 years. Pralines here are the original recipe, not the creamy kind, and they come in six sizes. You can buy them in batches ranging in price from $3 to $9 (or individual ones to munch as you meander for 50¢). The shop stays open from 10 a.m. to 5:30 p.m. every day except Sunday.

CANDLES: **French Market Candle Shop**, 824 Decatur St. (tel. 522-6004). There's a delightful collection of novelty (including animals) candles in this shop, along with a large stock of beautiful artistic shapes and sizes. Brass candlesticks and other candle-related items, as well. Hours are 9 a.m. to 6 p.m. daily.

Vieux Carré Candle Shop, 708 Iberville St. (tel. 525-5546). There's not much in the way of candles and the things that go with them that you won't find in this French Quarter shop. An impressive selection of sizes (from half an inch to several feet high) and some unusual candle holders. Open every day from 9 a.m. to 6 p.m.

CLOTHING: Perhaps as a leftover from their elegant past, New Orleanians love fashion, and shops around the city accommodate them by providing everything from high-fashion designer clothes to the latest "funky" styles. Men and women will find stylish garb to suit almost any taste readily available.

All American Jeans, 622 Canal St. (tel. 581-6666). Well, you know what you'll find at this address. And they have those beloved denims for the entire family. Hours are 10 a.m. to 5:30 p.m. Monday through Saturday.

Bela's Imports, 822 Chartres St. (tel. 522-0539), has one of the best selections of women's fashions I've run into for "the exciting and unique person," as they advertise. Here's where you'll find that distinctive blouse, skirt, robe, jacket, etc., at prices that are very, very reasonable. Hours are 10 a.m. to 6 p.m. seven days a week.

Gentlemen's Quarter, Ltd., in the Monteleone Hotel at 232 Royal St. (tel. 522-7139), has a terrific stock of men's wear, from casual sport coats and slacks right up to the most elegant dinner clothes. A real convenience is their same-day alteration service. Open Monday through Saturday from 10 a.m. to 6 p.m., from noon to 4 p.m. on Sunday. This, incidentally, is the largest men's shop in the French Quarter.

Lilly Pulitzer of New Orleans, 530 Wilkinson St. (tel. 522-4433), is another exclusive establishment specializing in colorful, sophisticated cruise and summer clothing for the entire family. The staff is conversant in French, Swedish, German, and Spanish. Open 9:30 a.m. to 5:30 p.m. Monday through Friday, 10 a.m. to 5 p.m. on Saturday.

Meyer the Hatter, 120 St. Charles Ave. (tel. 525-1048). Men will find distinguished headwear—one of the largest selections of fine hats and caps in the South—with labels like Stetson, Dobbs, and Borsalino in this fine shop which opened in 1894 and is now run by third-generation members of the same family. Open Monday through Saturday from 9:30 a.m. to 5:30 p.m.

Mignon Faget, Ltd., 710 Dublin St. in the Riverbend shopping center (tel. 865-1107). The original designs in this shop have all been made up in workrooms right on the premises (but they're also marketed all over the country). They reflect a feeling for the natural look, as does the beautifully crafted gold and silver jewelry fashioned in earth and sea forms. Hours are Monday through Saturday, 10 a.m. to 6 p.m.

Town and Country, 1432 St. Charles Ave. (tel. 525-9572). Opened almost a half century ago, this shop has a warm, friendly atmosphere that encourages leisurely examination of their fine fashions. There are designer collections, distinctive dresses and jewelry, and some truly smashing accessories. Hours are 9:30 a.m. to 5:30 p.m. Monday through Friday, until 5 p.m. on Saturday.

Uptown Izzy's is actually uptown, in the French Quarter, and in Metairie. All three shops sell designer fashions at discounts of 30% to 60%. There are classic styles as well as the latest fashions, and some of the best clothing buys in town. The uptown branch is at 8219 Oak St. (tel. 861-4833), with hours of 10 a.m. to 5:30 p.m., Monday through Saturday; in the French Quarter, they're at 833 Conti St. (tel. 524-4339), open 10 a.m. to 6 p.m. Monday through Saturday, 11 a.m. to 4 p.m. on Sunday; and in Metairie, at 3750 Veterans Blvd. (tel. 456-9119), open 10 a.m. to 6 p.m. Monday through Saturday, (until 8:30 p.m. on Thursday).

COSTUMES: These are just two of the shops specializing in Mardi Gras finery. One tip to remember is that New Orleanians often sell their costumes after Ash Wednesday and you can sometimes pick up a one-time-worn outfit at a small fraction of its cost new.

Garland's Mardi Gras Center, 831 Chartres St. (tel. 524-4384), carries sizes 2 to 50 and has a wide selection of new, ready-made costumes as well as used outfits. They also do custom costumes, and carry all accessories such as wigs, masks, hats, makeup, and jewelry. Hours are 10 a.m. to 5:30 p.m., Monday through Saturday.

Costume Headquarters, 3635 Banks St. (tel. 488-9523 or 488-6959), handles mostly rentals (which should be arranged well in advance of the big day), but do have a limited selection of costumes for sale.

FANS: Because I'm an incurable romantic, I can't think of a better cooling system than those slow-turning ceiling fans you see all over the South (and the energy saving over air conditioning is astounding!). So it was a real treat to see the marvelous old restored specimens in the **White Pillars Emporium,** 8238 Oak St., in the Carrollton section. Open Monday through Saturday from 10 a.m. to 5 p.m.

FOODS: Café du Monde, 800 Decatur St. in the French Market. If you want to try your hand at making those scrumptious beignets, you can buy the mix here. To make it complete, pick up a tin of their famous coffee. Open around the clock, seven days a week.

GIFT SHOPS: There are literally hundreds of gift shops in New Orleans, ranging from very expensive to junky. Herewith, the ones I found most attractive.

Dumaine Nostaligia Shop, 607 Dumaine (tel. 525-2244). Ah, those years from 1900 to 1950! They live again in this "Memory

Lane" shop, where you'll find such items as old slot machines, radios, telephones, art deco items, and Wurlitzer jukeboxes. Everything's authentic—no reproductions. It's open daily from 11 a.m. to 6 p.m.

Lemon Tree, 535 Wilkinson St. in the French Quarter (tel. 523-5134). This two-storied galleria has a wide selection of gifts, silver, chinaware, and antique furniture. You'll also find toys, candles, fancy soaps, and kitchen equipment. Open 10 a.m. to 6 p.m. daily.

Little Mex, 1017-21 Decatur St. (tel. 529-3397). I don't really know how to tell you about this amazing store—from a rather unimposing entrance, you walk into an interior that just goes on and on and on. And it's filled with just about everything under the sun. There are imports from all over the world—a huge selection from Mexico—leather goods, straw, wheat, and bamboo products, baskets (I bought a great one to carry an accumulation of purchases already made), metal sculpture, dolls, brass and copper items, and . . . well, all I can say is to be sure to allow some extra time for some of the best browsing in the French Quarter. Open 9 a.m. to 5 p.m. every day.

Pontalba Gift Shop, 900 N. Peters St. (tel. 522-4511). This shop has one of the widest varieties of gifts I ran across. Their handmade New Orleans dolls are a delight. Some items are costly, others quite reasonable, and the usual low-priced souvenirs are also on hand. It's open seven days a week from 9 a.m. to 5:30 p.m.

Pontalba Historical Puppetorium, 514 St. Peter St. on Jackson Square (tel. 522-0344 or 944-8144). There's an excellent puppet presentation of New Orleans history here (see Chapter VIII, "Seeing French Quarter Sights"), but you can also purchase puppets. In fact, they have the largest collection in the United States. Open every day from 10 a.m. to 6 p.m.

Santa's Quarters, 1025 Decatur St. (tel. 581-5820). If you're walking down Decatur Street in July and suddenly hear "Jingle Bells," you'll know you've found this year-round Christmas store. It's an enchanting place, with ornaments from around the world, all kinds of decorations, and so many Christmas ideas you may very well finish up all your holiday shopping months in advance. Open from 10 a.m. to 5 p.m. daily.

JEWELRY: Boudreaux's Jewelers, Inc., 124 Baronne St. (tel. 581-4441). In the downtown section of town, this fine shop was begun back in 1933 by Gil Boudreaux, Sr., whose sons carry on the same tradition of elegance today. The stunning store has the largest staff of artisans in the city, creating one-of-a-kind masterpieces that are sure to become heirlooms. It's open Monday through Saturday from 9 a.m. to 5:30 p.m.

New Orleans Silversmiths, 600 Chartres St. (tel. 522-8333). You'll find jewelry, both old and new, in gold and silver here, as well as a variety of reproductions of antiques. They also carry silverware and pewter. Hours are 9:30 a.m. to 5 p.m. Monday through Saturday.

Orleans Jewels, 622 St. Peter St. (tel. 523-1816). If the real thing is beyond your budget, you can purchase counterfeit diamonds here that *look* like the real thing. There are hundreds of rings, necklaces, and earrings, or you can buy loose stones for your own settings. Open Monday through Saturday 10 a.m. to 5 p.m., Sunday from 11 a.m. to 4 p.m.

LEATHER GOODS: **Rapp's Luggage and Leather**, 604 Canal St. (tel. 568-1953), carries an extensive selection of leather goods, from the most expensive designer luggage to duffle bags, wallets to attaché cases, and many other items you'd never expect to find in a leather goods store. Quality is high and prices reasonable. They can also repair luggage. Hours are 10 a.m. to 5:30 p.m., and there are branches at Uptown Square, 200 Broadway (tel. 861-1453); The Plaza in Lake Forest (tel. 246-0310); 3250 Severn at 17th Street, Metairie (tel. 885-6536); and Oakwood Shopping Center (tel. 362-5408).

PERFUME: **The Bourbon French Perfume Co.**, 318 Royal St. (tel. 522-4480), has been blending exquisite fragrances for over a century, and their perfumes are manufactured right on the premises here—a complete line of women's scents as well as European soaps and bath oils and fragrances for men. Hours are 9 a.m. to 5 p.m. Monday through Saturday, 10 a.m. to 5 p.m. on Sunday.

PIPES AND TOBACCO: **Ye Olde Pipe Shoppe**, 306 Chartres St. As I'm a lady pipe smoker (*please* don't write me about that— women have been smoking pipes for centuries!), Mr. Edwin Jansen's shop won my heart in about two seconds flat (or maybe it was Mr. Jansen himself). His grandfather, August, founded the place way back in 1868, and at one time repaired Jefferson Davis's pipes. Nowadays, *my* Mr. Jansen hand-makes beautiful briar pipes, repairs broken pipes, and sells pipe accessories and enough tobacco blends to keep you puffing all year long. This is not a fancy shop, but a warm, comfortable stopping-off place for pipe lovers. While you're there, take a look at the marvelous collection of antique pipes put together by his father and grandfather. In keeping with the character of this special place, the pipes aren't shown off in a velvet-lined display, just heaped in a glass case, making it sort of an adventure to run your eyes over one after the other, trying to imagine each in the fond hand of its original owner. Over the years, Mr. Jansen has developed a firm philosophy about pipes and their smokers and has written an excellent book about them. If pipes are your thing, don't fail to search this place out and spend some time with a kindred spirit. Open 10 a.m. to 5 p.m. Monday through Saturday.

TOYS: The Little Toy Shoppe, 900 Decatur St. in the French Market (tel. 522-6588). The dolls in this shop are some of the most beautiful I've ever seen, especially the Madame Alexander and Effanbee ones—and the New Orleans-made bisque and rag dolls. There's all manner of cuddly stuffed animals, dollhouses and furniture, toy soldiers, miniature cars and trucks. Stop by from 9:30 a.m. to 5:30 p.m. Monday to Thursday, to 9 p.m. on Friday and Saturday, and 10 a.m. to 9 p.m. on Sunday.

Chapter XII

SIDE TRIPS

NEW ORLEANS CAN SERVE as the hub for three interesting side trips. The banks of the Mississippi River are lined with great plantation homes; a little over 100 miles to the west is the heart of Acadiana, where the unique, delightful culture of the Cajuns lives on; and to the east is the resort-filled Gulf of Mexico coastline. While a day trip is possible to see some of the plantation houses which are open to the public, both the other trips will probably require overnight stops, and each is likely to lure you for more than just one night. I must warn you, too, that should you become hooked on the romanticism of the plantations, it is quite possible to keep rambling north of the River Road to visit those in the St. Francisville area, an exploration that also calls for an overnight stay—and I'll tell you about two of the old homes in which you can actually spend the night if you plan far enough ahead.

The Plantations

In the beginning, the planters of Louisiana were little more than rugged frontiersmen as they spread out along the Mississippi from New Orleans. Swamplands had to be cleared, with a mighty expenditure of sweat and muscle. And the indigo which was first cultivated as a cash crop had to be transported downriver to New Orleans before there was any return on all that work, no mean feat in itself. Even today, when you ride modern highways through some of the bayous, your imagination will almost automatically present a very vivid picture of what it must have been like for those early settlers.

Fields were cleared, swamps drained, and crops planted, however, in spite of all the obstacles. And rough flat boats and keel boats (with crewmen even rougher than their vessels) could get the produce to market in New Orleans—sometimes. Once on the river, if boats weren't capsized by rapids, snags, sand bars, and

EXCURSIONS FROM NEW ORLEANS 171

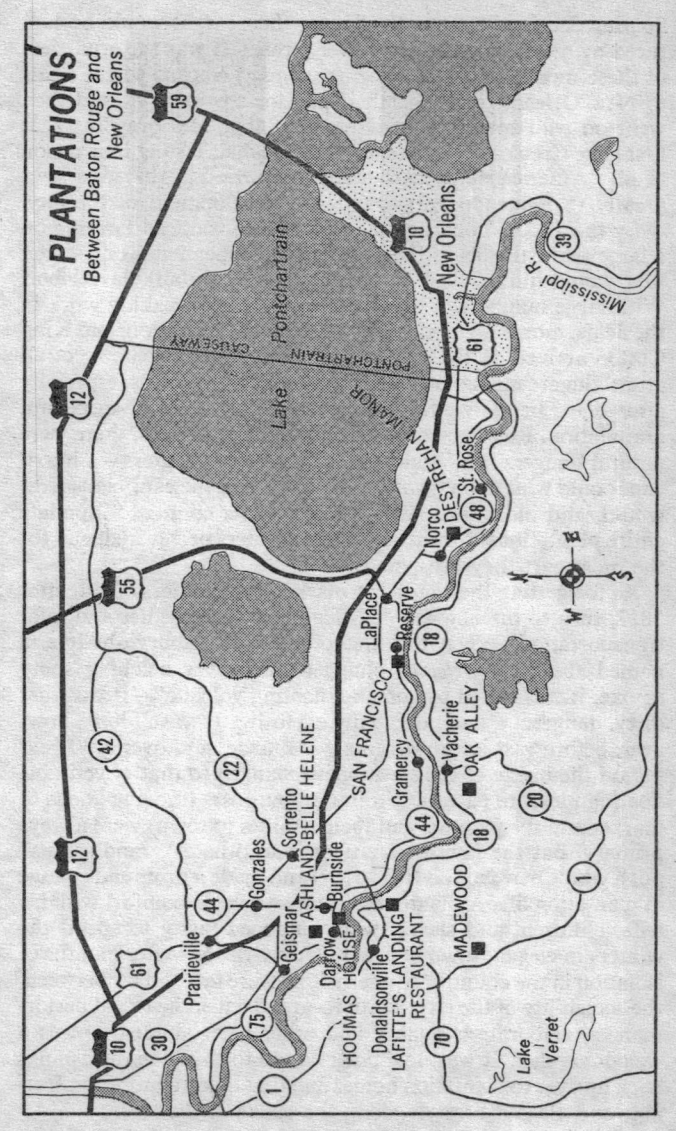

floating debris, there was the danger their cargos would be captured by murdering bands of river pirates. It was the crudeness of these men (and a few amazing women) who poled the boats to New Orleans, collected their pay for the journey, and then went on wild sprees of drinking, gambling, and brawling that first gave Créoles of the French Quarter their lasting impression of all "Americans" as barbarians, a conviction that was later greatly to influence the growth and development of the city.

By the 1800s, Louisiana planters had introduced farming on a large scale, thanks to their use of (and dependence on—a fact that would ultimately bring about their downfall) slave labor. With large numbers of blacks to do the back-breaking work in the fields, more and more acres went under cultivation, and King Cotton arrived on the scene to prove the most profitable of all crops. Sugarcane too brought huge monetary returns, especially after one Étienne de Bore discovered the secret of successful granulation. Rice became a secondary crop. Always, there were natural dangers that could spell disaster for planters—a hurricane could wipe out a whole year's work, and the capricious river would, and did, make swift changes in its course to inundate entire plantations. Nevertheless, the planters persevered, and for the most part they prospered.

As for getting their crops to market, the planters could, after 1812, turn to the new-fangled steamboat for speedier and safer transportation. When the first of these (Pittsburgh-built and named the *New Orleans*) chugged downriver belching sooty smoke, it was called by some a "floating volcano"—it was that dirty, dangerous, and potentially explosive. It wasn't long, however, before vast improvements were made, and over a 30-year period the image of the steamboats changed to that of veritable floating pleasure palaces. Utilitarian purposes (moving goods to market and the planters and their families to town) were always primary, but the lavish staterooms and ornate "grand salons" put a whole new face on river travel and made a profound change in plantation life. A planter could now travel in comfort with his wife, children, and slaves, which induced many to spend the winters in elegant town houses in New Orleans. After months of isolation in the country, where visitors were few and far between, the sociability of the city—with its grand balls, theatrical performances, elaborate banquets, and other entertainments—was a welcome relief. It was now possible too to ship fine furnishings back upriver to plantation homes and thus enjoy a more comfortable and elegant lifestyle along the banks of the river.

EXCURSIONS FROM NEW ORLEANS 173

Those wonderful floating pleasure palaces did, alas, add another element of danger to the lives of some planters. For along with the prosperous plantation families, northern merchants, carpetbag-carrying peddlers, European visitors, and poor immigrant families who made up passenger lists, came the most colorful and dramatic passenger of all—the riverboat gambler. Perhaps because they were natural-born gamblers (didn't they gamble on Mother Nature herself every year?), plantation owners were drawn like magnets to the sharp-witted, silver-tongued professionals. Huge fortunes were won and lost on Ole Man River, and more than once when cash, luggage, and jewelry were depleted, the deed to a plantation went on the table, to be raked in by a well-dressed, cigar-smoking pro. During one famous game, which went on for three days without interruption, it was said that over $37,000 in gold was on the table at one point. Thus, a planter might leave his plantation home a wealthy man and arrive at journey's end a pauper. And if the gamblers didn't get him, the steamboat captains might! As the vessels became grander and grander and more and more efficient, the captains and pilots took to racing each other—a hazardous practice that caused the loss of many boats and even more lives and fortunes.

It was during this period of prosperity, from the 1820s until the beginning of the Civil War, that most of the impressive plantation homes were built. They were the focal point of a self-sustaining community, and almost always were near the riverfront, with a wide avenue of oaks leading to a wharf. On either side stood a *garçonnière* (much smaller houses, sometimes used to give adolescent sons and their friends privacy; others were guest houses for travelers who stopped for a night's lodging). Behind the main house, the kitchen was built separately because of the danger of fire, and the overseer's office was close enough for convenience. Some plantations had, behind these two structures, pigeon houses, or dovecotes—and all had the inevitable slave quarters, usually in twin lines bordering a lane leading to cotton or sugarcane fields. When cotton gins and sugar mills came along, they were generally across the fields, out of sight of the main house.

What were they like, these main houses? Well, in the beginning, they were much like the simple "raised cottage" known as Madame John's Legacy, on New Orleans's Dumaine Street, with long, sloping roofs, with cement-covered brick walls on the ground floor, with wood and brick (brick between posts) used in the living quarters on the second floor. They suited the sultry

Louisiana climate and swampy building sites, and they made use of native materials. There's a distinct West Indies influence in houses of this colonial period, much unlike the grander styles that were to follow in the 1800s.

In the 1820s, homes were built that combined traces of the West Indian style with some Greek Revival and Georgian influences—a style that has been dubbed Louisiana Classic. Large rounded columns usually surrounded the main body of the house, wide galleries reaching from the columns to the walls encircled upper floors, and the roof was a dormered one. Upper and lower floors consisted of four large rooms centered by a wide central hall. Their construction was entirely of native materials, with a few imported interior details such as fireplace mantels. Remember, there were no stone quarries in Louisiana, and if stone were used (which wasn't very often), it had to be shipped from New England and transported up the Mississippi from New Orleans. The river, on the other hand, flowed through banks of clay, there were all those slaves, and bricks could be made right on the spot. Cypress too was plentiful—and more than that, the water-loving wood was perfect for the hot, humid climate, which could quickly deteriorate those woods less impervious to its destructiveness. Thus, the damp-resistant wood was used for house beams, and even for railings on the galleries (unlike the fancy cast iron so much used in New Orleans). To protect the homemade bricks from dampness, they were plastered or cement covered, and sometimes the outer coating was tinted, although more often it was left to mellow into a soft, off-white color. The columns were almost always of plastered brick, and very occasionally of cypress wood. Even their capitals were of these materials except for a rare instance when cast iron was used. These houses, then, took some features from European architecture, some from the West Indian styles which so well suited the location, and adapted them to local building materials.

By the 1850s, planters were more prosperous and their homes became more grandiose. The extravagance of Victorian architecture was embraced and given a unique Louisiana flavor; features of northern Italian villas crept in; and some plantation homes followed Gothic lines (notably the fantastic San Francisco Plantation, sometimes called "steamboat Gothic"). As planters and their families traveled to Europe more and more, they brought home elegant furnishings for the houses which had begun to grow in size as well as ornateness. European masters were imported for fine woodworking, until Louisiana craftsmen such as

Mallard and Seignouret developed skills which rivaled or surpassed those from abroad. Ceilings were adorned by elaborate "medallions" from which glittering crystal chandeliers hung, and on wooden mantels and wainscoting the art of *faux marbre* ("false marble") began to appear. In short, plantation owners seemed determined to make their country homes every bit as elegant as their New Orleans town houses. They were developing a way of life dedicated to graciousness and hospitality unlike any other in American history.

As they grew in opulence, the plantation houses expanded in size—some had as many as 30 or 40 rooms. Why so large? Well, partly because families were quite large in those days. But even more important, if there was to be any social life in the country, it had to come from days- or weeks-long visits from neighbors or friends. After all, travel being what it was, there just was no such thing as "popping in for a call." But there were other reasons too, and they had to do with that well-known southern pride. Madewood, for example, over on Bayou Lafource, was built for no other reason than to outshine the builder's brother, who had a beautiful home, Woodlawn, nearby! Two suitors of one young lady put up rival, massive houses in an attempt to win her affections. It was a simple case of antebellum "keeping up with the Joneses"!

But underneath their enormous wealth and power lay an economy built on the backs of slaves. It was, as world history has many times shown, an unhealthy foundation, and it crumbled, as was inevitable, with the beginning of the Civil War. Farming as it was then practiced was impossible without that large, cheap labor base. And, of course, as plantation owners went away to fight, management of the plantations deteriorated even where slaves stayed on during the war. During Reconstruction, lands were often confiscated and turned over intact to those unfit or unable financially to continue the large-scale operation, or broken up into smaller, more manageable farms. With increasing international competition, the cotton and sugar markets that had built such large fortunes started to crumble. And as industrialism moved south, there was no place for life as it had been lived in the golden plantation years.

It is hard to remember when you walk through the grand old homes left in the wake of the plantation era that the culture they embody had its beginning, reached a lofty pinnacle, and then died away in the span of less than 100 years! It has left as almost its only—and certainly its more eloquent—relic, houses the like of which will undoubtedly never again be seen.

What has happened to them since the beginning of this century? Several have been the victims of fire, others of floods. Some have been torn down to make way for such things as industrial plants. Others, too costly to be maintained in modern times, have been left to the ravages of dampness and decay. But for a few, fate has been more kind—wealthy families have bought the houses and restored them with love and affection, retaining their feeling for "the good life" and filling them with family heirlooms or treasured antiques. The encroachment of modernity is restricted primarily to the installation of plumbing and electricity. Some are used only as private residences, but you can visit others for a small admission fee (which, in some instances, supplements the owner's own resources to keep up the old house). Not one single home open to the public is owned by descendants of the original owners! Today's visitors are, then, truly indebted to those "outsiders" who have gone to such lengths to preserve one part of our heritage which might otherwise disappear completely.

All the plantation homes shown on the map on page 171 are within easy driving distance of New Orleans. How many you take in on any one day will depend, I suspect, on your endurance behind the wheel, your walking stamina (you'll cover a lot of ground touring the houses), and how early you set out. You'll be driving through "country" Louisiana, and I might as well warn you that some of what you'll see is really quite tacky—that modern, industrial economy just isn't pretty to look at! Also, don't expect to enjoy broad river views as you drive along River Road (the name given to the roadway on *both* sides of the Mississippi)—you'll have to drive up on the levee for that. You will, however, pass through little towns that date back to plantation days, and in your own car you'll have the luxury of turning off to inspect interesting old churches or above-ground cemeteries which can only be glimpsed from a tour bus window. Personally, I think it's a good idea to make your first plantation inspection via one of the excellent tours you'll find listed, then take the car exploring after you've gained some familiarity with the territory. Another advantage of the tours is the detailed background information furnished by guides—your own ramblings will be the better for it.

One more word about this particular group of homes: If you should happen to be in New Orleans on Christmas Eve and drive along River Road, your way will be lit by huge bonfires on the levees—they're to light the way for the Christ Child (an old Latin custom), and residents along here spend weeks collecting wood, trash, and anything that's flammable to make the fires blaze brightly.

Because not all Louisiana plantations actually bordered the Mississippi River (many were on bayous which also provided water transportation), some of the grand old homes have survived at locations too far away from New Orleans to be visited in a single day. I'm listing those separately, with the recommendation that you try to stay overnight at one of the several which offer guest accommodations. Failing that, I'll include accommodations in Baton Rouge and St. Francisville, either of which can serve as a convenient tour base.

A DAY TRIP FROM NEW ORLEANS: I'll start with the plantations nearest New Orleans and describe each, for ready reference, in the alphabetical order in which it appears on the map, although that is not necessarily the order in which you will view them.

Destrehan Manor

Twenty-three miles from New Orleans, on the River Road, is Destrehan Manor, La. 48, Destrehan, La. (tel. 504/764-9315). A free mulatto named Charles built this house in 1787. The wings on either side were added later, and it has in the intervening years undergone remodeling. Some of the largest live oaks in the state are on the grounds of the West Indies–style house. Its double galleries are surrounded by Doric columns which support the central structure's hipped roof. Inside, you can see the original woodwork and some interesting antiques. There's also a gift shop, and you can purchase light refreshments. The American Oil Company, which had bought the property, presented the house (in a state of deterioration) to the River Road Historical Society, and during its restoration some of the earliest methods of construction were uncovered. The society has left some glimpses of the construction open for visitors to see. Destrehan is the oldest plantation home remaining, and during its long lifetime its ownership has passed to several prominent residents of the area. It is open to the public every day from 10 a.m. to 4 p.m. at a $3.50 admission charge for adults, $2 for students, and free to preschoolers.

178 ARTHUR FROMMER'S NEW ORLEANS

Ormond

A mile and a half above Destrehan (not shown on the map, since it isn't open to public), look for Ormond plantation house, a two-story structure with columns and gallery and a wing on each end. The house has in recent years been bought and beautifully restored as a private residence, but its early history is one of tragedy. Built sometime before 1790 by one Pierre de Trepagnier on land granted him by the Spanish government, it has witnessed the mysterious disappearance of Pierre when he went off with a complete stranger and was never seen or heard from again, the wiping out of almost an entire family by yellow fever, and the murder of its owner during Reconstruction, when his body was found riddled with bullets and hanging from a live oak. From all appearances, it has now fallen on happier days and its future looks bright. You can't go inside, but it is certainly worth a slowdown and long look as you pass by.

San Francisco

This fantastic mansion on La. 44 two miles north of Reserve was built in 1856 by a man who was obsessed by the great pleasure boats on which he had traveled. He was determined to transmit their lighthearted joyousness into a house that would forever remind him and his many friends of the gaiety aboard the steamboats. So, beginning with the Gothic architecture then in vogue, he overlaid it with overtones of the river queens, and what he came up with has been called "steamboat Gothic," a term later used as a book title by novelist Frances Parkinson Keyes in which the house itself appears. Sadly, Valsin Marmillion did not live to see his dream house completed. His health and his finances (strained by the heavy construction costs) began to fail and he died, wryly calling the mansion "Sans Fruscin," which can be roughly translated as "my last red cent" (from whence comes its present name, a corruption of that term). His widow lived here only long enough to sell it, but the legacy left by her husband is a fantasy come true even after all these years. The three-storied, plastered brick house has broad galleries that look for all the world like a ship's double decks, and twin stairs lead to a broad main portal much like those leading to a steamboat's grand salon. Galleries are trimmed with lacy railings between the fluted columns, and over the front door there's a mirror that reflects the river. Inside, Marmillion created sheer beauty in every room through the use of carved woodwork and frescoes alive with flowers, birds, nymphs, and cherubs painted on walls and ceilings. Those marvelous frescos, glowing with wonderfully delicate colors, were done by Dominique Canova, who painted the rotunda of the famous St. Louis Hotel. San Francisco is now owned by the Marathon Oil Company, and its dazzling restoration includes furnishings of English and French 18th-century furniture and paintings. You can go through the house any day between 10 a.m. and 4 p.m.; admission is $4.50 for adults, $3 for ages 12 to 17, $2 for ages 6 to 11, and under 6, free. There's a small gift shop (tel. 504/535-2341).

Tezcuco

On La. 44, just upriver from the Sunshine Bridge (55 miles from New Orleans), Tezcuco was one of the last plantation houses built before the Civil War. Although small, the raised cottage was some five years in the building, using slave labor, wood from surrounding swamps, and bricks from kilns on the plantation. While the house follows the traditional floor plan of a central hall flanked by two rooms on either side, an unusual feature is the staircase leading to the gallery at each end, as well as the expected central stair. The grounds, densely planted with shrubs, wisteria, honeysuckle, and other native plants, contain huge live oaks draped with great cascades of moss, giving an almost ghostly appearance even in bright sunlight. There's a pleasant gazebo on the lawn, and a rather large giftshop in the basement. The house is closed to the public, so you won't find it on the map.

Oak Alley

On La. 18 between St. James and Vacherie, Oak Alley (mailing address: Rte. 2, Box 10, Vacherie, LA 70090; tel. 504/265-2151), is 60 miles from downtown New Orleans, and probably the most famous plantation house in Louisiana. It was built in 1839 by Jacques Telesphore Roman III and named Bon Séjour—but if you'll walk out to the levee and look back at the quarter-mile avenue of live oaks (estimated to be about 300 years old), you'll see why steamboat passengers quickly dubbed it "Oak Alley," a name which soon replaced the original. Those trees were planted, it is thought, by an early settler and so enamored of them was Roman that he planned his house to have exactly as many columns as there were trees, 28 in all. The fluted Doric columns completely surround the Greek Revival house and support a broad second-story gallery. Inside, the floor plan is traditional, even to the attic, with a wide central hall flanked by two large rooms. Until 1914, Oak Alley lay disintegrating, but that year Mr. and Mrs. Jefferson Hardin, of New Orleans, bought it and moved in. Then in 1925 it passed to a Mr. and Mrs. Andrew Stewart, whose loving restoration is responsible for its National Historic Landmark designation. Both the Stewarts have passed on now, but two of their staff, who have been here for years, stay on to guide visitors through the home. It is furnished just as it was during the Stewarts' lifetime—with a comfortably elegant mix of antiques and more modern pieces. It is open to the public from 9:30 a.m. to 5:30 p.m., and the admission is $4 for adults, $2.50 for students, $1.50 for children. Overnight accommodations are available in a two-bedroom cottage, with living room and kitchen, for $60. Also, there's a restaurant open for lunch, 11 a.m. to 3 p.m.

Lafitte's Landing Restaurant

At the foot of Sunshine Bridge on La. 3089 Service Road (just off La. 18), you'll find this huge raised cottage, built in 1797. It was said to be one of Jean Lafitte's hangouts, and today there's a good restaurant and lounge in the building, a good stopping point for lunch. Hours are 11 a.m. to 3 p.m. every day and 6 to 10 p.m. Tuesday through Saturday. Since hours can change, you might want to call 504/473-1232 and check or make reservations.

The Cabin

This is another good eating place appropriate to a day of plantation viewing. Located on La. 44 at La. 22, it is a slave cabin from the Monroe plantation, built about 1830. Nowadays it holds interesting antiques and good Louisiana food. Hours are 11 a.m. to 3 p.m. Monday through Thursday, to 10 p.m. on Friday and Saturday, and 6 p.m. on Sunday. If you want to call, the number is 504/473-3007 (not on the map).

Houmas House

Right on La. 942 near Burnside (mailing address: Rte. 1, Box 181, Corrent, LA 70723; tel. 504/473-7841), and 58 miles from New Orleans, this lovely old house had very humble beginnings in a two-room cabin built in the 1700s on land originally owned by the Houmas Indians. When the massive Greek Revival main house was built out front, the cabin was retained as the kitchen, and it survives today, with two rooms which have been added. The impressive main house is 2½ stories tall, with 14 columns on three sides supporting the wide gallery. At either side are hexagonal *garçonnières* (remember, those were for the young male family members or for travelers who were put up for the night), and a carriageway is formed where the old cabin is connected to the main house. The late Dr. George Crozat, of New Orleans, purchased the house some years ago and went about restoring it as a comfortable home for himself and his mother, bringing in authentic furnishings of the period in which it was built. The live oaks, magnolias, and formal gardens which surround Houmas House are magnificent and frame this house in a way that is precisely what comes to mind when most of us think "plantation house." It so closely fits that image that it's been used in the movies—you may, in fact, already have seen its exterior if you saw *Hush, Hush, Sweet Charlotte*. There's an interesting gift shop out back. Dr. Crozat's heirs now open Houmas House daily (except major holidays) from 10 a.m. to 4 p.m., and there's an admission fee for the guided tour of $4.50 for adults, $2.50 for ages 13 to 18, $1.50 for ages 6 to 12, under 6, free.

Ashland–Belle Hélène

On La. 75 between Geismar and Darrow (tel. 504/861-6423), about 70 miles from New Orleans, this huge house, taller than any other you're likely to see (its square columns are four feet square and some 30 feet high), was built in 1841 as a wedding present by Duncan Kenner, Confederate minister plenipotentiary to France, for his beautiful young bride. The galleries, surrounded by a colonnade of eight columns to a side, are 20 feet wide, the ground floor level paved with brick and tile. Originally, the thick walls (plastered brick marked off to resemble stone) were tinted a lemon yellow, the shutters were an aqua blue, and the pillars were white—a study in pastels. At the end of the large central hall there's a spiral staircase, and all the rooms have marble mantels. Kenner named his home Ashland, after Henry Clay's residence, and it became well known for its gracious hospitality and fine wine cellar. A lover of horseflesh, its owner also maintained locally famous stables. After the Civil War, the house was bought by a John Reuss, who renamed it Belle Hélène, after his granddaughter, but the original name was too closely associated with it to be dropped, hence it gained the double title. By the mid-1900s, the house was standing vacant, prey to the destructive forces of nature. Such was its visual appeal, however, that in 1957 it was used for scenes in *Band of Angels,* and *Beguiled* was filmed here in 1970. Partially restored and partially furnished, Ashland–Belle Hélène is now open only to groups by special appointment, but it is there for you to see from the outside.

Madewood

You won't want to miss this magnificent house on Bayou Lafourche, just below Napoleonville on La. 308, one of the best preserved of the plantation mansions (mailing address: Rte. 2, Box 478, Napoleon, LA 70390; tel. 504/524-1988). It was built by the son of a wealthy planter who had originally come from North Carolina in 1818. Madewood was the creation of the youngest of three brothers, and it was built for the sole purpose of outdoing his older brother's elegant mansion, Woodlawn. Four years were spent cutting lumber and making bricks, and another four in actual construction. It was finally completed in 1848, but its owner never got to gloat over his brother, for yellow fever carried him off just before it was finished. The large, two-story, Greek Revival house of stucco-covered brick is set on a low terrace, and on either side connecting wings duplicate its design. Inside, ceilings are 25 feet high, central hallways are huge, as are bedrooms, there's a carved, winding walnut staircase —and more than 20 rooms! And a tremendous ballroom. Outside, there's a carriage house and the family cemetery. Truly, it's more than worth the drive. It's open daily from 10 a.m. to 5 p.m. (except major holidays), and admission is $4 for adults, $2 for children under 12.

TOURS FROM NEW ORLEANS: As I said in the beginning, it's an excellent idea to take one of the plantation house bus tours from New Orleans before setting out on your own. Most of the tours visit only one or two of the houses I have described, leaving plenty for your private exploration. My experience has been that tour guides are exceptionally well informed, and the buses are an easy, comfortable way to get around in unfamiliar territory. Almost every tour company operates a River Road plantation tour—here are two I especially like.

The **Gray Line,** 1793 Julia St. (tel. 525-0138), has a 5½-hour

EXCURSIONS FROM NEW ORLEANS 183

River Road Plantations Tour. The two plantations visited are Oak Alley and Houmas House. All admissions are included in the $30 charge. Tours depart at 9:30 a.m., and they pick you up and deliver you at your hotel. The cost of lunch at a country restaurant, however, is not included and generally runs $5 to $6, sometimes more.

Southern Tours, 7801 Edinburgh St. (tel. 486-0604), offers a six-hour Southern Plantation Tour which visits San Francisco and Houmas House, with a lunch stop at a Cajun restaurant. Lunch is not included in the $30 tour charge, but all admissions are. Southern's tour begins at 10 a.m., and they too call for you and deliver you back to your hotel.

PLANTATIONS BEYOND THE NEW ORLEANS AREA: Most of the plantations described below are clustered in the area around St. Francisville, north of Baton Rouge. An overnight stay is a virtual necessity if you want to see any number of these houses, and you'll really get into the spirit of things if you plan your overnight at any of the accommodations described below. You may, however, wish to stay in St. Francisville itself, or even in Baton Rouge. At the end of this section, I'll tell you about accommodations in both places. If you plan to make Baton Rouge your base, the St. Francisville tour will cover approximately 100 miles, and you will want to set aside at least one full day, probably two. In Baton Rouge itself, there is one plantation home, and about 30 miles northwest, another, both of which you may want to include in your sightseeing.

The very first thing you should do is go by one of the **Baton Rouge Area Information Centers** to pick up their useful brochure "Baton Rouge, Heart of Plantation Country," which contains several driving tours in the city and surrounding area. One is in the Old State Capitol, North Boulevard and the River Road (tel. 504/383-1825), and is open Monday through Friday from 9:30 a.m. to 4:30 p.m., Saturday from 10 a.m. to 5 p.m., and Sunday from 1 to 5 p.m. The other is on the west side of the Mississippi at La. Hwy. 415 and I-10 Hwy. (tel. 504/344-2920), open 9 a.m. to 5 p.m. daily.

Magnolia Mound

This old home at 2161 Nicholson Dr. in Baton Rouge (tel. 504/343-4955) was built in the late 1700s. Its single story is nearly five feet off the ground and has a front porch 80 feet across. The hand-carved woodwork and thick plank floors inside are still in excellent condition. Magnolia Mound takes its name from the grove of trees on a bluff overlooking the Mississippi which is its setting. It is one of the oldest wooden structures in the state and is furnished in early Federal style. Costumed guides take you through. From Tuesday through Saturday, the house is open from 10 a.m. to 4 p.m., on Sunday from 1 to 4 p.m. Adults pay $4; students, $2; and children, $1.

Nottoway Plantation

To reach Nottoway Plantation (mailing address: P.O. Box 160, White Castle, LA 70788; tel. 504/545-2730) from Baton Rouge, take I-10 West to the Plaquemine exit, then La. 1 south for 18 miles. (From New Orleans, follow I-10 West to the La. 22 exit, then left on La. 70 across the Sunshine Bridge; exit onto La. 1 and drive 14 miles north through Donaldsonville.) This magnificent house has been likened to a castle, and you're likely to agree when you see its 22 enormous columns which support the original slate roof. Built in 1859, a blend of Greek Revival and Italianate, the house has 64 rooms and a total area of over 53,000 square feet. It was saved from Civil War destruction by the kindness of a northern gunboat officer who had once been a guest there, and kindness still blesses it, for the present owner has lovingly restored its rooms to their former glory. The white ballroom, with its hand-carved cypress Corinthian columns, archways, delicate plaster friezework, and original crystal chandeliers, is especially lovely. A restaurant serves lunch from 11 a.m. to 3 p.m., and you may stay overnight in one of those restored bedrooms (most have fireplaces) with its own private bath for $100 double occupancy, which includes a continental breakfast and tour of the house. Even if you're not staying, take the tour: 9 a.m. to 5 p.m. daily (except for Christmas), for which there is a $4 fee for adults, $2 for children 12 or under.

Parlange

To reach this plantation, one of the few that still functions as a working farm, drive 19 miles west on U.S. 190, then ten miles north on La. 1 (near New Roads; tel. 504/638-8410). Built in 1750, the house is one of the oldest in the state, and its two stories rise above a raised brick basement. Galleries encircle the house and there are two brick pigeonniers, one on either side. Indigo was planted here at first, then in the 1800s sugarcane became the plantation's main crop. During the Civil War, this house was host to generals from both sides (Gen. Nathaniel Banks of the Union and Gen. Dick Taylor of the Confederacy)—not, of course, at the same time. You can visit Parlange any day of the week from 9 a.m. to 5 p.m. There's a $4 admission charge for adults, $2 for children 6 to 12.

Asphodel

Located on La. 68 (south of La. 10 and north of U.S. 61), Asphodel is a charming example of the Greek Revival style popular in the 1800s. It was built about 1833 and consists of a raised central section with two identical wings, of brick covered with a smooth plaster made with sand from a nearby creek. Doric columns line the gallery of the central section and support its gabled roof. Each of the wings has its own small porch. Asphodel has been seen in such films as *The Long Hot Summer*. On the grounds, the old Levy house (built in the 1840s) was moved here in recent years and is now used as an inn and a very fine restaurant. Overnight accommodations are sometimes hard to come by because of its popularity, and reservations are also necessary, as a rule, for meals at the restaurant as well. For details on booking, see the end of this section. In addition to the mansion itself (now the private home of its current owners), there are leafy forest trails open to visitors. The house is open Monday through Friday from 10 a.m. to 4 p.m. and by appointment only on Saturday and Sunday for groups (call 504/654-6868). Admission is $4.

Oakley

Oakley Plantation (mailing address: P.O. Box 546, St. Francisville, LA 70775; tel. 504/635-3739) is on La. 965, three miles east of U.S. 61. This lovely old house is where John James Audubon came to study and paint the wildlife of this part of Louisiana. The house itself was built in 1799 and is a three-story frame house with the raised basement so typical of that era. The two galleries are joined by a curved stairway, and the whole house has a simplicity that bespeaks its age. When Audubon was here, he tutored a daughter of the family and painted some 32 of his *Birds of America* series. When you visit it today, you will see some original prints from Audubon's *Elephant Folio* and many fine antiques. A walk through the gardens and nature trails will explain why this location had such appeal for Audubon.

Oakley is, as a matter of fact, now a part of the 100-acre Audubon State Commemorative Area, a wildlife sanctuary which would have gladdened the naturalist's heart. In the kitchen building there is now a gift shop, but you can still see the huge old kitchen fireplace over which the family's meals were once cooked. The house is open from 9 a.m. to 5 p.m. Monday through Saturday, and from 1 to 5 p.m. on Sunday. There is a $2 (for four people in a car, 25¢ for each additional) charge to visit the grounds, and an additional $2 fee if you would like to tour the house. Those under 6 or over 61 are admitted free.

Rosedown Plantation and Gardens

Just east of St. Francisville on I-10 and U.S. 61, you'll find Rosedown (mailing address: Drawer M, St. Francisville, LA 70775; tel. 504/635-3110). This truly magnificent home was built in 1835 by a descendant of George Washington on land which was a Spanish land grant back in 1789 to one of the founders of St. Francisville. The two-story house, flanked by one-story wings, combines classic and indigenous Louisiana styles. There are the typical columns and wide galleries across the front, and the house is made of cement-covered brick. A wide avenue of ancient oaks, their branches meeting overhead, leads up to the house, and the formal gardens are as impressive as the house itself—as well they might be, since the French landscape architect who designed these gardens was the creator of those at Versailles. As is altogether fitting in such a garden, marble statues of gods and goddesses are dotted along the winding pathways. Inside, the house still holds the massive furniture of its original owner, as well as a winding stairway and many beautiful murals and paintings. Rosedown is one of the most beautiful examples of antebellum plantation homes, and whether you're into architecture, antiques, or horticulture—or simply a lover of beauty—you'll find this an interesting stop. The house is open from March through October from 9 a.m. to 5 p.m. every day, and from November through February from 10 a.m. to 4 p.m. There's a $6 admission charge for the house and gardens (children pay $3 for the house, but can view the gardens free with adults).

The Myrtles

Located on U.S. 61, a little over one mile north of La. 10 (mailing address: P.O. Box 387, St. Francisville, LA 70775; tel.

504/635-6277), this beautiful house was built in 1795. Its gallery measures 110 feet in length and the elaborate iron grillwork is reminiscent of French Quarter houses in New Orleans. The Myrtles is in an astonishingly good state of preservation, especially inside, where the intricate plaster moldings are still intact in each room, and silver doorknobs (glass-coated) and even colonial wallpaper in the entry hall are just as they were when the house was built. The 1½-story house is set in a grove of great old live oaks, as is only fitting for one which is locally believed to have at least one ghost. When this old home was restored in recent years, much attention was given to filling it with furnishings authentic to the period in which it was built. You can visit the Myrtles from 9 a.m. to 5 p.m. any day of the week except Christmas. Adults pay $4 admission; children, $2. Overnight accommodations are available with private or shared baths at rates of $55 to $80 double, which includes plantation breakfast and tour.

Afton Villa Gardens

Sad to say, there's no longer a great plantation home on this site (a little over three miles north of La. 10 on U.S. 61), but Afton Villa was one of the finest until it burned in 1963. Its alley of great oak trees (one of the longest known) is still there, as are the beautiful formal gardens with their boxwood maze and statuary. The Gothic gatehouse also remains. The gardens are a real delight, with something flowering almost every season. It is perhaps at its best, however, in March and April, when you can visit from 9 a.m. to 4:30 p.m. every day of the week. From May through December, the gardens are open Wednesday through Sunday only, those same hours. Admission is $4 for adults, $2 for children.

The Cottage

This rambling country home on U.S. 61 four miles north of La. 10 is really a series of buildings constructed between 1795 and 1859. For my money, this is *the* place to make your headquarters. The low, two-story house has a long gallery out front, a perfect place to sit and relax of an evening. The first house was built entirely of virgin cypress taken from the grounds. Many of the outbuildings date from 1811, when Judge Thomas Butler (of "the Fighting Butlers," so prominent in American history) acquired the property. The judge carried on the family tradition of involvement in national affairs, as did his children after him. In fact, after his victory at the Battle of New Orleans, Gen. Andrew Jackson, along with a troop of officers (including no fewer than *eight* Butlers!), stopped off here for a three-week stay on his way from New Orleans to Natchez. Among the historic treasures on the grounds is a shiny, custom-designed carriage made for the judge in 1820. There are several outbuildings still intact, one of them a miniature cottage which was Judge Butler's office until his death, after which it became the plantation schoolhouse. Only two of the original 25 slave cabins remain. The interior of the Cottage looks very much as it did when the Butlers lived here, with hand-screened wallpaper, an 1800s loveseat (with space for a chaperone), and needlepoint firescreens made by the ladies of the Butler family. This is a working plantation of some 360 acres. It takes little or no imagination when staying at the Cottage to feel that you've managed to step through a time warp back to the days when plantation homes were not "open to the public," but were the center of a gracious, now-vanished way of life. Even if you don't stay as a guest, do visit—hours are 9 a.m. to 5 p.m. daily, and admission is $4 for adults, $2 for ages 6 to 12, and under 6, free.

ACCOMMODATIONS: One of the state's outstanding luxury hotels is located on the shores of Capitol Lake in **Baton Rouge**. The **Inn on the Lake**, 1575 Riverside North, Baton Rouge, LA 70803 (tel. toll free 800/535-9988; or 504/346-1482), is just one block from the State Capitol complex, yet in a pleasant setting with such amenities as tennis, swimming, and a jogging path around the lake. Rooms are unusually spacious and beautifully decorated, and there's a gourmet French restaurant as well as a plush lounge overlooking the lake. Doubles are $95 to $135.

In Baton Rouge, there's the **Hilton at Corporate Square**, 5500 Hilton Ave. (tel. 504/924-5000). Rooms are all Hilton quality, there's a pool room and health spa, a lounge with entertainment and dancing, and a very good dining room. Doubles range from $75 to $90, and family rates are available.

If a motel suits you better, try the **Monarch Inn–Best Western**, 10920 Mead Rd. at the Sherwood Forest Boulevard exit off I-12 (tel. 504/293-9370). The nicely furnished rooms have some oversize beds, and there's a pool, dining room, and a lounge with entertainment and dancing on Friday and Saturday. Double rates start at $55.

EXCURSIONS FROM NEW ORLEANS 189

In **St. Francisville**, your best bet is the **Ramada Inn,** on U.S. 61 at the La. 10 junction (tel. 504/635-3821). Rooms are nice sized and furnished in typical Ramada Inn style. In addition to the dining room, there's a lounge with entertainment and dancing, and a swimming pool. Plantation tours are also available. Double rooms are $55 and up.

Plantation Accommodations

To really get into the spirit of a plantation homes tour, you can't do better than **The Cottage** (mailing address: Rt. 5, P.O. Box 425, St. Francisville, LA 70775; driving directions: U.S. 61 four miles north of La. 10; tel. 504/635-3674). A full description of the house has already been given above, but I probably should add that the owners have, rather whimsically, planted a few rows of cotton between the camellias and azaleas in the garden, so if you've never seen King Cotton in his native habitat, this is your chance. There are two rooms in the main house and three in the wing added in 1850, all furnished with lovely antiques (even some canopied four-poster beds). A highlight of any stay here is the early-morning (8 a.m.) serving of steaming chicory coffee, with fresh cream and sugar, on a silver tray with bone china cups—and it comes, in old plantation style, right to your bedroom door. Half an hour later, you sit down to a full plantation breakfast in the formal dining room—it's a splendid repast of hickory-smoked bacon, eggs, grits (naturally), coffee, and homemade biscuits—an absolutely perfect way to begin the day! Best of all, there's no extra charge—it comes with your room. A tour of the house and grounds is also included in room rates, which are $75 for doubles. This place is popular with weekenders from New Orleans and other neighboring towns, as well as tourists, which makes it essential to book as far ahead as you possibly can.

Another delightful plantation house that takes in paying guests is **Asphodel Plantation** (mailing address: Jackson, LA 70748; driving directions: La. 68, south of La. 10 and north of U.S. 61; tel. 504/654-6868). Read the foregoing description for full particulars, and you'll know that the house used as an inn is actually the old Levy House, built in 1840 and moved onto the grounds here in recent years. This old town house also holds the restaurant (which specializes in Louisiana dishes like red beans with ham and rice, shrimp créole, shrimp gumbo, chicken curry, and homemade bread that is famous throughout the state), the lounge, and the fireside sitting room. Some of the 20 guest rooms are in nearby cottages, rather rustic in appearance. No antique furnishings here, and furnishings are (in the words of one guest) a little spartan. Some have a sitting room area complete with fireplace. But the setting—ah, the setting!—you'll *know* you're in plantation country, and that's what matters. Incidentally, meals in that outstanding restaurant are surprisingly moderate. A marvelous plantation breakfast is included in the double room rate of $60 to $75 per night. Here too bookings *must* be well in advance, especially in the period from March to May.

See also the accommodations at Nottoway Plantation and The Myrtles (above). Both should be booked well in advance.

Cajun Country

Just what *is* Cajun Country? Well, its official name is Acadiana, and it consists of a rough triangle of Louisiana made up of 22 parishes (counties), from St. Landry Parish at the top of the triangle to the Gulf of Mexico at its base. Lafayette is its "capital," and it's dotted with towns with names like St. Martinsville and New Iberia and Abbeville and Jeanerette. Oh, you won't find its boundaries marked on any map with the name "Acadiana" stamped across it. And yet, there live within those 22 parishes (counties) a people whose history and culture and way of life is so distinctive that crossing them is not much different from stepping over the portals of another country. Even their language differs from that found anywhere else in the world.

And just *who* are these Acadians, or "Cajuns"? If you've gone through the standard American schooling, you probably already know something about them. Think back to the days you struggled through Henry Wadsworth Longfellow's epic poem *Evangeline*—remember how touched you were (unless you're the most stone-hearted of cynics) by that story of two lovers who spent their lives wandering the face of this land searching for each other after being wrenched from their own homeland? Evangeline and her Gabriel were Acadians, part of a tragic band of French Canadians who became the forefathers of today's Cajuns.

Their story began in the early 1600s, when colonists from France immigrated to the southeastern coast of Canada. There, in a region they named Acadia, they developed a peaceful, agricultural culture based on the simple values of a strong religious faith (Catholic), a deep love of family, and an abiding respect for their relatively small land holdings. Isolated from the

EXCURSIONS FROM NEW ORLEANS 191

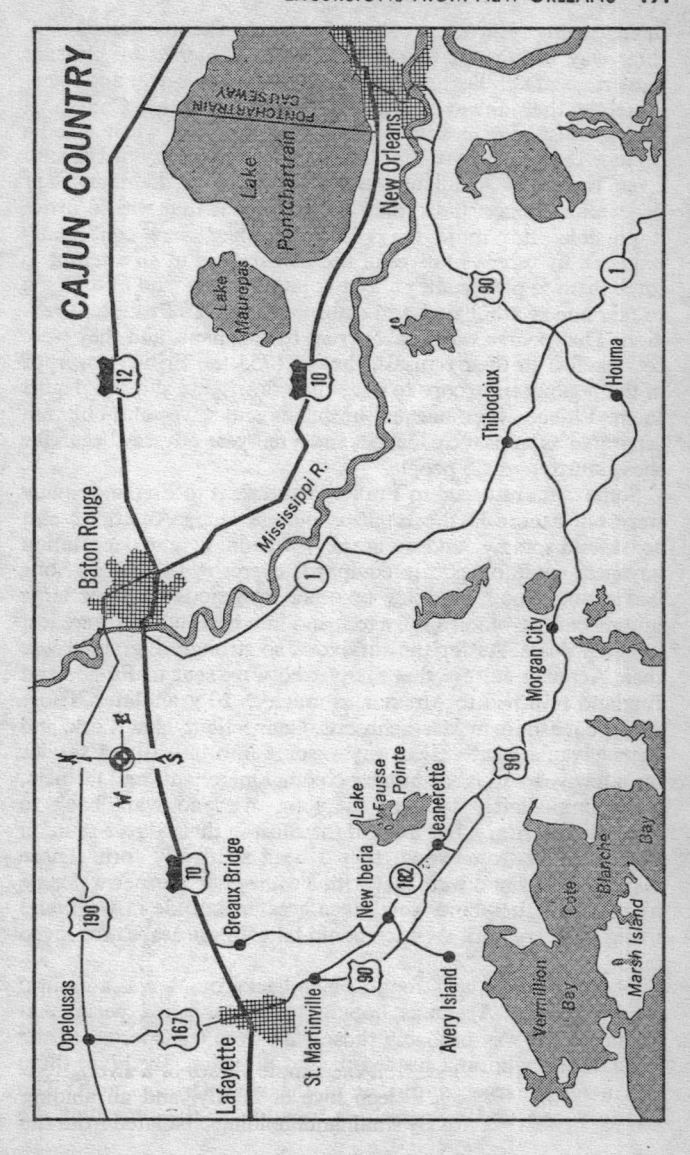

mainstream of European culture for nearly a century and a half, their way of life was one of hard work lightened by pleasant gatherings of families and friends when work was over and punctuated by their unwavering devotion to their Mother Church. It was a satisfying, pastoral existence until 1713, when Acadia became the property of the British under the Treaty of Utrecht. Even then, the Acadians were determined to maintain their peaceful existence under the new rulers, but that was to prove impossible. For more than 40 years, they were continually harassed by representatives of the British king in an attempt to force them to pledge allegiance to that monarch, and in so doing to renounce Catholicism and embrace the king's Protestant religion. That course was so abhorrent to Acadians, and they were so steadfast in their refusals, that in 1755 the British governor of the region sent troops to seize their farms and ships to deport them. Villages were burned, husbands and wives and children separated as ships were loaded, and a ten-year odyssey began for these sturdy, gentle people.

Some were returned to France, some went to England, many were put ashore in the English colonies along America's east coast, and some wound up in the West Indies. The deportation voyages, made on poorly equipped, overcrowded ships—none had enough food, clothing, or other provisions for their large human cargos—took a huge toll, and hundreds of lives were lost in the process. As for the survivors, so strongly ingrained was their Acadian culture that many who were sent to France and England returned to America as much as 20 years later. Those who went ashore in Massachusetts, Connecticut, New York, and Pennsylvania went varied ways—some into indentured service for a few years to labor-hungry colonial merchants and farmers, some immediately took to the long overland walk back to Canadian territory, but *all* held foremost in their aims a reunion with families from whom they'd been so rudely torn. Those taken to Maryland were met with a somewhat warmer welcome by colonists there and were given greater latitude in work and living quarters until they too could take up the search for loved ones.

Louisiana, with its strong French background, was a natural destination for Acadians hoping to reestablish a permanent home, and it was probably those who were transported to the West Indies who first headed in that direction. By 1763, there was a fairly large contingent in the New Orleans area. The territory was under Spanish domination at the time, but the shared Catholic religion and the natural industriousness of the newcomers made them welcome by the governing bodies, and many Acadians were given land grants in outlying areas. In 1765, one Bernard Andry brought a band of 231 men, women, and children to the region now known as Acadiana. Joseph Broussard, one of the Acadian leaders, was instrumental in making an agreement with one of the largest landowners to give each immigrant family the use of one bull and five cows with calves for six consecutive years. They agreed, at the end of that time, to return the same amount of livestock, plus one-half the increase or the money realized from the sale of one-half the increase.

The land on which they settled differed greatly from that they had left in Nova Scotia. The swampy land was low-lying and boggy, interlaced with bayous and lakes. No one has ever come up with an exact description of the bayous (called "bayuk" by the Choctaw Indians)—Longfellow's poem comes close when he relates that arriving Acadians

"Soon were lost in a maze of sluggish and devious waters,
Which, like a network of steel, extended in every direction.
Over their heads, the towering and tenebrous boughs of
  the cypress
Met in a dusky arch, and trailing mosses in mid-air,
Waved like banners that hang on the walls of ancient
  cathedrals."

Suffice it to say that a bayou is something less than a river, more than a creek, and it is sluggish, with little or no current. But the swamps were forested with live oak, willow, ash, and gum, and they were teeming with wildlife. Granted land that mostly bounded the bayous, the Acadians went to work with a will, building small levees, or dikes, along the banks, draining fields for small farms and pastures, and taking to the swamps to hunt and trap the plentiful game for food and furs. The isolation of their new home bothered them not one bit—it was perhaps the only thing this location had in common with the homeland they had left.

Always attuned to family closeness, sons would build homes close to fathers, and thus small settlements developed. The homes they constructed were marvelously adapted to the locale. From the swamps, they took cypress for their houses. To provide insulation between inner and outer walls, they again turned to natural materials, filling spaces with a mixture of mud and Spanish moss (*bousillage*). They pitched roofs high so the frequent rains would drain off, and they utilized the attic space thus created as sleeping quarters for the family's young men (this was called a *garçonnière*). And in order to get maximum use from every inch of interior space on the ground floor, stairways up to the *garçonnières* were placed outside on the front porch. The stairs did double duty as seating space when families gathered at one house (for that matter, so did the porch itself, which was many times used for extra sleeping space).

From their surroundings too came much of what has come to be known as Cajun cooking. Taking foods which could be locally grown, the Acadians based its preparation on their own French culinary heritage, threw in some of the Spanish treatment, added a bit of native Indian methods (they'd always got on well with local Indians, both in Nova Scotia and in Louisiana), picked up African secrets from blacks, and came up with a unique cuisine that is now justly famous. The dishes that evolved are based on a *roux*, made by combining oil and flour, which is slowly browned in a heavy pot. Into the roux go seasonings and native meat or seafood (sometimes both), and the mixture is left to simmer until (as one Cajun told me) it is "good." As a variation, okra is sometimes used to make gumbo instead of the roux. In that case, one final step is omitted—*filé* (ground sassafras leaves), which is added to all roux-based gumbo when it is served into the bowl (*never* during cooking), does not appear in the okra-based dishes. Served over rice, either version is delicious. Combining various meats and seafoods with rice and seasonings, the Acadians created jambalaya. And from the plentiful crayfish, they came up with crayfish étouffée, a rich blending of the small, freshwater cousin of the lobster with those delectable seasonings, again serving the result on a bed of rice. What all this adds up to is some of the best, and most unique, eating in the world—the food alone is sufficient justification for an expedition into Cajun Country! One final word about this wonderful feast: The Cajuns will invariably doctor any or all of these specialties with a dash of hot sauce (usually that produced on the large hot-pepper plantation near New Iberia, known to us all as "Tabasco")—if you follow their lead, do so with caution. When they say "hot," they mean *hot!*

Cooking is an important ingredient of any large family gathering whatever the occasion, whether it be to help one another with harvests or slaughtering, celebrate the end of such tasks, or just to enjoy a sociable hour or two together. Another ingredient, equally important, is the music, which any Cajun will tell you makes the food taste better. Its roots are probably those of medieval France, and it is almost wholly an orally transmitted art form (few Cajun melodies have ever been committed to paper). The simple lyrics and strains are either very, very sad, or very, very happy, and I defy you to listen to one of the gayer numbers and keep your feet still. From the time when they used only a fiddle and triangle, Cajun musicians have expanded and now play guitars, harmonicas, the accordion, and drums, but always with the distinctive sound of their special music. The best possible place to hear the music is at a *fais-dodo* (a term once used to tell the babies to "go to sleep" when they were stashed in a room apart from the one in which there would be dancing in someone's home). Nowadays, a *fais-dodo* usually takes place in a dance hall, a village square, or even in the streets, and if you're lucky enough to run across one, stop the car and join in—the Cajuns *love* company, and in no time at all you'll be dancing with the best of them. And if you don't just happen on a dance, look for the music in **La Poussière**, 1212 Grandpoint Ave. (tel. 318/332-1721), or in Breaux Bridge, **Grand Street Dance Hall**, 113 W. Grant St. (tel. 318/237-8513), in Lafayette, or any dance hall you pass, no matter its outer appearance. (If you can hear live music, don't hesitate to go in, for you won't be a stranger long.)

Special Note: If you become completely beguiled by this special music and the special people who play it—and if you're hardy enough for an early Saturday morning drive—there's a unique happening you won't want to miss in the little town of Mamou, some 53 miles northwest of Lafayette. Every Saturday, from 8 to 11 a.m., Cajuns from miles around congregate in **Fred's Lounge**, 420 Sixth St. (tel. 318/468-5411), for a live broadcast of music, local news, and commercials the likes of which you won't hear anywhere else. Never mind the early hour, the ambience is that of a nighttime get-together, with conviviality running high and the bar doing a brisk business. No slick broadcast, this—the "studio" is a roped-off section of the dance floor, the men behind the mikes and instruments are rugged Cajuns who work hard in the outdoors all week, and the audience crowds the floor dancing with friends and neighbors. To get there, take I-10 West to La. 13 North, and Mamou is about 11 miles due north of Eunice. It's a memorable experience! Incidentally, if you should meet Fred, his last name is Tate.

Well, that's Cajun Country and the people who inhabit it,

albeit in very abbreviated form. Just one thing remains to be straightened out, and it has to do with Mr. Longfellow and his poem. The real Evangeline was Emmeline Labiche, and her sweetheart was named Louis Pierre Arceneaux. And their story has a different ending from the one the poet assigned to his two lovers. Emmeline found her Louis Pierre, after many years of searching, right in Cajun Country in the town of St. Martinville. The real-life tragedy was that by then Louis had given up hope of ever finding her and was pledged to another. She died of a broken heart in Louisiana, *not* in Philadelphia as in the poem. With that set right, let's talk about the best way to explore Acadiana as a visitor and what you can expect to find there.

The map on page 191 shows a circular drive which could allow you to take in one or two of the plantation homes en route to Baton Rouge (if you take River Road instead of I-10 as shown here) before turning west on I-10 to reach Lafayette. The Interstate highway runs along the edge of Acadiana, but the little town of Breaux Bridge, just off it on La. 31, is real Cajun Country, and of course Lafayette is its heart. A return to New Orleans via U.S. 90 will take you right through the history, legend, and romance of this region. It's too long a drive for one day, and you'll want to book accommodations in Lafayette for at least a one-night stay. Using I-10, the distance from New Orleans to Lafayette is 134 miles; from Lafayette to New Orleans via U.S. 90 is 167 miles. You should know in advance, however, that this is true "wandering country," which explains why I wouldn't *dare* set out a step-by-step itinerary. I'll list some of the things to be sure not to miss, confident that you will find scores of other Cajun Country attractions on your own. Along the way, I'll mention some of the outstanding Cajun restaurants (but rest assured, it's almost impossible to get bad food out here), and tell you about places to stay overnight.

The best tip I can give you, however, is that you write ahead to the **Lafayette Parish Convention and Visitors Commission,** P.O. Box 52066 O.C.S., Lafayette, LA 70505 (tel. 318/232-3808) —they'll send you tons of detailed information to make your trip even more fun. They're open from 9 a.m. to 5 p.m. seven days a week, if you want to stop in while you're there.

If there is just no way you can find time to get out to Cajun Country for an extended visit, may I suggest that you take one of the excellent day tours listed at the end of this section. It's a good introduction to the area, and maybe on your next New Orleans visit (and rest assured, there will be another) you will be able to drive out for an in-depth exploration of this fascinating region.

If, on the other hand, you can get here during festival time (see Chapter X), you'll have a terrific time, right along with native Cajuns, who enjoy their festivals with real gusto.

BREAUX BRIDGE: Just off I-10 on La. 31, this little town, founded in 1859, prides itself on being the "Crawfish Capital of the World." Its famous Crawfish Festival and Fair has drawn as many as 100,000 to the town of 4500 permanent residents, and it's the most Cajun affair you can imagine, with music, a unique "bayou" parade, crayfish races, crayfish-eating contests, and lots more. It's such a splendiferous party, in fact, that it takes a full year to recover, so the folks at Breaux Bridge only hold it every two years—the next one is scheduled for 1986—and it's always held in early May. Lucky you, if that's when you plan to come. Otherwise, you'll have to be content with stopping by for some of the best Cajun eating to be found (see the "Where to Eat" section that follows for one very special recommendation).

LAFAYETTE: If you haven't written them in advance, make your first stop at the office of the **Lafayette Parish Convention and Visitors Center,** where the helpful staff will tell you everything you could possibly want to know about their region and send you out loaded with material to enlighten your stay. You'll find them by turning off I-10 onto U.S. 167 South (it's the first exit), which becomes U.S. 90, and the office is in the center of the median at 16th Street, just before the light at Pinhook Road (tel. 318/232-3737). They're open from 9 a.m. to 5 p.m. daily.

Acadian Village and Tropical Gardens

Just south of La. 342, on Mouton Road, you'll find a reconstructed (actually, a reassembled) Cajun bayou community at Acadian Village (mailing address: Rte. 3, Box 1976, Lafayette, LA 70505; tel. 318/981-2364). Houses, churches, and other buildings have been moved from original locations to this site beside a sleepy bayou. A footpath on its banks takes you past these historic structures, past workshops occupied by working craftsmen, and through the Around-the-World Gardens. The buildings hold a representative collection of Cajun furnishings, and the gardens have plants from most of the warm-weather areas of the globe. There's a gift shop too, where you can buy

Cajun handicrafts and an interesting selection of books on this unique culture. The village and gardens are open daily (except for holidays), from 10 a.m. through 5 p.m. Adults pay $2.50; ages 6 to 18 and over 65, $1.25; and under 6, free.

Judge Roy Bean's

This old Acadian building at 1304 Pinhook Rd., which dates from 1799, was once an inn. Built of cypress and handmade bricks, it has been beautifully remodeled and now is home for a fine restaurant, **Café Vermilionville** (tel. 237-0100), which specializes in Cajun and Créole cuisine. Lunch hours are 11 a.m. to 2 p.m. Tuesday through Friday, dinner from 6 to 10 p.m. Tuesday through Saturday. Sunday brunch, 10:30 a.m. to 2 p.m., features local Cajun bands.

The Lafayette Museum

Louisiana's first Democratic governor, Alexandre Mouton, once lived in the antebellum town house (built in the early 1800s) with square columns and two galleries which now houses the Lafayette Museum at 1122 Lafayette St. (tel. 318/234-2208). Its cupola, attic, and entire second floor, incidentally, were added in 1849. Inside, in addition to the antiques, paintings, and historic documents you might expect to find, there's a colorful collection of Mardi Gras costumes worn by Lafayette's krewe kings and queens. There's no set admission charge, but you're encouraged to leave a donation. Hours are 9 a.m. to noon and 2 to 5 p.m. Tuesday through Saturday, 3 to 5 p.m. on Sunday (except for major holidays, when it's closed).

Sans Souci Bookstore

That's right, a *bookstore*. And while the shop at 219 East Vermilion St. might be recommended solely for the great collection of books on Louisiana and the Cajuns, it is interesting too because of the building it occupies. This is one of the old "shotgun" structures, built before the Civil War. The term, of course, refers to the fact that the one-room house is so arranged that you can fire a gunshot through the front door and it would travel through every room in the house and straight out the back door. It is also one of the few residences in this country which have ever served as a post office, which this one did both during and after the war (Civil War, that is).

Cypress Lake

In the very heart of Lafayette, on the University of Southwestern Louisiana grounds, there's a lovely natural swamp environment. Although small, the effect is of being in the wild, and during warm months you'll actually see alligators. Water birds of several varieties, as well as turtles, are almost always on hand, and during the month of April the swamp is abloom with Louisiana irises. If you want to know more about the lake and how it is used as a teaching tool, contact the **University News Service,** University of Southwestern Louisiana, Lafayette, LA 70504 (tel. 318/232-3808). If you just want to get closer to the sort of swampland seen most often from highways which keep them a little remote, you'll find Cypress Lake next to the Student Union on the USL campus, between St. Mary Boulevard and University Avenue, Hebrard Boulevard and McKinley Street.

A Special Sports Note

If you're in Cajun Country between the first week in April and Labor Day and happen to be a devotee of the "sport of kings," you can enjoy an evening of racing at Evangeline Downs (three miles north on U.S. 167). Post time is 7:15 p.m. Thursday through Saturday, 1:30 p.m. on Sunday and on major holidays. General admission is $2, the grandstand is $2.50, and if you bring along a jacket and want to enjoy the clubhouse, it's $3. Don't bring the kids, though—no minors allowed. For current schedules and clubhouse reservations, call 896-6185.

OPELOUSAS: This town to the north of Lafayette, on U.S. 167, was the longtime home of an early American hero. Jim Bowie, a hero of the Alamo, lived here, and you can see a fine collection of his possessions and memorabilia at the **Jim Bowie Museum,** at 220 Academy St. (tel. 318/984-6263). It's open from 8 a.m. to 4 p.m. Monday to Friday, and it's free.

No matter what time of day you arrive in Opelousas, do drop in at the **Palace Café,** on the corner of Market and Landry Streets (tel. 942-2142), for a bite to eat. This is a family-run, old-style café that's been in business for over 50 years, and the home cooking just can't be beat. Gumbo in several versions, étouffée, all kinds of seafood, frog legs, steaks, fried chicken—well, the list of offerings is *extensive.* My personal favorites, however, are the Greek specialties on the menu, like the marvelous salad with feta cheese, black olives, green olives, anchovies, mixed green vegetables, and hard-boiled egg tossed with imported olive oil and vinegar (and, I'm convinced, a great deal of affection from Pete or Steve Doucas, the owners). Or the sticky-sweet, mouthwatering baklava, an unequalled pastry made with honey and pecan butter. Prices are very, very low (anywhere from $1.50 for a sandwich to $3.95 for that salad to $7.95 for a whopping seafood platter), service is friendly, and you'll be surrounded by locals who make this a regular eating place. They're open seven days a week from 6 a.m. to 10 p.m., until 11 p.m. on Friday and Saturday. Closed on holidays.

ST. MARTINVILLE: This historic old town goes all the way back to 1765, when it was a military station known as the Poste des Attakapas. It is also the last home of Emmeline Labiche, Longfellow's Evangeline. There was a time, too, when it was known as "la Petite Paris," when many aristocrats fled their homeland during the French Revolution and settled here, bringing with them the tradition of fancy balls, lavish banquets, and other forms of high living.

St. Martin de Tours Church

This is the Mother Church of the Acadians, and the building you see on Main Street was built in 1834, on the site of the original. It is also the fourth-oldest Roman Catholic church in Louisiana. Fr. George Murphy, an Irish priest, was the first to associate it with its patron saint, St. Martin, back in the 1790s, and there's a noteworthy portrait of the saint behind the main altar. You'll also see the original box pews, a replica of the grotto of Lourdes, an ornate baptismal font (which some say was a gift from King Louis XVI of France), and the lovely old altar itself.

Evangeline Monument

Longfellow's heroine is commemorated by a statute to the side and slightly to the rear of St. Martin's Church. It was donated to the town in 1929 by a movie company which came here to film the epic. The star of that movie, Delores del Rio, is supposed to have posed for the statue. Legend says that the real-life Evangeline lies buried here.

Evangeline Oak

On Port Street, where it ends at Bayou Teche, this ancient old oak is where her descendants say Emmeline's boat landed at the end of her long travels from Nova Scotia. Legend has it that it was here too that she learned of her lover's betrothal to another.

André Olivier Museum

Not a museum in the usual sense, this is a typical country store of the old days. If you're really interested, and the least bit friendly, you'll hear some colorful Cajun stories from the proprietor. Look for it on Bridge Street.

Longfellow-Evangeline Commemorative Area

Situated on the banks of Bayou Teche, just north of town on La. 31, 157 acres hold a park on land that once belonged to Louis Arceneaux, Emmeline's real-life Gabriel. The Acadian House Museum on the grounds dates from about 1765 and is typical of the larger Acadian homes, with bricks that were handmade and baked in the sun, cypress frame and pegs (instead of nails), and *bousillage* construction on the upper floor. You can also see the *cuisine* (outdoor kitchen) and *magazin* (storehouse) out back. Admission to the Acadian House is $2 for adults, $1 for students, and those under 6 are free.

As in Opelousas, I am going to recommend that you stop in at a local eatery, and while the menu is not as extensive as at the Palace, the **Thibodeaux Café & Barber Shop** is definitely not to be missed. It's on Main Street just across from St. Martin de Tours Church, and you'll find the tiny eating space a warm, homey, friendly place to relax from all that sightseeing. Best of all, you'll find good, home-cooked dishes—from gumbo or soup to complete dinners of local origin—at incredibly low prices. It's open for all three meals (and I heartily recommend breakfast here) on weekdays, breakfast and lunch on weekends.

JEANERETTE: This lovely little town on the banks of the Bayou Teche is filled with beautiful old antebellum homes, and is worth a visit just for the scenic beauty (as well as for an excellent restaurant described in the "Where to Eat" section that follows).

Albania Mansion

Just south of town on La. 182, the Albania mansion (mailing address: P.O. Box 389, Jeanerette, LA 70544; tel. 318/276-4816) is off the highway in a grove of trees which screen it from the road. This may be where you decide to spend your overnight, although the rental quarters are not "big house" rooms or filled with antiques (see the "Where to Stay" section that follows). The mansion itself, however, fits every plantation house image you've ever had, with large square columns which line the gallery of the "carriage entrance." The "bayou entrance" features a smaller set of galleries held by four pillars. The gabled house is centered around an impressive, three-story, free-standing spiral stairway. Built in 1837, the house contains eight marble mantels, and in addition to fine rosewood, walnut, mahogany, and cherry antiques (there's one entire room of Directoire furnishings), you'll view an incredible collection of old and rare dolls. There's a gift shop too. You can tour the mansion from 10 a.m. to 4 p.m. from Monday through Friday, and 2 to 4 p.m. on Sunday. Admission is $4.50.

IN AND AROUND NEW IBERIA: This interesting town had its beginnings in 1779, when a large group of Malagueños, 300 in all, came up Bayou Teche and settled here. It was incorporated in 1813, and its history changed drastically after the arrival of the steamboat *Plowboy* in 1836. New Iberia became the terminal for steamboats traveling up the bayou from New Orleans, and it promptly developed the rambunctious character of a frontier town. In 1839, however, yellow fever traveled up the bayou with the steamboats and laid low over a quarter of the population—many more were saved through the heroic nursing of a black woman called Tante Felicité who had come here from Santo Domingo and who went tirelessly from family to family carrying food and medicine (she had had the fever many years before and was immune). During the Civil War, New Iberia was a Confederate training center, and as such was attacked again and again by Union troops. Confederate and Union soldiers alike plundered the land to such an extent it is said that local Acadians threatened to declare war on *both* sides if any more of their chickens, cattle, and farm produce were appropriated! The steamboats continued coming up the bayou until 1947 (I'll bet you didn't know the steamboat era lasted that long anywhere in the United States). New Iberia has continued its growth and is known as the "Queen City of the Teche."

Shadows-on-the-Teche Plantation

This splendid home at 117 East Main St. (tel. 318/369-6446) was built in 1831 for David Weeks, a wealthy planter, and is beautifully preserved. It reflects the prevailing classical taste of the times and its columns and architectural features are of the Tuscan style. The two-story house is built of rose-colored brick and sits amid oak trees which were planted too close together for normal growth outward, and consequently grew to incredible heights. This is one of the most authentically restored and furnished homes in the state, and it is now the property of the National Trust for Historic Preservation. You can visit any day of the week from 9 a.m. to 4:30 p.m. for a $4 admission fee.

Tabasco Sauce Factory and Jungle Gardens

Avery Island, on La. 329, is underlaid by a gigantic salt dome, and the oldest rock salt mine in the Western Hemisphere is located here. But it is the fiery-hot peppers that grow especially well here that have brought its greatest claim to fame. The Tabasco sauce so loved not only by Cajuns but all over the world as well, is made by a closely knit family and equally close workers who cultivate and harvest the peppers, then nurse the sauce through a fermentation process first developed by the forefathers of Walter S. McIlhenny, third-generation president of McIlhenny Co. You can tour the new factory at no charge, then take driving or walking tours (for a fee) of the Jungle Gardens. They cover more than 300 acres, and there's something in bloom continuously from November through June. There's a Buddha from A.D. 1000 in the Chinese Garden, sunken gardens, a bird sanctuary, tropical plants, and great numbers of egrets and herons. Hours for the gardens are 9 a.m. to 5 p.m. every day. Admission is $4 for adults, $2.50 for ages 6 to 12. Tour the factory from 9 a.m. to noon and 1 to 3:45 p.m. Monday to Friday.

WHERE TO STAY: Lafayette makes an ideal base for exploring Cajun Country, but if staying on a real plantation has special appeal, there's one at Jeanerette.

In Lafayette

The new (in 1982) **Sheraton Acadiana Hotel,** 1801 Pinhook Rd. (tel. 318/233-8120), has some 300 guest rooms, most with wet bars and refrigerators. There's a plush lounge, award-winning restaurant, informal Café Raintree, New Orleans–style courtyard with swimming pool and hot tubs, and a Crown Service floor with concierge service. Doubles run $75 to $95 from January through July, $80 to $105 in other months.

The **Holiday Inn South–Airport,** P.O. Box 2668, Lafayette, LA 70502 (tel. 318/234-8521), is located on U.S. 90. There's a pool, playground, dining room, and lounge with entertainment and dancing. Rooms are about standard for this chain, which means comfortable and attractive. Double rooms cost $50 and up.

The **Ramada Inn,** 1810 Hwy. 167N, Lafayette, LA 70501 (tel. 318/233-5610), is located just one block south of I-10 (exit 103A). The Ramada has a pool, a coin laundry (handy if you have the kids along) and a dining room. There's a bar also, which stays open from 11 a.m. to 2 a.m. Double rooms (and they're quite nice) run from $45 up.

At Jeanerette

The **Albania Mansion,** P.O. Box 389, Jeanerette, LA 70544 (tel. 318/276-4816), has already been described above, but let me tell you about the old slave cabin in which you can spend the night (if you book far enough in advance, that is). It's built of cypress, with a tin roof that can get a little noisy if it rains—which doesn't bother me personally, since some of my fondest childhood memories are of rain drumming on a tin roof in the South, but I don't know how city folk would take to it. The little cabin is outfitted with a gas stove and refrigerator, a large sofa and trundle bed in the living room, a four-poster bed and rosewood dresser in the bedroom, and one of those days-of-yore claw-footed bathtubs in the bathroom. I find it delightful, and a completely different experience from "big house" guest quarters on most plantations. One big advantage, of course, is that you can do your own cooking, but I strongly recommend that you limit that to breakfast and hie yourself out to the excellent Cajun restaurants in the neighborhood for main meals (after all, you can eat your own cooking at home). Rates are $60 for doubles, children are not accepted, and accommodations are only available April through October.

WHERE TO EAT: As I said before, almost anyplace you stop will serve good food—it's one of the things that makes Cajun Country such a special place to visit. Indeed, this section would be much smaller if I could tell you where *not* to eat—then I could just skip the whole thing. However, the restaurants listed below are those I especially like, and like all recommendations in this book, they're a highly subjective list. You won't see some of the towns on the map on page 192, but never mind, you'll find them. Also, because of space limitations, these are not full-blown reviews, just a mention to point you in the right direction.

In Breaux Bridge

The **Crawfish Kitchen Restaurant,** I-10, exit 109 (tel. 332-2687), specializes in crayfish, cooked in a wide variety of dishes. Other seafood and steak are equally good. You'll find real Cajun Country cooking in this unpretentious eatery, which is open every day from 10 a.m. to 10 p.m. Prices, incidentally, are very reasonable.

Mulate's Restaurant, Highway 94, Breaux Bridge (tel. 318/332-4648), is a roadside café with cypress-board walls, where Cajun owner Kerry Boutte takes great care to make every dish authentic to his heritage. Stuffed crab is a specialty. Five nights a week, there's live Cajun music after 8 p.m. Mulate's is a good introduction to the Cajun world of friendliness, unique food, and music. Hours are 11 a.m. to 10 p.m., and prices are quite reasonable.

In Lafayette

Chez Pastor, 1211 Pinhook Rd. (tel. 234-5189), differs a little from most Cajun restaurants in that its decor borders on being "fancy." But at heart it's still the easy, informal sort of place where food and friendship prevail. Their Cajun canapes are terrific bite-size bits of boudin (hot smoked sausage) cooked and served in a cast-iron skillet. A wide range of seafoods, crayfish, and beef dishes are cooked in the Cajun manner with a touch of Créole in some. Prices are moderate. Every day except Sunday, Chez Pastor is open from 11 a.m. to 2 p.m. for lunch, 5 to 10 p.m. for dinner, and it's a great favorite with locals.

Prejean's, Highway 167 North (tel. 896-3247), is a place to experience as well as fill yourself with superb Cajun cooking. You'll almost always find a large gathering of locals in attendance here, either in the big main dining room or in the lounge with its oyster bar and marvelous stained-glass mural depicting a cypress shrimp boat on bayou waters. Other trappings in the rather plain interior consist of fish nets, crayfish traps, trawling boards, and similar items associated with the Cajuns' close affinity with fishing. In season, heaping platters of boiled crayfish come out of the kitchen in a continuous stream, along with shrimp, oysters, gumbo, and all sorts of other local dishes. On Friday and Saturday nights from 7 to 10:30 p.m. there's live Cajun music, which transforms all those happy diners into happy party-goers. Lunch is served from 11 a.m. to 2 p.m. Monday to Friday; dinner from 5:30 to 9:30 p.m. Monday to Thursday, until 11 p.m. on Friday and Saturday, and 5 to 9 p.m. on Sunday. Prices are in the $4.50 to $14.95 range.

Angelle's, on Highway 167 North, across from Evangeline Downs Racetrack (tel. 896-8416), is in a Cajun-style building with high-pitched roof and surrounding porch. It's a relaxed, friendly establishment which specializes in Cajun seafood dishes and steaks. Their crayfish dishes are also very good. Hours are 11 a.m. to 10 p.m. Tuesday through Sunday, and the attractive lounge is open from 5 to 11 p.m. those same days.

Don's Seafood Hut, 4309 Johnston St. (tel. 981-1141), has an excellent crayfish dinner that includes crayfish bisque, étouffée, fried crayfish tails, stuffed crayfish heads, and crayfish salad. Try it, you'll like it. And your check will be around $16 for a crayfish dinner. Hours are 11 a.m. to 10 p.m.

In Jeanerette

Just about one of the best places in Cajun Country to eat is in this little town, about a mile off the new Highway 90 on La. 182 (old Highway 90). The **Yellow Bowl**, Highway 90 (tel. 276-4416), is a bit eccentric when it comes to hours, so I suggest that you call ahead to be sure they'll be open—and if Cajun food is what you came for in the first place, you'll be well advised to plan your arrival in Jeanerette during their hours of operation! Normally, they're open from 11 a.m. to 10 p.m. Wednesday through Sunday. It's really an engaging place, with a crayfish dinner that surpasses many another. Étouffée is good here too, as are the fried crayfish and crab patty. The moderate price range of $7 to $15 makes the food taste even better, somehow.

TOURS: And what if you simply cannot spare the time to wander around Cajun Country? Well, you can still go home with at least a taste of this totally different region that is New Orleans's neighbor. If you have a day for out-of-town activities, one of these tours will give you a glimpse of how and where the Cajuns live.

Jacco Tours, 1515 Lafitte St., New Orleans (tel. 568-0141), has an excellent "Swamp Parade" tour which departs at 9 a.m. for a six-hour trip to Cajun Country. You'll be picked up by minibus, cross to the West Bank, drive the old Choctaw trail through the Lafourche-Delta swamp, visit a plantation and a Cajun village, be taken by boat down a bayou, eat lunch at a Cajun restaurant, and return home via the ferry by minibus. The cost? $35 plus the cost of your lunch (about $8, more or less).

The **Bayou Jean Lafitte,** 2340 International Trade Mart (tel. 586-8777), a modern passenger ship, departs daily at 11 a.m. from the Toulouse Street wharf across from Jackson Square for a 5½-hour Bayou Cruise. The 45-mile route takes you back into the intrigue and charm of Bayou Barataria, where Jean Lafitte and his notorious buccaneers once thrived. A professional guide fills you in on the history of the region. There's a snackbar, cocktail bar, and gift shop on board. Adults pay $13; children, $6.50; and under-6s sail free.

The Gulf Coast

East of New Orleans stretches the sunny Gulf Coast, a resort area that not only features all the water sports, but adds lots of golf, tennis, and, after dark, enough spice to liven up the day's relaxation. Within easy, and pleasant, driving distance of New Orleans, the small towns along the gulf have personality, charm, and—I must add reluctantly—a touch of commercialism that comes from having so many diversions packed into such a comparatively small area. Nevertheless, because those diversions are centered in historic old towns that have never grown into cities, there's none of the frantic, "enforced joy hour" feeling that pervades so many "high-rise" resort areas. Instead, a leisurely "Old South" atmosphere prevails, and a few days spent winding down along the gulf is the perfect end to a New Orleans visit.

Closest to the city is the Mississippi coast, and the two have close historical ties. The Spanish were the first Europeans along here, when DeSoto explored the coastal territory in the early 1500s, but it remained for the French to make the first settlements. Sieur d'Iberville (brother of New Orleans's founder, Bienville, did just that in 1699 at what is now Ocean Springs, calling the little post Fort Maurepas. On the site of present-day Mobile, Alabama, Fort Condé was established in 1702. When Bienville set out for the Mississippi a few years later to plant the French flag at New Orleans, the Fort Maurepas headquarters were moved to a location near where the Biloxi Lighthouse stands. Along the Pascagoula River, some 300 German colonists moved onto land grants in 1718 and set about farming, with the village of Pascagoula as a focal point. Through the years, these little settlements along the Gulf Coast changed hands time and time again, with rulers sometimes French, sometimes Spanish, sometimes English, and finally, American.

Your drive will be along beautiful bays and a long stretch of man-made beach. Offshore, the coastal islands are administered by the National Park System to offer all sorts of recreation and a bit of sightseeing. And although almost any of the resort towns would make a good vacation base, because they are close together, I'll confine my accommodations recommendations to Biloxi, Pascagoula, and a spiffy resort on the eastern side of Mobile Bay (with one or two suggestions for Mobile itself). The suggested restaurants are only the tip of a culinary iceberg—fresh seafood is found all along the coast in an amazing variety, with more eateries (that range from the most elegant to some that are not far from waterfront shanties) than you'll be able to sample. And since this is a resort area, prices are more sensitive to change than in other locations, so please bear in mind that those quoted are *at the time of writing*—some fluctuations due to seasonal influences or our old bugaboo inflation can be anticipated.

WHERE TO STAY: My personal recommendations follow, but no matter what your choice, reserve ahead if you can, for during the summer season it is quite possible to find almost every room booked, especially on weekends, when residents of Mississippi and its neighboring states head for the gulf. As I've said before, prices quoted are those in effect *as we go to press* and are subject to change. Also, you should know that prices go up rather sharply during the Christmas and New Year's holidays and during Mardi Gras week.

In Biloxi

To my mind, the most elegant place to stay in Biloxi is the **Broadwater Beach**, P.O. Box 127, Biloxi, MS 39533 (tel. 601/388-2211), which has a long track record in offering the best at the beach (such a long record, in fact, that I remember it from the days of my youth). Set in 33 acres of landscaped, wooded grounds, it offers every facility you can think of: lighted tennis courts, two 18-hole golf courses, a putting green and driving range, lawn games, Ping-Pong, and two pools plus a wading pool. The dining room is excellent, and there's entertainment in the attractive lounge. Rooms are large and brightly decorated, and for sheer luxury, there are cottages scattered about the grounds. Doubles run from $75 to $100; cottages considerably more.

The **Royal d'Iberville**, 3420 W. Beach Blvd. (tel. 601/388-6610), also has large rooms, many with balconies, extra basins in separate dressing rooms, and oversize beds. There are lighted tennis courts, swimming pool, hot tub, and golf privileges at a nearby course. The dining room is above average, and the lounge has dancing and entertainment. Doubles are in the $65 to $75 range.

In Pascagoula

Nearly as romantic as the legend of the Singing River is **Longfellow House**, 3401 Beach Blvd. (tel. 601/762-1122). The main house, once called "Bellvue," was built in 1850 by slave traders from New Orleans. Since then, it has been a girls' school (run by a headmaster who turned out to be something of a scoundrel), fallen into the hands of wealthy northerners who had a penchant for drink, been the property of a sea captain, and finally the happy home of a plantation owner and banker and his family. Somewhere along the way, Henry Wadsworth Longfellow was supposed to have stayed here, and some say he wrote "The Building of a Ship" during his stay.

Today, the house itself is used only for the dining room (a lovely, sunny room overlooking the wooded grounds), the popular lounge (which has entertainment that draws many locals as well as guests), offices of the inn, and private parties in the upstairs rooms. Guest rooms are in one- and two-story cottages scattered along pleasant walkways through vast lawns and planted gardens. Rooms are much larger than most luxury hotels, and nicely furnished, either opening onto or overlooking the landscaped grounds. There's a pool, golf, tennis, racquet ball, shuffleboard, sailing or boating, and charter-fishing trips can be arranged. For all the feeling of elegance and pampering by the friendly staff, rates are a surprisingly low $70 for doubles, $90 for a cottage which will accommodate four.

In a more moderate price range, the **La Font Inn**, on U.S. 90 East (tel. 601/762-7111), is a large, pleasant motel just off the highway, with spacious rooms overlooking the pool, steam baths in some rooms, and oversize beds in many. A lifeguard is on duty at the pool in summer, and there's a playground and wading pool for the young folk. The dining room is reasonably priced and very popular with natives. Doubles here start at $55.

In Mobile

The **Malaga Inn**, 359 Church St. (tel. 205/438-4701), is a small, utterly charming hotel consisting of restored 1862 twin town houses, with a garden courtyard and fountain. Many of the original furnishings are in evidence in public rooms. Guest rooms are nicely furnished, many with oversize beds. There's a pool and an excellent restaurant (see "Where to Eat"). You really can't do better if the graciousness for which the South is noted is what you're after. Double rates start at $50, children under 12 stay free in a room with their parents, and all rates increase slightly during Mardi Gras.

The **Best Western Admiral Semmes**, 250 Government Blvd. (tel. 205/432-4441), is a large, attractive motor hotel conveniently located to downtown. Rooms are spacious and decorated in above-average "motel decor." There's a pool, restaurant, and lounge. Doubles run from $50 to $60, and children under 12 stay free with their parents.

At Point Clear

At the **Grand Hotel**, Point Clear, AL 36564 (tel. 205/928-9201), the key word is "luxury." From the warm, awe-inspiring lobby that rises two stories high and is centered by a huge fireplace and filled with brass, porcelain, and antiques, and paneled and beamed by cypress, to the cypress-paneled rooms and cottages, quiet elegance holds sway. The dining room makes each meal an experience, especially if you get there early enough to sit next to the glass-walled end that overlooks the bay. As for facilities, there's a little bit of everything: a 27-hole championship golf course, deep-sea fishing, sailing, waterskiing, a pool and a beach area, bowling on the green, shuffleboard, skeet and trap shooting, a recreation hall, dancing and entertainment in the Bird Cage cocktail lounge, and if you have a favorite activity I've left out, it's probably there too. The hotel will also arrange sightseeing tours. The Grand Hotel operates on a modified American plan (breakfast and full-course dinner included in rates), and offers rooms in the main building, the Bay House, and cottage units for two to eight people. Rates, per person, for double occupancy range from $80 to $105 in spring and fall to $90 to $125 in summer and winter. Singles run higher, and cottage rates vary from $140 to $370. They offer a wide variety of golf and family package plans.

WHERE TO EAT: As you can probably guess, fresh seafood stars on most menus along the Gulf Coast.

In Biloxi

Mary Mahoney's Old French House, 138 Rue Magnolia (tel. 374-0163), is in a converted house and slave quarters that date from 1737. It fairly oozes charm, with fireplaces, antiques, a patio for cocktails and courtyard dining. Of course, you can't eat charm, and at this place the food measures up to its surroundings. Try the baked shrimp Dolores or the red snapper. Semi-à la carte prices range from $4 to $8 at lunch, $8 to $20 at dinner. Hours are 11 a.m. to 10:30 p.m. every day except Sunday and Christmas. It's a good idea to reserve.

White Pillars, 100 Rodenburg Ave. at West Beach (tel. 432-8741), is in a restored southern mansion set back from U.S. 90. Gourmet cuisine stars here, with specialties such as eggplant Josephine, and trout en papillotte. In addition to the main dining rooms, there's enclosed patio dining, and entertainment and dancing every night except Sunday. White Pillars has one of the largest wine selections on the Gulf Coast. Hours are 5 to 11 p.m., and it closes on major holidays. This is another place reservations are in order. Prices are in the $10 to $20 range.

For more casual dining at family-oriented prices, you can't do better than the **Sea 'n' Sirloin**, on the beach across from the Royal d'Iberville. It's a big place right on the water, with wide windows to let you enjoy the view as well as the food. The à la carte menu has shrimp boiled in the shell, oysters on the half shell, fried crab claws, blackened fish, and a host of other specialties that range from $4 to the top $18 (for the sea 'n' sirloin special—"sea" being lobster stuffed with crabmeat). The excellent salad bar has some 25 items, and there's an extensive wine list. This is definitely a place to bring the family! Hours are 11 a.m. to 10 p.m., seven days a week.

In Pascagoula

At the **La Font Inn**, on U.S. 90 East (tel. 601/762-7111), Sunday dinner is an event, with a fixed-price menu ($8.50 for adults, $7 for children) that features baked ham with wine sauce, fresh crabmeat Newburg, veal scallopine, and roast leg of lamb. Vegetables are really fresh and nicely prepared, and the price includes five courses. Other times, dinner prices run $7 to $15. Breakfast hours are 6 to 10 a.m.; lunch, 11 a.m. to 2 p.m.; dinner, 6 to 10 p.m.

In Mobile

The **Malaga Inn**, 359 Church St. (tel. 438-4701), features gracious dining in a Spanish setting. There's background music, and jacket and tie are a must in the evening. Specialties here include escalope de veau au parmesan, lump crabmeat pestalozi, and steak peperonata, as well as other continental dishes, all exceptionally well prepared and served. The dining room is open for all three meals, with breakfast running $4 to $6; lunch, $5 to $8; and dinner, $8 to $18. They also serve children's plates from $4.

Constantine's, in the Rodway Inn, 1500 Government St. (tel. 471-5371), has been in Mobile since 1934, run by the same family, and so well run that when I was an Alabama resident years ago it was a foregone conclusion that any trip to Mobile meant dinner there. Their specialties are prime ribs, steak, and—best of all, in my opinion—fresh gulf seafood. They serve all three meals at moderate prices. Hours are 6 a.m. to 11 p.m., and dress is casual.

NOTES

NOTES

NOTES

NOW, SAVE MONEY ON ALL YOUR TRAVELS!
Join Arthur Frommer's $25-A-Day Travel Club

Saving money while traveling is never a simple matter, which is why, over 22 years ago, the **$25-A-Day Travel Club** was formed. Actually, the idea came from readers of the Arthur Frommer Publications who felt that such an organization could bring financial benefits, continuing travel information, and a sense of community to economy-minded travelers all over the world.

In keeping with the money-saving concept, the annual membership fee is low—$15 (U.S. residents) or $18 (Canadian, Mexican, and foreign residents)—and is immediately exceeded by the value of your benefits which include:

(1) The latest edition of any TWO of the books listed on the following page.

(2) An annual subscription to an 8-page quarterly newspaper *The Wonderful World of Budget Travel* which keeps you up-to-date on fastbreaking developments in low-cost travel in all parts of the world—bringing you the kind of information you'd have to pay over $25 a year to obtain elsewhere. This consumer-conscious publication also includes the following columns:

Travelers' Directory—members all over the world who are willing to provide hospitality to other members as they pass through their home cities.

Share-a-Trip—requests from members for travel companions who can share costs and help avoid the burdensome single supplement.

Readers Ask . . . Readers Reply—travel questions from members to which other members reply with authentic firsthand information.

(3) A copy of *Arthur Frommer's Guide to New York*.

(4) Your personal membership card which entitles you to purchase through the Club all Arthur Frommer Publications for a third to a half off their regular retail prices during the term of your membership.

So why not join this hardy band of international budgeteers NOW and participate in its exchange of information and hospitality? Simply send $15 (U.S. residents) or $18 U.S. (Canadian, Mexican, and other foreign residents) along with your name and address to: $25-A-Day Travel Club, Inc., 1230 Avenue of the Americas, New York, NY 10020. Remember to specify which *two* of the books in section (1) above you wish to receive in your initial package of members' benefits. Or tear out this page, check off any two books on the opposite side and send it to us with your membership fee.

FROMMER/PASMANTIER PUBLISHERS Date_____
1230 AVE. OF THE AMERICAS, NEW YORK, NY 10020

Friends, please send me the books checked below:

$-A-DAY GUIDES
(In-depth guides to low-cost tourist accommodations and facilities.)

☐ Europe on $25 a Day	$10.95
☐ Australia on $25 a Day	$9.95
☐ England and Scotland on $25 a Day	$9.95
☐ Greece on $25 a Day	$9.95
☐ Hawaii on $35 a Day	$9.95
☐ India on $15 & $25 a Day	$9.95
☐ Ireland on $25 a Day	$9.95
☐ Israel on $30 & $35 a Day	$9.95
☐ Mexico on $20 a Day	$9.95
☐ New Zealand on $20 & $25 a Day	$9.95
☐ New York on $35 a Day	$8.95
☐ Scandinavia on $25 a Day	$9.95
☐ South America on $25 a Day	$8.95
☐ Spain and Morocco (plus the Canary Is.) on $25 a Day	$9.95
☐ Washington, D.C. on $35 a Day	$8.95

DOLLARWISE GUIDES
(Guides to accommodations and facilities from budget to deluxe, with emphasis on the medium-priced.)

☐ Austria & Hungary	$10.95	☐ Cruises (incl. Alaska, Carib, Mex, Hawaii, Panama, Canada, & US)	$10.95
☐ Egypt	$9.95	☐ California & Las Vegas	$9.95
☐ England & Scotland	$10.95	☐ Florida	$9.95
☐ France	$10.95	☐ New England	$9.95
☐ Germany	$9.95	☐ Northwest	$10.95
☐ Italy	$10.95	☐ Southeast & New Orleans	$9.95
☐ Portugal (incl. Madeira & the Azores)	$9.95	☐ Southwest	$10.95
☐ Switzerland & Liechtenstein	$9.95		
☐ Canada	$10.95		
☐ Caribbean (incl. Bermuda & the Bahamas)	$10.95		

THE ARTHUR FROMMER GUIDES
(Pocket-size guides to tourist accommodations and facilities in all price ranges.)

☐ Amsterdam/Holland	$4.95	☐ Mexico City/Acapulco	$4.95
☐ Athens	$4.95	☐ Montreal/Quebec City	$4.95
☐ Atlantic City/Cape May	$4.95	☐ New Orleans	$4.95
☐ Boston	$4.95	☐ New York	$4.95
☐ Dublin/Ireland	$4.95	☐ Orlando/Disney World/EPCOT	$4.95
☐ Hawaii	$4.95	☐ Paris	$4.95
☐ Las Vegas	$4.95	☐ Philadelphia	$4.95
☐ Lisbon/Madrid/Costa del Sol	$4.95	☐ Rome	$4.95
☐ London	$4.95	☐ San Francisco	$4.95
☐ Los Angeles	$4.95	☐ Washington, D.C.	$4.95

SPECIAL EDITIONS

☐ How to Beat the High Cost of Travel	$4.95	☐ Marilyn Wood's Wonderful Weekends (NY, Conn, Mass, RI, Vt, NJ, Pa)	$9.95
☐ New York Urban Athlete (NYC sports guide for jocks & novices)	$9.95	☐ Museums in New York	$8.95
☐ Where to Stay USA (Accommodations from $3 to $25 a night)	$8.95	☐ Guide for the Disabled Traveler	$10.95
☐ Fast 'n' Easy Phrase Book (Fr/Sp/Ger/Ital. in one vol.)	$6.95	☐ Bed & Breakfast-No. America	$7.95

In U.S. include $1 post. & hdlg. for 1st book; 25¢ ea. add'l. book. Outside U.S. $2 and 50¢ respectively.

Enclosed is my check or money order for $_____

NAME_____

ADDRESS_____

CITY_____ STATE_____ ZIP_____